CW00954261

IS CAPITALISM OBSOLETE?

IS CAPITALISM OBSOLETE?

A Journey through Alternative
Economic Systems

GIACOMO CORNEO

TRANSLATED BY DANIEL STEUER

Harvard University Press

Cambridge, Massachusetts   London, England

2017

First published as *Bessere Welt: Hat der Kapitalismus Ausgedient?
Eine Reise durch alternative Wirtschaftssysteme* © 2014
Goldegg Verlag GmbH, Berlin and Vienna

LIBRARY OF CONGRESS CATALOGING-IN-PUBLICATION DATA
Names: Corneo, Giacomo G., author.
Title: Is capitalism obsolete? : a journey through alternative economic
systems / Giacomo Corneo ; translated by Daniel Steuer.
Other titles: Bessere Welt. English
Description: Cambridge, Massachusetts : Harvard University Press, 2017. |
"First published as Bessere Welt: Hat der Kapitalismus Ausgedient? Eine
Reise durch alternative Wirtschaftssysteme by Giacomo Corneo (c) 2014
Goldegg Verlag GmbH, Berlin and Vienna." | Includes bibliographical
references and index.
Identifiers: LCCN 2016057809 | ISBN 9780674495289 (alk. paper)
Subjects: LCSH: Comparative economics. | Macroeconomics. | Capitalism.
Classification: LCC HB90 .C67 2017 | DDC 330.12—dc23
LC record available at https://lccn.loc.gov/2016057809

CONTENTS

PREFACE

CAPITALISM IS UNPOPULAR. It was unpopular from the very beginning, and continues to be so now. By the same token, its enthusiastic proponents have almost always and everywhere been a small minority. Today is no exception: according to recent opinion polls in Germany, for example, less than half the population believes a market economy is the best possible economic system. If we substitute the term "a market economy" with "capitalism," the polls indicate even less support for the present economic order.

However, while capitalism's lack of popularity is obvious, its critics' ideas about what an alternative economic system might look like are nebulous. This is actually a surprising fact, given that humankind has been thinking about this question for a considerable amount of time. Past efforts have yielded many detailed suggestions about how production and consumption could be organized within society to allow everyone to lead the good life. This book therefore pursues a basic question: Is there a superior alternative to capitalism at all, and if so, what does (or would) it look like?

In search of answers, I invite the reader along on a trip around the most promising alternative ideas that have so far been conceived, from Plato's ideal Republic to the latest suggestions regarding unconditional basic income provisions, stakeholder grants, and shareholder socialism. In each case, I first describe the principles of the proposed alternative economic system, and then look at how it would work in practice, to find out whether the results would be better than those achieved by capitalism in its present form. The economic system that serves as a standard of comparison is the kind of social market economy we find today in Germany and other continental European countries.

I should point out that the intention here is not to present a history of ideas. The focus, rather, is on the longing for a more humane, more just, and more efficient economic system. Enormous social energy lies dormant in this longing. If this energy is to be converted into reasonable and fruitful political action, we need unprejudiced and rational discussion about the best available alternatives to the present system. My main objective is therefore to lay open the inner logic of the most interesting blueprints, so their economic viability can be put to the test. Accordingly, the coherence of these suggestions and the effects to be expected from their possible realization take center stage. The aim of this journey through unfamiliar economic systems is to show the extent to which a system beyond the social market economy is practically possible.

Of course, a journey into the unknown is always at the same time a journey into oneself. In the same way, the comparison of alternative systems provides a perspective from which the current system can be better understood. The comparison teaches us how it functions, what its limits are, and what its so-far-unexplored possibilities might be. This is another objective of this book: by way of comparisons with alternative economic systems, I want to identify measures that would help transform the social market economy into a more humane, more just, and more efficient system.

This book is aimed at a wide readership and therefore does not presuppose any specialist economics knowledge. I try to present the insights that economic analysis can provide in ways that are generally accessible, without compromising the rigor of the argument. Although footnotes and additional references could be added to almost any paragraph, I intentionally do without them to allow the text to read more fluently. Pointers to further literature and to literature quoted in the text can be found in the References section at the end of the book.

Giacomo Corneo,
Berlin

PROLOGUE:

A FATHER AND DAUGHTER DEBATE

ONE DAY, an ongoing email exchange between father and daughter took an unexpected turn.

Daughter: . . . And yes, I did look through that eco-
    nomics textbook you handed me as I left. No need to
    return to that subject, if you don't mind.

Father: Well, but . . . does that mean your thinking
    has changed about it?

Daughter: Ha—not much, unfortunately. Actually, not
    at all! I think I even laughed out loud when I got to
    the part where the invisible hand of the market
    keeps everything running efficiently and abuses in
    check. What world do these people live in? In the
    world I'm in, nothing seems to be keeping bankers
    from targeting 25 percent return on equity and
    helping themselves to gigantic bonuses. Or doing
    all kinds of creative accounting that somehow goes
    undiscovered till the bank ends up in a mess. Or
    then escaping any need to pay for their gross errors,
    because the state, of course, bails them out—the
    same heavy-handed state, incidentally, that all

these distinguished gentlemen can't stop howling about.

That's how things really go in a market system, along with all the crazy justification of "incomes in line with the market." That's another whole class of wrongs perpetrated by invisible hands!

Father: Well, the "invisible hand of the market" is only a metaphor . . .

Daughter: Except that it isn't—it's that thieving banker's hand quite literally sneaking into the taxpayer's wallet. And what is the consequence of all this? The money for satisfying real, basic needs is missing.

Therefore, please call it "capitalism," and not "the market economy"! At least that makes clear in whose interest the system operates: in the interest of capital.

And don't forget that the comfortable and cozy existence of the Western European middle classes is in no way representative of everyday life under capitalism. For most people in Africa, Asia, and Latin America, living under capitalism means nothing but exploitation and misery!

Father: It's easy to rant and rave about capitalism in general. But what is it exactly that you are criticizing?

Daughter: If you really want to know, I am happy to explain. But you'd need to take some time for this, because there's a lot to criticize about your economic system . . .

Father: No problem. Go on, I'm curious!

Daughter: OK, your economic system is wasteful, unjust, and alienating. And wastefulness, injustice, and alienation are not the result of some natural law. They are the result of particular social rules, the rules of capitalism. And keep in mind that the capitalist economic system is the product of a relatively short period in history. Just as it once emerged, it will one day decline and be replaced with a better set of rules. We can fight against capitalism and replace it—and it is up to us to do that. Human beings get to decide how to bring about a better world. Now, let me elaborate.

First Charge: Wastefulness

Capitalism wastes our resources on a grand scale. It would be possible to achieve much greater wealth for everyone with the same resources. I guess that's what you economists call "inefficiency." So, in a nutshell, capitalism doesn't even satisfy the most basic requirement of an economic system.

The evidence is clear. Start with unemployment: About a tenth of the world's population that is fit and wants to work is denied the possibility to do so! At the same time, production facilities and machines lie idle. We suffer from a lack of housing and yet many apartments are owned by speculators and left intentionally empty. That's hardly one of your "highly efficient market processes," is it?

Or take a look at how capitalism treats the natural environment. Is the destruction of a sound environment and of natural resources efficient in economic terms? The rain forests are cleared, the oceans exhausted, and the atmosphere polluted with emissions. There is no self-regulation. Capitalism brings nature to the point of collapse. We are heading for a climatic catastrophe that will see whole countries and coastal cities submerged. This really is an amazing example of "efficiency," isn't it?

And have you ever thought about the use of food under capitalism? In the developing world, millions of people are starving. Meanwhile, in the West, *just*

as many suffer from obesity. This is an actual sta-
tistic I read in the news. Be honest: does this constitute a rational allocation of food?

According to cold economic logic, we would also have
to put the imperialist wars that are constantly produced by this allegedly wonderful system under the
heading of wastefulness. They are attempts by states,
or alliances of states such as NATO, to gain advantages for their elites through the use of military
force—for instance, by taking control of foreign oil
reserves. Highly valuable resources are invested in
such wars which could be put to productive use. The
waste is gigantic. In the United States alone, the
government spends about five percent of gross domestic product on the military. That amounts to more
than 700 billion dollars each year—an incredibly large
sum. Just imagine: that's more than twice the overall
gross domestic product of Bangladesh, a country with
a population of 160 million people. Think how much
suffering could be avoided with the help of these resources—and instead, they're being used to increase
the suffering. That's right, to increase it! Because,
sadly, as we have witnessed in the past, every now and
again the U.S. government clears out its weapons ar-
senal by ordering the bombing of whole countries like
Vietnam or Iraq, to do the arms industry a favor.

Second Charge: Injustice
Let's move on to the supposed "distributive justice"
of capitalism—another joke, since in fact it is an
affront to justice. A just distribution would involve paying attention to the individual needs of
human beings and rewarding them on the basis of
their individual merits. But distribution within our
capitalist system pays attention to neither needs
nor merits. The unjust distribution between indi-

viduals who had the bad fortune to be born in poor nations and those who had the good fortune to be born in rich ones is especially scandalous. The discrepancy in wealth between these two groups is so immense that no one can possibly believe that it is the result of differences in need or merit.

And even within Europe, levels of income inequality are unacceptable. Just take a look at Germany. A single household from the top one percent receives *eight times* the average household's income!

The argument that this imbalance serves some kind of positive function for society, because of the incentives resulting from it, must surely be a fairy tale invented to keep voters happy. Incentives to do what? Just imagine how people like that hedge fund manager, John Paulsen, became rich. Compare the salaries and the social usefulness of all those gamblers in the financial markets with what hospital nurses earn and do.

Third Charge: Alienation
This particular point is difficult to substantiate with figures. Let me try to explain it, anyway. Under capitalist conditions, people are encouraged to set goals for themselves that are just simply incompatible with meaningful personal development. The system practically lures them into leading pitiful existences, whether we're talking about work, consumption, or political participation.

Take work, for a start. Work should actually enable you to cultivate your personal abilities and give you opportunities to cooperate in fulfilling ways with others. But under capitalism, work forces you to carry out monotonous routines as a dependent individual whose aims are limited to jostling others aside at the workplace and to cheating the company and its customers as soon as the opportunity arises.

The whole sphere of consumption should also support personal development and foster mutual human support. Instead, people blow their money in acts of competitive consumerism orchestrated by the marketing industry. Occasionally, the sheer proportions of this consumerism push thousands of families into insolvency, as in the subprime crisis that hit the United States in 2007.

A political democracy should rest on "domination-free discourse" and give all citizens the same possibilities for exerting political influence. However, for most, it takes the form of a pure spectator democracy in which citizens' power of judgment is weakened rather than strengthened.

I know what you're thinking: you keep repeating that we should wait patiently for reform. But what have the last sixty years, with all their reforms, achieved for all of us Europeans? The incidence of unemployment, environmental disasters, and war has not dropped at all. Income inequality has not decreased, either—and, despite all the promises, children from working-class families still face far worse prospects than children from middle-class backgrounds. Precarious employment conditions are more widespread today than they were sixty years ago. I have to think this is why men identify so much with their cars. It's because they can't bear to identify with what they do and what they are. And, oh, one last thing: political participation. It hasn't increased. If anything, it has decreased.

I say, if sixty years of reforms under ideal conditions only managed to reproduce wastefulness, injustice, and alienation, then another sixty years of institutional window dressing will hardly make a difference.

From which it follows, quite obviously: capitalism must be abolished!

Father: Oh dear, I didn't expect quite such a tirade! But I will bravely respond, starting with your last point concerning reforms. Your claim (with which, incidentally, I don't agree) that the decades since the Second World War have not seen any improvements with respect to wastefulness, injustice, or alienation does not necessarily mean that the reforms that were made were useless. After all, we do not know what would have happened without them. Presumably, the exploitation of the environment, the concentration of wealth, and the disenfranchisement of the people would have gone much further. In that case, it would make sense to keep believing in reform!

You also forget that, during these decades, wealth has increased in general, and education and health provision have improved substantially for large parts of the population. Obsolete, authoritarian relationships within marriages, in families, and at the workplace are, for the most part, things of the past. I'm not saying we've reached the stage where perfect wisdom prevails, but these are all important contributions to the quality of life.

Nevertheless, I do think you are essentially right when you say capitalism is an inefficient, unjust, and alienating system. Do I surprise you? Look, I'm even prepared to discuss whether social progress is too slow and whether perhaps radical change is a risk worth taking. But such a discussion only makes sense if we can establish some clarity about what shape this change might take.

It would be somewhat premature to conclude from the weaknesses of capitalism that the system should be abolished. Don't forget, you may find yourself *worse off* as a result of change. An imperfect system should only be abolished if there is another system that can be put in its place—one that we have strong confidence will, indeed, be superior to the old one.

And we should be wary of comparing real conditions with ideal conditions, because otherwise we end up committing a genuinely dangerous "nirvana fallacy."

So, what do we really need? You have given me an idea. We should do a rational analysis of all the serious suggestions for alternative economic systems our species has managed to formulate so far. After all, people have racked their brains over these questions for a long time. Then, once we have taken a good look at these suggestions, we will be able to make a judgment on whether or not capitalism has run its course.

I'm getting right to work on this. Prepare yourself for an exciting journey beyond capitalism! I'll be in touch again tomorrow . . .

PHILOSOPHERS AND FAILURES
OF THE STATE

THE GREAT GREEK PHILOSOPHER PLATO, a disciple of Socrates, wrote his work *The Republic* in the fourth century BCE, making it the oldest preserved treatise on an ideal polity. It has had lasting influence on the development of Western philosophy, as well as on literature about political utopias.

In Plato's times, political economy did not exist. Thus we would in vain search the text of *The Republic* for concrete suggestions on how to design an economic system in an efficient, just, and humane way. We know, however, that every economic system interacts in crucial ways with a political system, and therefore that we cannot answer the question of what a better economic system might look like without investigating the relationship between these two spheres. It is precisely this crucial interface that forms Plato's starting point.

We should keep in mind that capitalism, or rather such capitalism as was associated with trade in the ancient world, is not abolished by Plato. His ideal polity does not therefore count as one of the stops on our journey through proposed alternative economic systems beyond capitalism. But for very good reasons Plato's polity belongs at the threshold where this journey begins, because familiarizing ourselves with it will increase our determination to set off on this expedition.

A PROBLEMATIC INTERFACE

Most economists describe the capitalist economic system as a combination of a market system and private ownership of the means of production. The most disgraceful collective misdeeds seem to emerge not *within* this economic system, but rather at the interface between the economic system and the political system. To the present day, imperialist aggressions, in which capitalist circles lead whole countries into war, remain the most horrific examples of the significance of this interface. Financial crises provide other such examples. At least since the Great Depression of 1929, it has been well recognized that the financial sector, if it is not regulated, exponentially aggravates the overall risk of economic crises. This is why, for instance, high equity ratios should be legally required, and also transparency regarding the accounts of financial intermediaries. In the years leading up to the latest crisis, however, politicians everywhere were enticed by the financial lobby into deregulating more and more, or into regulating ineffectively. For a long time, the success of this financial lobby brought high rates of profit to the financial industry and hefty bonuses for the financial managers. Then the crisis came, and demonstrated that these income gains did not correspond to an exceptionally high level of value creation, but rather to a gigantic amount of value being wiped off the books by misguided real estate investment.

Given the scope of the effects that bad politics can have under capitalism, it is important to ask whether the deficiencies for which capitalism is blamed by its critics could not simply be overcome by radically changing the way in which the activities of the state are organized—that is, without touching the core elements of the capitalist economic system (namely, markets and private property). If that were possible, the whole discussion of what to put in capitalism's place would become superfluous and we could save ourselves the round-trip through alternative economic systems.

From this perspective, Plato's *Republic* could well be read as an invitation to cancel the journey because, essentially, his suggestion is to keep capitalism, and at the same time to completely decouple the political sphere from the economic sphere. In Plato's ideal state, there is, on the one hand, a majority of the population which enjoys the economic freedom of the market while forgoing the right to have any political influence—in other words, while forgoing democracy—and, on the other hand, a group of benevolent and wise men who live outside of capitalism and take care of the political affairs for the rest of the population.

Would this be a feasible way to cure our society's ills?

POLITICAL ECONOMY AND GOVERNMENT FAILURE

To properly appreciate Plato's design, it is useful first to briefly sketch the approach taken by today's political economy. Political economists assume in their studies a capitalist economy and a state monopoly on violence for the protection of individuals and their property. Depending on the distribution of property rights, on individual preferences, and on natural and technological factors, the capitalist order leads to a specific allocation of resources. By "allocation of resources," we should imagine some exact determination of who produces what and how, and who consumes what. In other words, the allocation of resources is the overall result of the workings of an economic system.

In cases where the economic activity of the government is limited to the protection of property rights, and where these can be traded freely by all economic subjects, economists speak of a *laissez-faire* system. But this is a special case of capitalism that has never actually quite existed in reality, because those who govern like to intervene in economic affairs. For that matter, economic theory shows that the allocation of resources under such a laissez-faire system would almost always prove suboptimal and would be, in principle, improved by introducing state activities into the system. Intelligent regulation of the financial sector by the state, for example, helps to prevent macroeconomic crises. A tax-transfer system helps to protect individuals against poverty. If the laissez-faire system fails to provide particular goods or does not achieve a satisfactory income distribution, an expansion of the activities of the government beyond its protection of property rights can in principle yield better social results. It is at this point in the line of argument, however, that modern-day political economists typically issue a warning:

government failure can have even more serious consequences for society than market failure.

And this brings us right back to the problematic interface highlighted above. For government failure is an expression of the difficult relationship between the economy and politics. This difficult relationship can essentially be explained with two general properties of polities. First, a polity is not a collection of like-minded individuals possessed by a single will. On the contrary, it consists of individuals and groups who hold different opinions and often have vastly divergent interests. This plurality of interests should be taken into consideration when making political decisions that affect many individuals and groups, so that a beneficial balance of interests can be achieved. Second, the technical advantages of the division of labor, with which we are familiar from the organization of production processes, also apply to state activities. The prospect of sizable efficiency gains causes a polity to grant a certain group the right to make decisions in the name of the polity in general, and to watch over the implementation of these decisions. The members of this group are called politicians.

These two properties—conflicting interests within the polity and the delegation of collective decisions—imply that state power always carries the threat of causing more or less harm to a smaller or larger group of the population.

To protect itself against state failures, a polity may agree on a constitution which limits the authority of those who govern—by, for instance, declaring certain rights of the individual to be inviolable. In that case, certain arrangements must be put in place to make sure that those who govern will actually abide by the constitutional norms. One such arrangement would be the establishment of a constitutional court.

Once the limits of state intervention are defined by the constitution, a polity is faced with the question of how it will arrive at collective decisions. In general, political institutions should achieve two things. They should take care that the various interests existing in society are adequately represented, and they should make sure that those who govern do not use the state to exploit the rest of the population. The question is how this might be done under capitalist conditions.

LOOKING AT CAPITALISM FROM A CRITICAL PERSPECTIVE

A political economist who is critical of capitalism is someone who denies the possibility of finding political institutions that can satisfactorily solve the problems of collective decision-making mentioned above as long as the economic system is organized in capitalist fashion. Such an economist believes in particular that capitalism does not allow for genuine democracy. But it is best if we let a hypothetical representative of that position explain what exactly this means. Here might be the words of a political economist who is critical of capitalism:

> In a modern economy, capital income typically constitutes about a third of national income. As a third of national income is garnered by a much smaller part of the population, capitalists live under income conditions that are altogether different from those experienced by most other citizens. First, the average income of a capitalist is a multiple of the average income in the population overall. Second, the larger part of a capitalist's personal income is income from capital, while for the rest of the population, income from labor is by far the more important part. Because of these different income conditions, capitalists often prefer policy options which run counter to the interests of a vast majority of the population—namely, options which raise profits for firm owners and other income from capital at the expense of the welfare of the majority of the population. Such options include using the military to intervene in oil-rich countries and tolerating tax havens.
>
> If our alleged democracies really advanced the interests of the majority of the population, then their governments would never pursue such policies. The contrary is the case: behind a democratic façade, the interests of the capitalists prevail over those of the majority.
>
> Why is this possible? Although the capitalists are a minority, they have two advantages over the majority. First, because there are fewer of them, it is easier for them to coordinate their actions. The modern corporation already provides an institutional

framework within which capital investors can agree on strategies for exerting political influence. Even larger networks emerge through ownership chains and cross-shareholding. In Germany, for example, these networks are reflected in the composition of supervisory boards which promote the development of common positions and initiatives. The majority of the population, by contrast, suffers from the phenomenon of free-riding. Because political or social commitment from an individual incurs tangible costs for him or her but contributes only minimally to the collective cause—let alone the individual's personal gain—there is no material incentive to engage in collective matters.

Second, due to their wealth, capitalists are able to finance effective political lobbying. Wealthy individuals, corporations, associations, and foundations can thus influence the results of democratic processes of decision making. They can, for instance, make generous donations to support the election campaigns of particular candidates or parties. They may be in a position to offer lucrative posts to former holders of political office, or to arrange for them to give highly paid lectures. They can also finance media corporations, think tanks, and research institutions, all of which may in turn influence the opinions of decision-makers and voters in particular ways. What results is a systematic distortion of the democratic process which ignores the interests of the majority and undermines political equality.

At the root of this problem lies the uneven distribution of capital and the unrestricted right to income from capital. In principle, a far-reaching redistribution of wealth, through the high taxation of inheritance and of income from capital, could solve this problem. But in practice this does not happen, for the simple reason that such measures require collective decisions that would need to be taken within the democratic process—and that very process is systematically distorted in favor of the interests of capitalists. The abolition of capitalism, by contrast, would solve the problem at the root.

Reading the ancient Greeks, we also see some of them expressing this view that democracy carries within it a dangerous plutocratic tendency. Plato considers the combination of Athenian capitalism and democracy to be fundamentally unstable. As we'll see, however, his solution is the abolition not of capitalism, but of democracy.

PLATO'S DESIGN

According to Plato, the ideal polity is, first of all, a just polity—but, to him, justice means something different than what most people today understand it to be. For Plato, a polity is just when each person in it does what he or she can do best, and thus helps the overall community.

The starting point for Plato's reflections is his observation that human beings have different natures. One person is more talented at this activity, while another is more talented at that. Justice means for him that every human being pursues a profession that is at the same time a vocation. In the ideal polity, the division of labor will therefore be organized in perfect harmony with the distribution of natural talents.

This demand for justice also applies to the function of ruling, which Plato considers to be the most important activity in a polity. Plato is of the opinion that some people are particularly suited for ruling, by virtue of possessing certain traits. They are better than others at identifying and implementing measures which create sustainability for the polity. Thus, his maxim that labor should be divided in accordance with varying talents provides the justification for having a suitable group of professional politicians framing and making the big decisions. In an ideal situation, the just division of labor is fully realized. The ideal polity is therefore, according to Plato, nondemocratic; in such a polity, the majority of the population has no right to modify the decisions of the rulers, or to dismiss the rulers and replace them with different ones.

From the perspective of political economy, we might of course object to this by pointing out that the absence of democratic control makes government failures even more likely. Where there is no threat of rulers' not being reelected, it is even easier for rich merchants to manipulate those rulers. Plato seeks to mitigate this risk in two ways. First, in his ideal state, professional politicians are physically separated from the rest of the population as early as possible in life, and comprehensively taught only to act for the common good. Second, professional politicians are not allowed to own any private property or engage in any market-economic activities.

Thus, to avoid any failures of the state, Plato suggests creating an impenetrable barrier between the economy and politics. Most people—the majority class of workers—take care of the processes of production and exchange which secure the material reproduction of society. These processes take place within the framework of a regulated market economy that maintains the principle of private property. Political decisions, however, are taken by a preeminent council of experts recruited from the class of the so-called guardians.

Guardians and working people represent the soul and the body, respectively, of the Platonic polity, and Plato is almost exclusively interested in the soul. He does not make any innovative suggestions regarding the organization of economic processes. Markets, money, and private property continue to determine the everyday life of working people. And in terms of economic policies, Plato seems to recommend a pragmatic course. On the one hand, he warns against legislation that is overzealous in wanting to regulate markets. In his opinion, too much state regulation tends to inhibit the division of labor within the polity to an unnecessary degree, and thus to create privileged positions within the social fabric. On the other hand, he recommends distributive policies that prevent a social division into poor and rich.

Thus, we can define Plato as an opponent of democracy as well as an adherent of the market economy, making it clear that these two positions are not necessarily mutually exclusive.

In Plato's ideal state, the guardians devote themselves to strategic questions regarding the polity. In his time, that mostly meant questions about war or peace. Their power is great because they take on all of the tasks of today's parliamentarians, members of government, and constitutional judges. They also appoint the army. In this ideal state, there is no such thing as today's separation of powers, with its "checks and balances." To make sure that guardians fulfill their tasks in the best possible way, Plato makes detailed suggestions as to how they are to be selected and trained, and according to which basic rules their lives are to be organized.

A POLITICAL ELITE WITHOUT PRIVATE PROPERTY

The guardian class of the ideal state is not just an assemblage of wise and benevolent political leaders. They form a separate community of individuals who live permanently together—usually throughout their whole lives—and devote their entire existences to public service. We have to imagine the guardians as a community living in physical separation from the rest of society. They live and eat together, and among themselves they share everything. They do not earn their living through subsistence production, because they should not waste their valuable time on manual labor. They are provided with food and everything else they need by the producers.

Plato is of the opinion that the guardians should live as simple a life as soldiers in the field—they are meant to be a "low-cost, high-quality" political class. We should note that the individual guardian does not receive a salary from the rest of society that he or she can spend at will. Rather, all of the guardians' property is communal property. They collectively decide on their consumption, and each of them receives items to be consumed according to a process of rationing. Services used by the individual guardians are also rationed.

Why does Plato not allow the guardians to hold private property? One of the reasons is that he wants to make optimal use of human talents. The guardians are meant to dedicate themselves exclusively to the interests of the polity. In the absence of private property, they will not be tempted to betray their mission and focus instead on the accumulation of private wealth. We might respond to this by saying that, to avoid the possibility of such a betrayal, it is only necessary to prohibit the guardians from undertaking any activities in addition to those concerned with advancing the interests of the polity. It is difficult to ensure that such a prohibition is actually observed, however, because there are ways of keeping secondary incomes and privileges secret—ways that make it impossible for courts to produce legally watertight proof of them. Indeed, today, the private remuneration of politicians for promoting particular interests mostly takes forms that do not allow for legal objections to be raised. By contrast, the prohibition of private property, and the general community of goods among the guardians, makes it impossible for any of them to be bribed. Thus, the community of goods among the guardians serves the purpose of separating out political and economic power. The state cannot develop into a plutocracy—that is, into a form of state in which the rich and wealthy exercise political domination. Some of the worries of those political economists who are critical of capitalism are thus taken into consideration.

Another reason for abolishing private property among the guardians, in Plato's view, is that this will promote social cohesion. If an individual guardian gets rich at the expense of the polity, this will provoke resentment on the part of the other citizens—and especially on the part of other guardians. Sooner or later, the guardians will be scheming to get the better of one another, and as a group they will appear as "hostile masters of the other citizens instead of their allies." It will no longer be possible to speak of an ideal state at all; devastating social unrest and political upheaval will be in the offing.

THE GUARDIAN CLASS AS A UNITARY BIOLOGICAL ENTITY

It may appear unduly harsh not to allow politicians any private property just to avoid the possibility of bribery. But other suggestions by Plato for promoting the unity of the guardians are still more extreme. The guardians are not only meant to live and eat together; to a certain degree, they are expected to become a unitary biological entity.

There is no gender discrimination within the class of guardians; women and men alike may rule in Plato's republic. It is expected that they will have children, and that typically these children will also become guardians. Sometimes children from the guardian class are moved to the class of producers, and, conversely, children from the class of producers may be promoted to the guardian class. For the most part, however, the political elite is simply recruited from the children of the political elite.

This might not strike us as particularly unusual. Today, the social permeability of the elite class is also low, and institutions such as elite universities and foundations supporting the supposedly gifted and talented tend to lead to members of the elite marrying within their class. But Plato's rules are even more extreme than that; for the guardians, the institution of the family is to be abolished altogether.

Marriage, in the sense of a contract that binds for life, is entirely absent for the guardian class. They are allowed neither to marry nor to found families. The older guardians interfere massively in the determination of what pairings should produce children, in a manner "comparable to horse-breeders in the case of horses." And once the children are born, they are separated from their parents at the earliest possible stage and brought up together with the other children.

This is heavy stuff. What is the logic behind it? As the children are quickly separated from their biological parents, the true family relations are obscured—and that is precisely what Plato wants. Given this lack of knowledge, every child regards every other as a sibling, and sees a potential parent in every one of the guardians; similarly, adults regard every child as their own. This is meant to strengthen the feeling of unity within the guardian class. Once again, unity among the political leaders is seen as necessary for creating a sustainable polity—this is Plato's central concern.

EXCURSUS: THE GENETICALLY DETERMINED ALTRUISM OF THE GUARDIANS

How effective would this deceptive strategy actually be in fostering an altruistic attitude—that is, an unselfish way of thinking and acting—among the guardians?

Let us take a look at Plato's extraordinary demand through a particular lens—namely, that of modern evolutionary theory, which explains altruism among related animals with reference to their genetic affinity. Because a gene of a particular animal can often also be found in the animal's relatives, the gene will multiply at a relatively high rate if it induces the animal to help its relatives, compared to a gene which engenders a purely egoistic form of behavior. Thus, natural selection has favored genes that cause altruistic behavior within families.

Just how pronounced this altruism will be depends on the genetic affinity between the individuals. Biologists measure this affinity using an index for blood relation ("relatedness"). Roughly speaking, this index corresponds to the proportion of shared genes, excluding those that all individuals of the same species have in common. At the same time, the value of this index corresponds to the likelihood that a "rare" gene will be found in two individuals, because they both would have inherited it from a common ancestor. The genetic affinity between full siblings is exactly one-half; between first-degree cousins it is exactly one-eighth.

The altruism brought about by natural selection could only develop to the extent that the individuals were able "correctly" to apply it— meaning to the extent that they were able to recognize genetic affinity. Thus, the more closely related an individual estimates another individual to be, the more intense the altruism should become.

By artificially producing uncertainty regarding biological descent within the guardian class, Plato changes these altruistic relations in two respects. On the one hand, the intensity of the altruism among blood relations decreases, because they cannot be certain of being related. On the other hand, altruism emerges among individuals who are not biologically related, because they suspect that they may be blood relations. As a consequence, altruistic tendencies are redistributed. Instead of fewer but more intense altruistic relations, every individual develops numerous, less intense altruistic relations. If we wanted to use an image, we might say that a coarsely meshed net of strong wire is replaced with a finely meshed one made of thin wire.

How much genetically determined altruism among the guardians would result from Plato's trick?

The answer depends on the number of guardians. Let us take as an example a hypothetical first generation of adult guardians that consists of $n/2$ men and $n/2$ women who are not related to each other and who produce children who also become guardians. If the biological parenthood of the second generation is unknown and purely determined by chance, the expected degree of relatedness between any two children will be $1/n$. Thus, altruism in the second generation will be less intense the more potential parents there are—which is to say, the more current guardians there are. If the intended strength of altruism is to correspond to that between second cousins, n should equal 32; in the case of 128 guardians, the strength of the altruism would correspond to that between third cousins.

These quantitative illustrations suggest that the trick of keeping natural relations secret would produce only a rather modest gain in genetically determined group cohesion, if we assume a group of several hundred guardians.

In any case, in Plato's ideal state, the abolition of the family does promote unity among the guardians by removing nepotism and the favoring of one's own children. And it removes the chance of rivalries and conflicts between family clans among the guardians.

The prohibition of marriage and family also has an effect similar to that of prohibiting private property. Scholars of family economics, such as the late Gary Becker (recipient of the Nobel Memorial Prize in Economics), describe a "marriage market" in which individuals compete for access to a scarce resource: desirable partners in life. If the guardians joined this market, enmities would arise not only among the guardians themselves, but also between the guardians and the class of producers. As the guardians represent a comparatively small group, they would often find attractive partners in the rest of the population. Competition between guardians and producers could not possibly work, however, because the former would be both players and referees. The producers would therefore suspect that certain political measures were not being taken in the interest of the common good, but to promote the interests of the guardians at the expense of the producers.

EDUCATION OF THE GUARDIANS

According to Plato, members of the political leadership must be carefully selected and educated. In the ideal state, their long education begins during early upbringing. The participants in this program are the children of the guardians and the most promising children from the producer class, who are integrated into the guardian community. This cannot easily happen against the will of their parents, however, and therefore a career as a guardian must be shown to be more attractive than existing alternatives. This is another reason why individual producers must not become much richer than the average person.

The aim of the educational program for the selected children is for them later to become rulers who are competent and love the polity. Up until the age of twenty, they receive a comprehensive education of body and mind, which is rigidly codified in a program to which the educators must closely adhere. Once the candidates for the position of a guardian have reached the age of twenty, a selection takes place, and only those who are still promising candidates at this point are admitted to the following course of study. Those selected must delve deeply into mathematics and the sciences for ten years. Then, at the age of thirty, another round of selection takes place, and the best candidates are allowed to turn their minds to philosophy for another five years.

The education of the guardians ends only when they reach age thirty-five. They are now well prepared and trained to lead the state as philosophers, although, to begin with, only in military terms and not yet in political terms. For the first fifteen years, every guardian does military service. The length of this period can be explained by the fact that the city of Athens was continually at war during Plato's times. Thus, the guardians practice their actual political profession only from their fiftieth year onwards; and the remaining life expectancy was probably not very long in those days. We may assume Plato was of the opinion that only individuals of this age would have acquired enough experience, and freed themselves sufficiently from their passions, to be good politicians.

Even when they have reached the age at which they can take office, the guardians do not act solely as professional politicians. After a few years in political leadership, they enter into a phase of learning during which they again dedicate themselves to philosophy. Periods of practice and theory repeatedly alternate. During the learning phases they also take care of the selection and education of the next generation of guardians—"comparable to horse-breeders in the case of horses."

A USEFUL MYTH

The ideal polity sketched by Plato can be summarized in a few lines. The overwhelming majority of individuals—the class of producers—take care only of their private affairs, and seek happiness in that realm. Collective matters that require governmental regulation are dealt with by political leaders who are wise and benign and therefore make the best possible decisions for the collective. The political leaders are drawn from the guardian class, which consists of those most gifted for that profession, and whose members live according to special rules separately from the rest of the population. Every guardian renounces private property and the possibility of having a family, lives communally with the other guardians, and is from a very early age onwards educated strictly with the future mission of becoming a political leader in mind.

A danger of this social model is that the class of producers might refuse to accept the power of the guardians. Plato highlights this point himself, and suggests a way of dealing with it. Seen in the context of Plato's philosophy more generally, the claim of the guardians' authority constitutes a problem. The guardians are philosophers who have seen the light of truth and have returned to the humans "in the dark cave." The producers, by contrast, are not philosophers, and therefore have only a fragmentary understanding of the world. They will not immediately realize the truth of the guardians, that they are wise and pursue only policies that are best for the polity. Just as a young son defies his benign father, a people may not accept the paternalistic authority of the guardians without some friction.

Somewhat hesitantly—as if he were ashamed of it—Plato therefore suggests legitimizing the constitution of this state, allegedly the best possible one, with a "necessary lie" in the form of a myth. According to this myth, all human beings descend from Mother Earth and are therefore brothers. The emotional bond of brotherhood is to help to unite all human beings, who would otherwise enjoy entirely different privileges as producers and guardians. Further, the myth says that God will see to it that humans inherit certain materials from Mother Earth. These materials, which are added to their souls in different proportions, are gold, silver, iron, and copper. Through these different admixtures, God means to indicate which role each human being has. Gold in the soul of a human being, for instance, indicates that he is to be a guardian, while copper marks a farmer. Everyone should adhere to these signs, which, in cases in which there is any doubt, are to be read by the guardians. If people do not follow God's command to adopt the roles that correspond to their particular mixture of materials, the state will perish.

Plato is convinced that the producers will accept the authority of the guardians if they can be made to believe in this myth.

UNAVOIDABLE DECLINE

Despite all these arrangements, Plato does not believe that his ideal state would be able to exist indefinitely, were it to become a reality. The risk of its degenerating into a military dictatorship, of the kind Plato was aware of from the case of Sparta (the authoritarian state that defeated Athens when Plato was still a young man) is too high.

The decline of the ideal state follows necessarily from Plato's theory of ideas. Ideas are eternal. If the ideal state is realized in practice, it becomes part of reality and thus subject to change. Starting out from perfection, any change can only mean deterioration. Thus, at some point, some fateful flaw will emerge in the real state of the philosophers. Perhaps the guardians will neglect the education of the next generation of guardians, resulting in a corrupt guardian class whose members begin to strive for personal honors. Soon thereafter, the guardians will want the right to own private property in the form of money, houses, and land. And once private property has been reintroduced into the guardian class, divisions and conflicts will arise, both among the guardians and between the guardians and the producers. The state will degenerate, ultimately becoming a tyranny that is permanently at war.

Even though he believed that, in the long term, his state of philosophers would decline, Plato thought it important to aspire to this form of state. Indeed, Plato promoted his ideal constitution, and visited Greek settlements in southern Italy where he hoped to be able to experiment with putting it into practice. But his hopes were ultimately disappointed; no attempt at realizing his ideal constitution was ever made.

TRACES

Plato's reflections on the ideal polity have nevertheless over many centuries left traces in the development of actual institutions. In particular, his message about a power elite whose members should lead modest lives, without property and according to strict rules, and whose legitimacy should ultimately rest on their ethical and intellectual superiority—without the need for democratic approval—found favor with certain movements within the Catholic Church.

An impressive example of the realization of some, though not all, elements of the Platonic constitution is the Jesuit state that, between 1610 and 1767, stretched across a vast area in and around present-day Paraguay. In this state, the padres corresponded to the guardians, and the remaining population consisted of the indigenous people. This was no small-scale experiment; in its heyday, almost 150,000 people lived in this Christian and socialist state. Clearly, its constitution was strongly influenced by Plato's *Republic*. But there are also unmistakable parallels with the work of an Italian admirer of Plato—the Dominican monk Tommaso Campanella. A few years before the Jesuit state was founded, Campanella had composed *La Città del Sole* (The City of the Sun), which portrays a utopia where the priests, rather than the philosophers, exercise political leadership.

Unlike Plato's guardians, the padres of the Jesuit state also took part in manual labor and were raised and educated in the conventional way. But they dominated the indigenous people in a paternalistic fashion, and did not possess individual wealth. There was no private ownership of the means of production whatsoever in the Jesuit state. In fact, the Padres oversaw a communist economic system which functioned without money or markets, and which survived twice as long as the Soviet Union.

Interestingly, the Paraguayan experiment did not perish due to a degeneration of the political leadership, or due to economic inefficiency. The existing studies of it rather indicate that remarkable social and economic results were achieved, and that nowhere else in South America were the Indians better off after the arrival of the Europeans than in the Jesuit state. The fate of this state was sealed, instead, by political agreements between the two colonial powers, Spain and Portugal. The padres were ordered by their superiors to leave the area and hand it over to the nephews of the conquistadores, who then ran it into the ground pursuing standard European colonial policies. Within a few years, the majority of the indigenous population of Paraguay had been wiped out. The flourishing agriculture and fine crafts that had emerged thanks to the audacity and industriousness of the padres also disappeared.

THE PHILOSOPHER KINGS: A THOUGHT EXPERIMENT

Let us return to the problem of government failure that we highlighted at the very beginning of this chapter. Government failures are no less disastrous today than they were in Plato's time, and if they could be avoided without throwing into question the viability of capitalism as an economic system, then the charges brought forward by the critics of capitalism could be mostly invalidated. Plato's *Republic* offers a recipe for doing so that consists of two main ingredients: first, the complete elimination of the personal economic interests of politicians, because they are not allowed to own private property; and second, the comprehensive education of these politicians from an early age, so that they become wise and benign. If those who govern cannot get rich, they will have no incentive to exploit the population. If they are wise, they will be competent in governing. If they are benign, they will be a force for prudence and benevolence across all of society.

Let us imagine, then, that a United States of Europe is to be organized according to Plato's model. An uninhabited area is found where some pleasant living quarters and working space for the professional politicians can be constructed. In this reclusive space, the politicians draft all the laws according to which the rest of the population must live. Some committees dedicate themselves to matters concerning all of the federation, others to matters concerning country-specific policies, and still others to regional and local policies. All the proceedings are streamed live on the internet to allow anyone who is interested to follow exactly how political decisions are made.

The politicians of these United States of Europe are not allowed to have any money or private property, and they live communally. As in Plato's ideal state, their lifestyle is neither luxurious nor impoverished. They commit themselves to governing together for the well-being of Europe, and are educated and trained to do so. As children, they are selected to become members of this class on the basis of entry examinations that are organized solely by the politicians themselves.

Although these modern guardians are professional politicians, they are altogether different from the politicians we know today. They are compassionate technocrats and practically-minded moral philosophers. They organize our collective concerns in the best way possible, so that we nonpoliticians do not have to bother ourselves with them. We can simply enjoy life; meanwhile, the politicians can implement prudent foreign policy for us, can intelligently regulate the financial sector, and can make optimal decisions in all other policy areas.

THE MIRAGE OF THE BENEVOLENT DICTATOR

If this pleasant prospect were a realistic possibility, there would be no good reason for embarking on an exhausting tour of the economic alternatives to capitalism; the only thing requiring radical change would be the way in which political decisions are made. But unfortunately it is not a realistic possibility.

The root of the problem is the mistaken epistemology on which the alleged agreement between the governing guardians is based. Plato conceives of the guardians as true philosophers who have all gained knowledge of the same world of ideas, and therefore share the same basic normative conceptions. In reality, philosophers are constantly arguing among themselves. This fact is grounded in the nature of their subject; philosophical theories consist neither of logical and mathematical propositions, the validity of which can be proven, nor of propositions that are empirically refutable.

Even economists, who often feel committed to making their theories empirically verifiable, vehemently disagree about which policies should be implemented. The lack of agreement results in part from the limitations of the analytic instruments they have for measuring the effects of policy decisions. This is mainly a technical problem and, given the comparatively young age of the discipline, it might be remedied over time. What cannot be remedied, however, is disagreement over the evaluation of political measures, because every individual has a different understanding of what the common good is. This is not specific to philosophers or economists, but a general characteristic of pluralistic societies.

The idea that entrusting a group of wise individuals with political leadership is a viable alternative is therefore misleading. Who should these wise individuals be? Just as different people have different ideas about what the common good is, so there is no agreement over who is wise; neither concept can be objectively determined. The difficulty does not lie in the details, but in the central fact of differing general worldviews and fundamental value judgments. Let us take as an example the question of what constitutes a just distribution of income within society. John Rawls and Robert Nozick, who both died in 2002, were preeminent theoreticians of this question. Rawls answered the question with reference to a maximin rule, according to which the optimal arrangement of income inequality in a society is the one under which the individuals who are worst off fare best compared to other ways in which inequalities might be organized. Nozick provides us with a comprehensive theoretical justification for a minimal state that does not engage in any redistribution. Both of these theories have many adherents among scholars all over the world, but their conclusions with regard to distributive policies are diametrically opposed, and would push our society in completely different directions. There is no scientific test that can tell us whose theory is right, and who, therefore, is wise.

Or take foreign policy. Consider the difference it would make if one defined the followers of Nietzsche as wise, and therefore as rulers—or by contrast, put followers of Erasmus of Rotterdam in charge.

In pluralist societies like ours, there is no single school of thought whose followers all citizens would happily accept as authoritative. The impossibility of arriving at a shared definition of the common good deprives Plato's ideal state of its legitimacy. As a consequence, citizens must make use of their own understanding, take responsibility, and reject immaturity. That was the motto of the Enlightenment and it is no less correct now. There are no angels we can entrust with taking collective decisions; there are only human beings. Freedom and equality, therefore, belong inseparably together, and force us to take the inconvenient path of democracy.

HOLDING ON TO DEMOCRACY

In his ancient age of trade capitalism, Plato already recognized that private property and markets produce a constellation of interests, and that any attempt to reconcile those must transcend the sphere of the purely economic and have major implications for the process of political decision-making. He did not expect that anything good would come of that, because he thought it likely that the particular interests of the economically powerful would prevail at the expense of the interests of the polity. He therefore suggested a radical separation of the political and economic spheres. In the absence of any financial interests of their own, and given full authority, benevolent experts were meant to create appropriate laws that would protect the citizens against the excesses of capitalism and provide for stability.

We can well understand why the ancient Greeks rejected Plato's suggestion, for it did not contain any mechanism for resolving conflicts between the rulers and those ruled, or within the political class. The most likely outcome would have been violent repression by the strongest. In the case of an erupting conflict, some guardians would have transformed the state into a military dictatorship, and under the conditions of this dictatorship there would have been no place for Plato's constitution and the myth of brotherhood, which would have set a limit to the arbitrary rule of those in power.

The consequences of a modernized version of Plato's state today would not be much different. Many people would in principle be prepared to hand their right to political participation over to a group of benevolent and wise individuals; it would, after all, be extremely convenient. But their caveat would be that the benevolent and wise sages must be *their* sages. And we should not forget that one man's benevolent sage is another man's villain.

Our first attempt at improving the world, with Plato's help, yet without changing anything about the economic system, must thus be considered a failure. Faced with the choice between capitalism and democracy, Plato wanted to give up democracy. We, however, want to hold on to democracy and find out what can be achieved if we give up capitalism. It is now time to explore the best possible alternatives.

UTOPIA AND COMMON OWNERSHIP

SO, HAS CAPITALISM RUN ITS COURSE?
The first destination on our journey beyond capitalism is a faraway island. At the beginning of the sixteenth century, the English scholar and statesman Thomas More published an exquisite work about this island, bearing the radical title *Utopia*. The word is formed from the Greek "ou-topos," which literally translates as "nowhere." The book is written in the form of a report given by a traveler about an unknown country whose institutions work so well that the country should serve as the model for the whole world. Although the polity of Utopia shares some features with Plato's ideal state, More's work is informed by an entirely different spirit—namely, that of humanism. In contrast to Plato, More does not aim to build a stable polity that measures up to an eternal idea of justice; rather, what is close to his heart is the wish to promote man's natural "pleasure." This makes building Utopia a far more appealing project than instituting the Republic.

Reading between the lines of this five-hundred-year-old work, we discern the fundamental conviction that the human beings produced by an economic system are more important than the goods and services it produces. A similar theme will recur in later critiques of capitalism, where it is expressed in terms of the aim of overcoming alienation and promoting human flourishing. On the happy island of Utopia, work, consumption, and democracy are spheres of self-regulating participation, personal development, mutual aid, and not least, a happy sociability.

The polity of Utopia differs from Plato's ideal state in two key respects. The first difference concerns the economic system. More extends the prohibition of private property, which, for Plato, applied only to the guardian class, to all of society. With this move, More also entirely abolishes the market system. Capitalism gives way to a society-wide system of common ownership. The second difference concerns the political system. The dictatorship of the philosophers is replaced with a democracy, presented as an original combination of grassroots organization and charismatic leadership.

THE QUESTION OF COOPERATION AND ALLOCATION

Utopia, it turns out, contains a significant contribution to our search for an economic system that would be superior to capitalism. Here we find a detailed description of an alternative economic system that follows a set of rules completely different from those of capitalism.

In what follows, we shall examine Utopia and other promising alternatives to capitalism with regard to their economic feasibility. For each of these alternatives, we want to present a reasoned evaluation of whether or not it would be capable of producing at least roughly the same amount of prosperity as today's system, because an economic system that is likely to lead to a drop in the level of prosperity would find few supporters—thus, it would lack the requisite political backing.

But how are we to arrive at a reasoned evaluation of whether a mechanism as complicated as an entire economic system would actually work?

At this point, we would do well to pause for a moment and reflect on the question of what it is that economic systems are meant to achieve in general. The word "economy" is derived from the Ancient Greek "oíkonomos," which refers to the management of a household's affairs. "Oíkos" was the term for the household. As an economic unit, a family faces two fundamental problems that it encounters again and again in ever varying forms. First, there are various tasks that must be performed conscientiously by the members of the family if it is to function well in economic terms. As well as working within the household, parents must put forth efforts to achieve sufficient income and to avoid getting into unsustainable debt. Children must pitch in at home and also do the schoolwork required for their education. All this assumes that each member of the family is motivated to perform the relevant tasks. But these individuals all have wills of their own, and these individual wills may cause problems for the family. Thus, the first fundamental economic problem of the family concerns its members' preparedness actually to join in the effort.

Second, the family must determine who will perform which tasks. The parents must discuss what outside work they might pursue, and whether to look for full- or part-time jobs, as well as how to share the work of the household. Regarding investments in children's education, decisions must be made that will influence their future professional opportunities. Agreements must be reached on how much income should be saved, and how the remaining income should be spent. In short, the family must continually decide how its available resources (limited time, energy, money, and so forth) will be used. Thus, the second fundamental economic problem of the family concerns the efficient use of its resources.

As a community with joint income and consumption, a family must ultimately take care to foster its members' willingness to cooperate and make the right use of its resources. The situation is similar in the case of an economic system. Although an economic system comprises a community much larger than a single family, the functions it must perform for that community to prosper correspond to those of a household system. An economic system must assure that individuals are genuinely motivated to carry out the tasks given to them, and that these tasks are economically reasonable. Thus we arrive at criteria that will help us judge the possible alternatives to capitalism. To be economically feasible, an alternative economic system must pass two tests: a cooperation test and an allocation test.

The first test asks whether a particular alternative to capitalism can provide sufficient economic cooperation among the members of the polity. Here, the questions in particular are whether individuals are prepared to participate actively in the production process, in accordance with their skills, and whether they are prepared to adapt their consumption to the limits set by the overall available resources (because a society cannot consume more than it produces). When applying this test, we must consider personal motives and establish whether the economic system in question motivates individuals to carry out their economic tasks to the best of their abilities.

The second test asks whether an alternative economic system is capable of bringing about a comparatively efficient allocation of resources. Here, the focus is on how the resources of a whole economy—such as human talents and labor power, as well as natural resources—are deployed vis-à-vis the alternative ways they could be. What consumer goods are produced? Is consumption or investment more favored? Are certain sectors of industry, or regions of the country, more or less supported? Are resources deployed to meet as many needs as possible, or is society wasting its resources?

To be preferable to capitalism, an alternative system must be able to solve both the problem of cooperation and the problem of allocation. It must be able to motivate individuals to act in economically meaningful ways and it must ensure that the use of available resources is temporally and spatially efficient.

Thomas More's presentation of Utopia is exceptionally well suited to be a starting point for a detailed analysis of the cooperation problem. The following reflections will focus on that aspect.

ECONOMIC SYSTEMS AND HUMAN CHARACTER

By placing these two criteria—incentives for cooperation and the allocation of scarce resources—at the center of our investigation, we open ourselves up to a criticism. Aren't we ignoring the most important characteristic of economic systems—namely, the kind of human beings they produce? Thus a clarification is in order; we must show that our approach is justified even if it is true that the effect an economic system has on human character is highly important.

Findings in the neurosciences suggest that the institutions that regulate the economic life of a society exert an influence on the development of its members' characters. A good economic system should therefore also have the property of producing "good human beings." In this respect, capitalism is not considered to be a good economic system by many of its critics, according to whom capitalism promotes human character traits that are incompatible with leading a good life.

A social psychologist critical of capitalism might make an argument along these lines:

> The combination of private property and the market system creates economic inequality and material insecurity. People who live under conditions of income inequality and material insecurity concentrate their attentions and energies on the generation of income and on the prudent use of it. This promotes avarice, jealousy, and greed, which in turn keep people from leading good lives. Market economies lead to a corrupting effect on all relationships between human beings. In a market, people encounter each other as buyers and sellers (or, in the case of the labor market, as capitalists and laborers) who have diametrically opposed interests when it comes to setting prices (or wages). Thus individuals face each other as adversaries in these negotiations. Moreover, people in capitalist systems experience conflict not only with their counterparts across the bargaining table, but also with the parties on their own side of the table, who become their competitors. As Plato observed so early on, the market system produces enmity instead of brotherhood.
>
> In the context of market transactions, both buyers and sellers hope to achieve better positions for themselves than they could achieve without market exchanges. The inherently hostile interactions between buyers and sellers therefore take place behind a shabby veil of politeness and create an atmosphere of false pretense that pervades all human relationships.
>
> To create better conditions of exchange for themselves, market participants dissemble, lie, and issue threats; the biggest rewards go to whichever side is best at cheating the other. As a selection mechanism, capitalism thus favors those who are best

at tricking other people. Those without scruples, who regard others only as means toward their own ends, are rewarded with higher income and hence more prestige and power. Such characters then become models for everyone else, and their attitude toward others becomes the norm and is taken for granted. As a result, capitalism promotes the fundamental attitude of a battle of "all against all," while any altruism or empathy is condemned to wither away.

The methodological argument that underlies this reasoning is clear: if economic institutions have an influence on human character, then this suggests that they should also be described in terms of that influence and be judged accordingly. The argument seems convincing not only because it is nicer to live among altruists than among egoists, but also because the long-term results of an economic system can be predicted more accurately when its influence on human character is taken into account.

While this approach is justified in principle, the problem with it is that we have too little knowledge about the ways in which different, and in particular not yet existing, social institutions can be expected to change the human character.

Let us take as an example More's hypothesis that a system of common ownership would produce better humans than the institution of private property. There is no proven theory from which the correctness of this hypothesis could be inferred. And unfortunately, the empirical evidence of what effects the institution of common ownership has on social psychology is far from being as unambiguous as utopian thinkers would like it to be. Consider the numerous small-scale utopian experiments of the last two hundred years, from Robert Owen's New Harmony commune, founded in 1825, and Charles Fourier's Phalanxes, to the hippy communes of the 1970s. All started out with great enthusiasm, but in the end were undone by their members' desires for power, jealousies, and laziness. Similarly, the Kibbutz movement in Israel had to give up, relatively quickly, on radical attempts to prohibit private property among members, and was not able to expand beyond rather narrow limits. Or look at China in the aftermath of Mao's cultural revolution. The generation emerging out of the Chinese people's communes created the most economically successful example of predatory capitalism to date. Even from the European monasteries, the most enduring institutions in which private property has been more or less abolished, come reports of deceit and malice that would seem to give the lie to the proposition that human beings who join a monastery become more altruistic.

Thus we must note that, so far, no solid basis of empirically provable facts has been established to support the hypothesis that common ownership "improves" human beings. And likewise, we can look at the other side of the coin: the hypothesis that private property and markets have a corrupting effect. That theory, perhaps too strongly influenced by observations of certain sectors of the market system, such as perceived excesses in the financial and insurance industries, also seems far-fetched. The anonymity of the market, in particular, prevents an overstretching of the limited capacities individuals have for cultivating meaningful interpersonal relations. The clearly defined responsibilities associated with private property might even foster some of the more desirable aspects of the human character, such as the ability to take responsibility for oneself. And intense market competition often produces a welcome disciplining effect, as potential fraudsters are aware that being found out as a liar will mean no one will want to do business with them. Honest people, by contrast, profit when they are able to earn the trust of other market participants, because it opens up more business opportunities.

To sum up, we can do no more than cautiously speculate about the alterations in human character that might result from systemic changes to the economy. Any claim about the superiority of a particular economic system that is based solely on its posited implications for human character is therefore not very convincing. To be on the safe side, it is wise always to proceed on the assumption that alternative economic systems—at least to begin with—must function with human beings as they are today. And this is what I shall do from here on, unless otherwise stated.

SPATIAL PLANNING ON AN ISLAND
THAT LIES NOWHERE

Let us return to Thomas More. In his description of Utopia, he places great emphasis on spatial planning within the polity. The idea that spatial and social order should harmonize was widespread in Renaissance culture, and it continues to inspire architects and urban planners to the present day. It therefore seems appropriate to provide a short description of the physical landscape of this island before embarking on the actual discussion of its political and economic system.

If we were traveling by plane, we could easily identify Utopia due to its peculiar shape, that of a crescent moon. At its broadest part—the middle—the island measures some two hundred miles across. More than twelve million people live on it, distributed across fifty-four almost identical cities all roughly equidistant from each other.

Such geometrical regularities characterize not only the network of settlements on the island but also the spatial arrangement of the cities. On Utopia, the spatial organization is the same in each of them. They are divided into four sections of equal size, with about sixty thousand inhabitants living in each section. A large square can be found at the center of each section. This square is a space for social interaction, and also of central importance for the workings of the economy, because it serves the purpose of collecting and distributing all newly produced articles of daily use.

The urban population lives in elegant, three-story, terraced houses. Each house faces the street at the front and has a garden at the back that is clearly visible from the next street. A traveler would be amazed at the wonderful sight afforded by the Utopians' gardens. Their condition of being so well kept is owed to a spirit of competition, with each street's residents vying with others to have the most beautiful gardens.

Each house in the city is occupied by just one family, but it is a large family. As a rule, it consists of about forty individuals, of which between ten and sixteen are adults. The large proportion of children reminds us of the fact that childhood mortality was extremely high in More's times. The people who live together in a house need not be related in the strictest sense, as there are forms of adoption, which we shall examine later. The family is a community permanently living together, and it plays a central economic role in Utopia. Each family is headed by a father and a mother of the house; they are responsible for it, and represent it to the outside world. The father and mother of a house are usually each the oldest member of their sex living in the house.

The doors of the houses are designed so that they cannot be locked. The inhabitants allow anyone to enter, as the Utopians do not have private property and the houses themselves are also common property. The families are allocated their houses by lot, and every ten years houses are redistributed by families' drawing lots again.

COLLECTIVE DECISION-MAKING

Most political decisions in Utopia are made through a system of indirect democracy within a federal structure. The system works from the bottom up. Every city is divided into four quarters as equal in size as possible. Within each quarter, subgroups are determined made up of thirty neighboring families—thus each subgroup consists of roughly 1,200 individuals, of which more than half are children. Every year, each subgroup elects a representative, called a philarch. Given a population of 240,000 inhabitants per city, this adds up to two hundred representatives for each city. These philarchs perform various public functions. In particular, they elect the prince of the city, who corresponds to a modern mayor. The right to nominate candidates in this election lies with the people, with each of the city's sections electing one candidate. Out of these four, the prince is then determined in a secret ballot at an assembly of the philarchs.

A prince is elected for life, unless there is a suspicion that he is seeking to enslave the people in some way, in which case he can be removed from office. The elections that determine the prince of a city are therefore taken very seriously by the Utopians—they are not repeated every four or five years. Another consequence of this rule is that the office holder is not tempted to act in a shortsighted way, with the date of the next election in mind. Lifelong office also means that lucrative jobs after the office holder's period in office, such as becoming the head of a large foreign bank, for instance, are not in the cards. This rules out one of the routes through which financially powerful enterprises and associations can purchase political influence.

In every city on Utopia, public matters are discussed every three days by the prince together with twenty archphilarchs. The latter represent the philarchs, and while their term of office is just one year, they are rarely replaced. Apart from that, every city has a senate, which deliberates over collective concerns and passes resolutions. It consists of philarchs who serve in rotation. There are also people's assemblies at which certain public matters are discussed. Every year, each of the fifty-four cities sends three experienced citizens as representatives to the island's supreme council. The council's seat is the capital of Utopia, Amaurot.

THE ECONOMIC SYSTEM

The economic system of Utopia does not know the central institutions of capitalism—private property and markets—because it is a system of common ownership. Within our system, private property and markets serve the purpose of resolving the twin problems of cooperation and allocation. Private property motivates people to produce, exchange, and be cautious in their consumption. Markets coordinate the economic decisions of households and enterprises. If a polity abandons these institutions, it will need others to perform the same functions.

More explains only how economic cooperation comes about on Utopia. In this context, he needs to argue against the belief that private property is necessary to instill economic reason in people, a belief that was as widely held then as it is now. The common view of the matter is that whoever has no personal reason for earning a living will not make any effort, and in the long term will become lazy; whoever does not need to pay for what he consumes will become wasteful. If everything belongs to all, where should appropriate incentives regarding work and consumption come from?

AGRICULTURAL PRODUCTION

Two areas of industry are responsible for most of the production on Utopia: agriculture and the crafts. The agricultural labor performed by the Utopians is done as a citizen's duty. Around every city there is arable land assigned to the city for agricultural production. The rural population lives on farms of about forty people each. This is not a permanent peasant population, however, because agricultural labor is organized on a principle of rotation. Every citizen, at some point or other in life, is sent to the country and must work on a farm for two years. Those who take a liking to farm work may stay on longer. More's reasoning behind this arrangement is that agricultural work is not interesting enough to attract enough volunteers, and therefore a citizen's duty based on legal compulsion is required.

This arrangement resembles military service or other nonmilitary kinds of national service in some modern societies, and can be understood as forming a part of a social contract. The Utopian citizen's duty concerns agriculture because this was the foundation of a nation's economy in More's time. In a Utopia of today, such a duty would perhaps be introduced for other areas and jobs that are at present indispensable yet do not attract enough volunteers.

In contrast to houses in the city, the farmhouses are often inhabited by two families at the same time. First, one half of family B moves from the city to the countryside, where they live for one year with half of family A, who have already been there for a year. At the end of the year, the members of family A return to the city, and the second half of family B moves in. After another year, the first half of family B returns to the city and is replaced with twenty members of family C, and so on. This makes sure that new arrivals are not left to their own devices, but are surrounded by people who have already worked the land for a year and can instruct them in the necessary skills. In this way, the rotation in the performance of agricultural tasks can take place with minimal training costs.

Agricultural production is organized by the philarchs of the farmers—that is, of those families currently living in the countryside—in agreement with the urban authorities. The city provides to the farmers free of charge everything they need that cannot be produced in the countryside, such as some consumer goods and tools for agricultural production. In the harvest season, the requisite number of harvest helpers are sent to the country. The farmers retain that part of the harvest they need for subsistence and agricultural production, and pass the rest on to the city.

THE CRAFTS

The other important economic sector for Utopia is craft production. Each citizen learns a craft and practices it. The choice of craft is freely made, but usually citizens learn their fathers' crafts. Anyone choosing another occupation must leave their house and be adopted by another family whose members practice that desired craft. Each family living together in one house therefore specializes in just one craft, and its members comprise an independent enterprise. The family is thus the fundamental unit of Utopia's production system.

The altruism intrinsic to families simplifies the running of the production process and hence becomes beneficial to the entire economy. Every inhabitant of Utopia must be embedded within a family to enjoy all political and economic rights and fulfill all political and economic duties.

Utopians are given fairly light workloads, to grant them sufficient free time for education, the arts, hobbies, and social life. Craftsmen work six hours per day—three in the morning and three in the afternoon. This is sufficient for covering all of society's needs for consumer goods, because there are no unproductive aristocrats or royal courts that have to be maintained, and also because all women also practice a craft.

The two periods of work are separated by a generous lunch break, long enough for a meal and two hours of rest. Usually, the meals are taken together. Each philarch, representing thirty families, has a hall at his disposal where his families may eat. This is also where dinner takes place, accompanied by music. Each hall has a chef who is responsible for overseeing food preparation. Utopians are also allowed to cook and eat at home but, given the delicious food on offer at the hall, doing so is rarely their preference.

Not all inhabitants of a city who are fit for work have to be craftsmen or cooks. In every city, nearly five hundred people are exempt from the duty to work and take up tasks in research, religion, or politics. These people form the ranks of learned men. Individuals join these ranks having been recommended by priests, and subsequently elected by the philarchs in a secret ballot. As long as a learned man is successful, he is freed from manual labor. If he fails to live up to the hopes that were placed in him, he is relegated to the rank of craftsman.

The ambassadors, priests, archphilarchs, and prince are usually selected from the ranks of the learned men. The priests, it should be noted, may belong to any of several religions, and the temples are shared by all religions. There is freedom of religion in Utopia, and the priests are elected by the people. Their task is first and foremost to teach the children. They are allowed to marry and start families. Women are equally able to join the priesthood, and they are neither advantaged nor disadvantaged in the selection process.

UNPLEASANT WORK

Unfortunately, there are some types of work that are indispensable for the satisfaction of important social needs that carry with them significant physical or psychological dangers. The citizens of Utopia are not expected to engage in such activities. As examples, More mentions the slaughtering of animals (which gradually blunts that most human of all feelings, empathy), and the cleaning of the communal dining halls. On Utopia, such activities are carried out by slaves.

Of course, Utopian slaves are not private property; they perform services for all. Nevertheless, some readers may be surprised about their presence in a text purporting to depict a humanist utopia. Where do the slaves come from?

More mentions three foreign sources and one domestic source for the slaves. First, prisoners of war are made slaves if they come from a state that launched a military attack on Utopia. Second, if necessary, Utopia acquires slaves from abroad by cheaply buying convicts who have been sentenced to death in their countries. Third, some foreigners voluntarily apply to become slaves; life as a Utopian slave is preferable to life in their home country. Finally, citizens of Utopia may themselves be consigned to slavery if they have committed serious misdeeds. This form of punishment is also important for the economic system because it represents the maximum penalty for those who do not abide by the rules of the system of common ownership.

These various types of slaves are treated in different ways. The foreign slaves who come voluntarily, for instance, are treated almost identically to normal citizens, and are allowed to return to their home countries at any time. By contrast, enslaved Utopians who have committed misdeeds are treated harshly. Despite having been educated according to the high moral standards of their country, they chose to betray them.

The presence of slaves shows how alien the idea of technological development was to More. If he had made the acquaintance of his contemporary, Leonardo da Vinci, he might have seen the opportunity to have machines instead of slaves relieve the burdens of unpleasant work. But without slavery he would also have had to think of a different punishment for those who do not abide by the rules of the system of common ownership. We will return to this point later, because the threat of punishment is closely related to the problem of cooperation.

DISTRIBUTION OF GOODS

How do goods pass from Utopia's producers to its consumers? The mechanism is very simple. Each family produces a particular kind of goods and brings them to public warehouses at the center of their quarter of the city. There, all goods produced by craftsmen and foodstuffs delivered from the surrounding countryside are gathered together. From these large warehouses the families of the quarter take what they need. But only the fathers of the houses may freely enter the warehouses; they check the supplies in the warehouse and take home what their families need—no more and no less.

If one of the island's cities has a certain good in abundance that is scarce in another city, then it passes that stock on to the other city as a gift. All in all, Utopia produces more than its inhabitants consume, indicating a high level of prosperity. The surplus is exported and exchanged for gold, silver, and iron. Iron needs to be imported because there is no ore on Utopia. Gold and silver are amassed by the state because of their usefulness in foreign affairs, particularly for bribing foreign enemies and recruiting foreign mercenaries during war. Utopians despise war as something altogether brutish. To avoid foreign attacks, they diligently train themselves in military discipline and pursue a sophisticated foreign policy.

UTOPIA AND THE PROBLEM OF COOPERATION

No unemployment, a high level of prosperity that is equally distributed, universal and lively social participation, and genuine political freedom—these are impressive achievements, at least if we ignore the existence of slavery. More named the island "Nowhere," not "No way," indicating that he probably considered the design of Utopia's institutions more than mere indulgence in fantasy. Could Utopia's economic system actually have worked in the way he described it?

As we've noted, for an economic system to function properly, it must pass the cooperation test. It must have rules that guarantee that individuals are prepared to take part in the production process, and its rules must encourage individuals to limit their consumption in accordance with the constraints of the overall economy. To what extent can Utopia's economic system—common ownership without private property and without markets—fulfill these fundamental requirements?

We know, of course, how capitalism brings about cooperation in the activities of production. Cooperative behavior, for most of the people who have lived under capitalism so far, is encouraged by a very simple and brutal rule: "He who does not work, does not eat." By this rule, the majority of people fit to work are forced by the institutions of capitalism to participate in the social process of production. Those who do not abide by it, and who rather help themselves to the private property of others without the owners' consent, are pursued by the police and live more or less on the margins of society. Such individuals are called thieves.

Under capitalism, individuals sell their labor power for a wage and then use those earnings to buy what is needed for their and their dependents' subsistence. The Utopian system, by contrast, grants the working individual—or, more precisely, the male head of the working household—direct access to the needed goods. Under capitalism, those who refuse to work will starve because they have no money. On Utopia, nonworkers also have to reckon with harsh consequences: they are persecuted by the state and may face enslavement. Thus, both economic systems feature strong incentives to take part in the production process.

Nevertheless, to be economically meaningful, incentives must do more than ensure that people merely turn up at their workplaces physically. While that might allow them to say in a formal sense that they participate in the production process, any genuine solution to the cooperation problem must bring about their active participation. This is why Marx emphasized that, under capitalism, what is sold is not labor but labor power. For a certain period of time—say, forty hours per week—employees place their labor power at the disposal of an employer, but this alone does not solve the cooperation problem. There is still a need to ensure that the employed laborer actively engages in the work to be done, and delivers actual labor of a quantity and quality that satisfies the demands of production. Utopia, with its system of common ownership, has the same challenge. To pass the cooperation test, its rules must make sure that those fit to work actually do so to the best of their abilities.

INCENTIVES TO WORK UNDER CAPITALISM

Under capitalism, firms use a broad range of methods to encourage their employees to put in the desired effort. Some methods we might characterize as providing psychological inducements and rewards. Large-scale firms, for instance, often try to make affiliation with their enterprise central to workers' sense of identity. Small-business owners trying to motivate good work often attempt to cultivate esprit de corps among their employees, and to build personal bonds with them. Other methods provide more material incentives and disincentives, using classic carrots and sticks like pay raises and threats of job loss to influence behavior. Of these two broad categories, the latter methods are far less available in a system of common ownership like Utopia's. Let us therefore consider their significance in more detail.

The decisive stick wielded by capitalism is the threat of dismissal in cases where an employee's performance falls below an employer's expectations. This threat, however, performs its "educational" purpose only if there is a meaningful level of unemployment in the economy. If a dismissed employee can immediately find another comparable job, dismissal entails no real penalty. Further, it is necessary that the employers observe the employees closely enough to establish with sufficient certainty if a particular employee is really slacking off. Whether this criterion is fulfilled depends on the nature of the job and the extent of the employee's underperformance. In some labor relations, the threat of dismissal plays only a subordinate role, because there are many uncertainties involved and employers do not want to risk committing the error of mistakenly dismissing good employees. In countries such as Germany, the force of this threat is also limited by the existence of laws providing legal protection against unfair dismissal.

There may be several reasons for an employer's lack of information regarding the actual performance of an employee. Usually it is hard to measure the employee's actual input into the production process, especially in such a way as would suffice as evidence for lawful dismissal in front of a labor court. More often than not, employers gain insight into the actual participation of employees only by observing outputs of the production process—that is, the amount of goods produced or services performed. Just measuring the results of a production process, however, doesn't mean that accurate information has been obtained about the effort put in by an employee. First, if there are multiple employees involved in the same production process it is difficult to tease out their individual contributions. Second, productivity measurement is subject to error at the best of times, and often key aspects of production output simply cannot be measured at a reasonable cost. This applies not only to the quality of the product, but also to the wear and tear to the machinery and other tools caused by the employee. Third, many accidental factors, which are independent of the employee's efforts, and which cannot be precisely established by the employer, can also influence production output.

In the case of tasks that are relatively easy for the employer to monitor and that offer the employee little room for maneuver, the threat of dismissal often suffices as a disciplining measure. Nevertheless, a certain room for maneuver always exists. Even work at an assembly line, or a harvest, can be performed with varying degrees of care without the employee's needing to be afraid of immediately being fired. In the case of tasks that are more difficult to monitor and that offer the employee greater room for maneuver, the threat of dismissal clearly is not enough. Employers therefore use the positive incentive of higher remuneration in the form of bonuses, salary increases, and promotions within the hierarchy of the enterprise, all of which are predicated on perceived increases in performance.

Thus, linking the remuneration of employees to their measured performance is a central instrument used by capitalists to create the desired incentives within the production process and thus to solve the cooperation problem. It is an effective but by no means perfect instrument, as it has certain deficiencies even when looked at from the narrow perspective of whether it promotes efficiency. In particular, it forces employees to bear an income risk that could better be borne by the employer. If you think about it, making wages dependent on production results allows unpredictable factors and errors of measurement to have important effects on an employee's income. That introduces a level of uncertainty which puts a strain on the employee. And therefore, the income risk ends up raising the labor costs of the enterprise, because the employee has to be compensated for taking this risk. Under capitalism, the degree to which remuneration is tied to performance is thus a balancing act between two effects: the desirable creation of incentives, and the undesirable shifting of risk to employees.

THE LIMITED IMPACT OF A DUTY TO WORK

Returning to Utopia, there is no possibility of its institutions solving the problem of cooperation using threats of dismissal or performance-related pay systems, because there people know of neither unemployment nor money. Instead they rely on an official duty to work—a law demanding that all those fit to work must conscientiously practice their occupations. Local authorities—the fathers of the houses and philarchs—make sure that this rule is being followed. Any violation represents an abuse of the system of common ownership and is punished by the state, with the city's senate deciding on the severity of the sentence. As private property does not exist, a financial penalty is not an option. The worst sentence that may be handed down is being made a slave.

Thus, Utopia solves the cooperation problem through a system of control that makes use of the local embeddedness of its citizens' lives. Every person does their work in the context of a large family, and each family is closely connected with its neighboring families through social and political institutions. Each group of thirty families elects its own representative, the philarch, who is at the same time one of them and the bearer of an office—that is, a representative of the general system of common ownership. He also acts as the inspector of families' houses as places of artisan production, and is responsible for ensuring that families make sufficient contributions to overall production. Thus, a philarch inspects thirty small-scale enterprises comprising a total workforce of about four hundred adults. On a given day, he might visit one enterprise in the morning and another in the afternoon, in which case it would take him fifteen working days to inspect all of the enterprises in his jurisdiction. If he finds that the duty to work is being neglected, he notifies the police and the judiciary springs into action. Among the Utopians, this threat replaces the capitalist threat of dismissal. The problem of cooperation is further addressed by social pressures to work and social disdain for freeloaders.

Whether these sticks are enough for Utopia to pass the cooperation test is not immediately clear. A skeptic might object that, at best, Utopia's institutions are able to solve the cooperation problem only to the extent that blatant violations of the work ethos would be avoided, but that they could not raise the level of performance beyond that. As a result, Utopia's warehouses would be mostly empty. In the view of such a critic, Utopia would fail the cooperation test. This is what the skeptic would say:

> For a philarch to be able to detect violations, it must first be determined what constitutes a violation; there must be requirements to be fulfilled by the producers. The authorities might, for instance, determine minimum quantities to be produced, depending on the type of craft and the size of the enterprise.
>
> If these minimum quantities are set too low, however, a substantial amount of productive capacity will remain unused. If they are set too high, taking average values from the past as a guide, it will be difficult to guarantee that the requirements are being adhered to, because if a lower quantity is produced, that does not automatically mean that the family who produced it was lazy. Various accidental factors, such as illness of a family member, could have negatively affected the result. Thus, to avoid injustices, the norms for production would need to be fairly modest—that is, close to the lower limit of what can reasonably be expected.
>
> In any case, such a system would lack any incentives for the producers to raise their performance above the fixed minimum level and to realize their full potential. Penalties may keep performance from falling below a certain norm, but they offer no upside productivity boosts; for that, one would need "negative penalties" that depend on actual output. This is exactly what bonuses and promotions achieve within the capitalist system. Money as a universal medium of reward allows for finely graded remuneration that depends on actual performance, and also allows for the flexible adaptation of incentives to changing circumstances. Neither is possible in the Utopian system, given its lack of a monetary economy.
>
> It is also questionable whether the philarchs themselves would be sufficiently motivated to control their craftsmen. They have only very weak incentives to do so, and may even have

some disincentives. Reporting idlers will no doubt cost them some votes when they stand for reelection. Therefore some authority would be needed to monitor, at the level of the quarter of the city, whether the aggregate production of the families working under the supervision of a particular philarch equaled the required minimum. But again, for the same reasons mentioned above, such an authority would be limited in its impact; at best it could compel philarchs to exercise a minimum of control. The best one might expect, then, is that the Utopians keep to comparatively low labor productivity norms without making full use of their capacity for production.

The story grows still worse when we recognize that these weak incentives on the side of production correspond to strong incentives on the side of consumption. Under capitalism, disposable income levels limit the claims to consumption, and market incomes establish a relatively close connection between an individual's contribution to the creation of social wealth and the consumption possibilities that individual receives from society. For Utopians, such a connection does not exist, because every family may take from the public warehouses whatever it needs—independent of the contribution the family has made. Why would the father of a family not take the greatest amount of consumption goods he can possibly carry, or the rarest goods of the highest quality?

COOPERATION IN THE SIXTEENTH CENTURY

The results that a particular economic system can yield depend not only on its fundamental rules, but also on the general conditions under which it operates, and especially its level of technological development. The common ownership conceived by More might well have worked under the technological conditions of his time, at least in the sense that those living in such an economic system would have been sufficiently motivated to act in an economically reasonable manner—that is, at least well enough to solve the cooperation problem. This seems possible for three reasons.

First, it is safe to assume that the craftsmen on Utopia enjoy working. Where workers hold positive attitudes towards their work, their strong intrinsic motivation can make additional incentives superfluous. On Utopia, we may expect to see people taking that high level of professional pride and general pleasure in their work, because they choose their occupations precisely according to these criteria. They practice a particular craft because they like it, often following a family tradition, and not because they want to earn as much money as possible. Extrinsic incentives for work should also be unnecessary because the working hours are so short. Laboring just six hours per day probably means ending one's workday before boredom, stress, and weariness set in. With such short hours, work is rarely experienced as a heavy burden— especially if, as on Utopia, the occupation is freely chosen, the working hours are comfortably arranged, and work takes place in pleasant company within one's own house. Imagine no need to commute.

Free occupational choice raises the question, of course, of how Utopia manages to fill all jobs adequately. In the absence of a labor market, how does it attract enough takers for work that is relatively unattractive, but not unattractive enough to be consigned to slaves? It is a good question, but because it relates to the economic problem of allocation it can be left to a later chapter. Here, let us just point out that in comparison to today, the economy of More's times was far less complex, and much less information would have been needed to solve the allocation problem.

Second, Utopia would appear to be a place that offers few alternatives for spending one's time. We are told that there are no pubs or clubs on Utopia. As the cities are to a large extent identical, we can guess that tourism plays only a minor role. Even if it held some attraction, traveling requires permission and is subject to strict rules. And in More's time, there are, of course, no electronic devices on which to play games, chat, and surf the Internet. Given these conditions, we can easily imagine that work is not considered a bitter necessity, but rather a welcome and popular pastime—and the temptation to shirk is weak.

Third, there is little reason to consume more than one's share on Utopia. On their visits to warehouses, consumers find no luxury goods to covet. To the contrary, luxury is ridiculed on Utopia. Gold and silver are used for making chamber pots and for the rings and chains that

must be worn by criminals as punishment. Out of the pearls and dia-
monds they occasionally collect, the Utopians make toy jewelry for
small children. Just as nowadays girls stop playing with their dolls when
they grow up (showing that they are no longer children), the older youth
of Utopia move on from their pearl and diamond playthings. The gar-
ments of the Utopians, which families produce for themselves, are very
simple and are everywhere much the same. Products in the warehouses
of the Utopian cities are also very limited in their variety.

These three factors set crucial limits to the temptations individuals
might have to exploit the system of common ownership. The fact that
every worker has strong local attachments also creates social pressure
not to behave selfishly. Pressure, too, comes from that ultimate threat
faced by shirkers—the prospect of being made slaves. All this taken
together suggests that the economic system of Utopia was indeed a
practicable alternative to the early capitalism of the sixteenth century,
regardless of what More himself thought about this question.

This conclusion is of little help to a critic of modern capitalism, however, because the factors mentioned above that speak in favor of Utopia's economic viability would be highly problematic as elements of an
alternative economic system today.

One problem is that, if the dominant factor in every worker's choice
of profession is their sheer love of that line of work, there is great potential for an inefficient division of labor. And given the current level of
technological development, a division of labor that is at least halfway
efficient is a necessary condition for achieving prosperity.

There is another problem, too. To arrive at similar levels of restriction
regarding people's alternative uses of leisure time, and regarding the
goods and services available for consumption, would require a drastic
narrowing of the range of potential human activities and thus of the
freedom and development of individuals. Such restrictions might have
been acceptable in an economy based on the technological conditions
of the Renaissance—at a time when only a small minority had experienced anything like a profligate life. But now we are considering a
hypothetical system of common ownership in the twenty-first century.
What people today would accept a substantial renunciation of their
accustomed leisure activities or consumption? Even politicians of green

parties seem unable to give up the conveniences of a bourgeois lifestyle. No system of common ownership in the twenty-first century would get far trying to artificially limit how people's free time could be spent or cull the diverse delights of the consumer world. But if these were all left in place, then the temptations for individuals to abuse common ownership for their personal interests would be great.

IS COMMON OWNERSHIP CONCEIVABLE IN THE TWENTY-FIRST CENTURY?

Let us now move to a level of abstraction from the particular rules of Utopia and consider what they might suggest for a comprehensive system of common ownership that we might wish for ourselves today. In this system, which might hypothetically spread over just one country, a whole continent, or the whole world, the norms for labor and claims to goods and services could be decided democratically. Work norms would establish how long and with what intensity an individual must work. These norms would not be uniform. To be just, work norms would need to vary depending on profession, industrial sector, and place, as well as on the worker's age and health. The consumption norms would be equally differentiated. They would determine the final use of material goods and immaterial services depending on relevant household characteristics.

The work norms should bring about an efficient use of a society's labor capacity. The norms for consumption should ensure a balanced consumption structure that takes the needs of all individuals into account. The two types of norms should be consistent with each other, as a population cannot consume more than it produces. All norms should be designed so that such a balance is achieved for any good and any service. When the technological conditions or demographic structures change, the norms should be adapted accordingly to make sure that they always achieve an overall economic balance.

Let us assume that such just and efficient norms for labor and consumption have been established in a democratic decision-making process, so that our society-wide system of common ownership would produce general prosperity, if only all individuals would adhere to them. In that case, the economic viability of our system of common ownership would depend solely on individuals' willingness to cooperate—that is, to abide by those norms. In theory, this willingness could be enforced through legal requirements and the police. But, as we saw in the case of Utopia, these are not suited to motivate individuals to engage in highly productive labor and cautious consumption. Legal requirements and police may at best guarantee that cooperation does not fall below a minimum level. This, however, would not be enough to create an attractive alternative to capitalism, because a low level of cooperation ultimately means a low level of prosperity.

There are more attractive means available, however, than legal requirements and the police for upholding demanding norms for labor and consumption in a society-wide system of common ownership. Two mechanisms in particular are worth considering. First, motivation to cooperate may come from social norms, so that members of the system act on the expectation of general reciprocity. They cooperate because they want to maintain the cooperation of all others. Second, cooperative actions could spring from an internal sense of values. Individuals have a deep sense of what is right, and are able to hold a high opinion of themselves when they adhere to it. Rather than give that up, they might reject temptations to take advantage of the system of common ownership for their own purposes.

What are the conditions under which such mechanisms could solve the problem of cooperation in a society-wide system of common ownership? The following chapter attempts to answer this question.

3

COOPERATION, RATIONALITY, VALUES

WE ARE IN THE YEAR 2050. Few people remember the bleak days of capitalism. For a long time now, everything has belonged to everyone. Money, markets, and profit-hungry corporations no longer exist. Demanding norms for labor and consumption have been democratically established; they apply to all of the planet's inhabitants and are voluntarily adhered to by everyone. Although no one is forced to do so, everyone works to the best of their abilities for the common good, and everyone voluntarily limits their consumption in such a way that all can satisfy their needs to the same degree.

Is this an altogether unrealistic scenario?

This chapter aims to provide some deeper insights into the mechanisms that could solve the problem of cooperation among the members of a free, society-wide system of common ownership. In contrast to the prior two chapters, this argument will not be based on a particular text, but will consider the fundamental factors that determine whether an economy organized in this way could work or not. Thus, the question to be answered is: What are the conditions under which the members of an economy based on common ownership would put in the necessary effort, despite not being paid for it and not being subject to any sort of police compulsion? These conditions will turn out to be less restrictive than one might think.

If the economy of a whole nation functioned as a free system of common ownership, then it would be a bit as though it were

Christmas every day. Every day, the members of the community would freely give their labor and would be presented with goods that others have produced with their labor. Christmas works even with people who have been socialized under capitalism: Every year, almost everyone gives one or more gifts, even though no one is forced to. It probably happens more frequently that someone picks the wrong present (a case of misallocation) than that someone of whom a present is expected neglects to give one (indicating a lack of cooperation).

This analogy with Christmas is apt because common ownership can only work if the willingness to give gifts becomes a fundamental attitude among its producers and consumers. The question then becomes: Under what conditions does such an attitude develop?

A person giving a gift to another person might be doing so for any number of reasons. We can divide these reasons into three categories. First, a gift may come straight from the heart: the giver is interested in the well-being of the recipient and truly wishes to make that person happy. In this case, the gift arises out of love, friendship, or sympathy for the other person. Second, a gift can be given for strategic reasons; the giver expects it to produce some advantageous reaction. The expectation might be that the recipient will reciprocate with a valuable gift in the future, or even that others will reward the giver's observed act of generosity. Third, a person may bestow a gift out of a sense of moral duty; not to act in this way would leave him or her feeling guilty.

In a system of common ownership, the requisite cooperative behavior might in principle be driven by these three types of motivation. Individuals would contribute labor to the community in that case because they loved its members, or expected individual advantages in return, or felt morally obliged to do so—and perhaps all three reasons would factor into their behavior. Rather than assume that all these motivations would be active at the same time, however, it is useful to look at them one by one, and to examine their individual plausibility. After evaluating the limits of each of the motivations in isolation, we can take their interplay into account and try to ascertain their overall potential.

CHARITY: GIVING FROM THE HEART

Would it be possible to support cooperation within a society-wide system of common ownership solely with the power of charity? This would mean that every member of the community would be prepared to give simply out of the goodness of his or her heart: to share and to make sacrifices for others without in any way demanding things in return—that is, without making claims on any goods or services.

It is useful to distinguish between two forms of charity: concrete and abstract. Everyday life is full of examples of concrete charity. These are cases of a pronounced and permanent altruism shown toward concrete individuals, in particular toward family and friends, to whom our gifts are given. This does not concern only material gifts, but also the kind of personal attention that is shown to someone in difficulty.

Although this concrete form of charity is probably the most important source of human happiness, it could hardly amount to a solution to the cooperation problem in a society-wide system of common ownership. The reason is simple. In a technologically highly advanced and globalized economy, few people know whom they actually make happy with the product of their labor—that is, to whom they would actually give their gifts.

Most people working in a complex economy with a pronounced division of labor would find it impossible to identify who exactly was using the products they produced. Some of these "recipients" of products would not yet even be born at the time the producer made the good they would one day use—think, for example, of highways and houses, which are used over many generations. Where it is not clear who the recipient of a gift is, the idea of charity toward known individuals does not enter into the equation, because its necessary object is missing. Thus, concrete charity cannot serve as the general motivating force for economic behavior.

To sustain generous behavior, therefore, in our hypothetical system of common ownership in the twenty-first century, we would need abstract charity. Producers and consumers would need to be inspired by a generalized love for mankind to make sacrifices for people they do not know.

In theory, this is conceivable—and to be sure, most of the relief and charitable organizations that support people in need all over the world depend on this kind of charity. This shows that incipient forms of the sort of altruism we seek for our system of common ownership already exist in our current society. Yet, we must also admit that such altruism is not universally present and that it tends to be reserved for people in the most extreme need. It is hard to imagine that our abstract love for all inhabitants of the planet would prove so motivating that we would get up early every day to perform even the most tedious aspects of our work. We could probably think of several other things we would rather do. If the members of the community we are imagining are made of the same stuff as us, it is doubtful that their abstract charity would be sufficient to solve the problem of cooperation.

Individuals who make sacrifices out of charity throughout their lives are usually considered saintly; they are seldom found on this earth. We should therefore not rely solely on charity to make sure that a global system of common ownership passes the cooperation test.

SOCIAL NORMS: I GIVE SO THAT YOU SHALL GIVE

As mentioned above, there are two further mechanisms that could solve the problem of cooperation in a system of common ownership: social norms and internalized values. The former work by engaging individuals' desires to conform to social conventions; the latter guide individuals to act according to the ethical principles they personally embrace. Turning first to social norms, let's consider how a society might cultivate a strong, broad expectation of mutual gift-giving or reciprocity.

I'll scratch your back, if you'll scratch mine: reciprocal behavior is an everyday occurrence. Friendliness is rewarded with friendliness. This helps to maintain cooperation among individuals without depending on money. Community groups, clubs, associations, and other initiatives in which we participate without expecting payment all function on this basis. Nevertheless, there are many cases in which cooperative behavior would be beneficial for all but does not occur. Just think of the trash left behind in public parks, or of the deteriorating public infrastructure in some developing countries, where the users are charged with its upkeep in the absence of the state's administration taking responsibility. Hence, there must be factors that favor the emergence of norms that demand cooperation, and other factors that obstruct their emergence. To identify these factors has always been one of the most important aims of the social sciences.

At first glance, social norms appear to be the results of habit and imitation: People behave with decency because others do, and because this is how people behaved in the past. Habit and imitation no doubt bring about a certain inertia in social behavior. Nevertheless, there are many examples of norms being eroded and replaced by different ones, and so there must be something other than routine that is decisive in securing the persistence of social norms. This factor is the calculated advantage for the individual in following the norm; conversely, it is precisely when individual actors realize that it is better for them to violate a social norm that even long-standing norms begin to deteriorate. The first deviators may signal to the others that it might be advantageous for them to violate the norm, too—and so it only takes a few individuals to throw social routines into question, to destroy norms, or even to prevent them from forming.

These reflections suggest a way of finding out which social norms will survive in the long run. Stable norms are rules for behavior that are obeyed even by those who rationally examine whether they would be better off if they followed a different pattern of behavior. Strategic thinkers examine not only the immediate consequences, but also the indirect consequences of their behavior. Thus, someone may consider that his or her violation of a social norm may lead other individuals to violate the norm, and that adhering to a norm may lead others also to adhere to it. Precisely such reasoned expectations regarding reciprocal behavior may sustain a norm of gift-giving in a system of common ownership.

Gifts between Egoists

Which conditions would lead rational individuals in a system of common ownership to spend their time and energy working for the community on the basis of a social norm? Again, it is useful first to look at the efficacy of such a norm without taking the other two possible motivations (altruistic inclinations and moral principles) into account. As a point of departure, let us imagine some hypothetical rational individuals who strive only for a high level of prosperity for themselves and whose actions are exclusively based on a purposive rationality.

The fundamental conclusions of recent research on this problem can be illustrated by means of a simple thought experiment. Let us consider the case of a system of common ownership that consists of just two families, the Smiths and the Greens. The Smiths live in the city, the Greens in the countryside. The Smiths practice a craft, the Greens, agriculture. Each family promises that it will bring anything it produces that exceeds its subsistence needs to a warehouse at the edge of the city at the end of a specific period—say one month—at which point the other family will be able to collect the excess production. In short, the families promise to give gifts to each other. The Smiths give household items and tools, and the Greens give agricultural produce. If they put in the appropriate effort, each is capable of delivering the necessary goods to cover the other's needs. But will they keep their promises? Will they pass the cooperation test?

Let us imagine, further, that the warehouse is divided in two, and that each section can be locked. Each family has the key to one of the sections and can deposit its products in it at any time. At the agreed time, the two families exchange the keys and each has free access to the goods provided by the other.

At the beginning of the time period, the Smiths and the Greens plan their productive activities. At that point, each of the families has two options. They can either intend to produce enough to cover the needs of the other family as well, or they can organize their production so that only their own subsistence is covered—an option that, of course, requires less effort. Let us call the first option "cooperation" (C) and the second "shirking" (S). In the case of just two families, these two options result in four possible outcomes for our hypothetical system of common ownership.

In the first outcome (C, C), each of the families puts in the effort to produce for the other family and profits from the products delivered by the other family. In this case, the system of common ownership has passed the cooperation test.

In the second outcome (S, S), neither of the families does anything for the other. Both lack necessities. The result is that the cooperation problem has not been solved; the system of common ownership has failed.

In the third outcome (C, S), the first family has made an effort for the second and has been exploited. Despite putting in serious efforts, the cooperating family lacks necessities. The cooperation problem has not been solved.

In the fourth outcome (S, C), the opposite of the previous situation happens. The first family has shirked work while the second has cooperated. Again, the cooperation problem of common ownership has not been solved.

In terms of the material well-being of the families, it is clear that the first family's is highest in the fourth scenario (featuring low labor efforts, and high level of provision for itself) and lowest in the third scenario (featuring high labor efforts and a low level of consumption). Between these extremes are the scenarios of mutual cooperation and mutual shirking, with the well-being of the families being greater in the case of mutual cooperation than in the case of mutual shirking. Thus, from the perspective of the first family, the fourth outcome is the best, the first outcome is the second best, the second outcome is the third best, and the third outcome is the worst. An analogous ranking of preferences, only in reverse order with respect to outcomes 3 and 4, applies to the second family.

It is helpful to assign an index of well-being for each of the families to each of the outcomes, reflecting what they receive in each case. The payoff for each family in the advantageous case of their shirking and the other family's cooperating (S, C) will be represented by the Greek letter α. Mutual cooperation (C, C) will yield β. Mutual shirking (S, S) will yield γ. And the worst payoff, where the family cooperates but the other family shirks (C, S), will be represented by the letter δ. The preference rankings for the families, then, can be expressed as a series of "greater thans": $\alpha > \beta > \gamma > \delta$. Figure 1 sums up this thought experiment.

The Greens' Well-Being

The Smiths' Well-Being

	Greens cooperate	Greens shirk
Smiths cooperate	β	α
Smiths shirk	δ	γ

	Greens cooperate	Greens shirk
Smiths cooperate	β	δ
Smiths shirk	α	γ

Figure 1. Payoffs to Two Families under Four Scenarios
The matrices show the various payoffs the Green and Smith families may receive depending on their behavior. The top right-hand quadrants show that the Greens receive the highest well-being result, α, if they cooperate while the Greens shirk, while the Smiths receive the lowest result, δ, under those conditions.

Now, what happens if one of the families soberly examines whether it should adhere to the norm of cooperation? The answer is unambiguous. Regardless of what the other family chooses to do, it is always advantageous for the family to shirk—so, common ownership is doomed to fail. The Smiths, for instance, may think: "If the Greens put in extra effort for us (the left-hand column of the matrix), we receive a payoff of α if we choose to shirk, while we only receive β if we behave cooperatively. If, however, the Greens decide to shirk (the right-hand column), we receive γ if we also shirk, and only δ if we choose to cooperate. Regardless of what the Greens decide, we are always better off shirking, because we save ourselves the extra productive effort required to cover the Greens' needs. Thus, we should only work for ourselves."

Because the Greens reach the symmetric conclusion, no cooperation at all would take place in this system of common ownership. Both families would break their promises and the two sections of the warehouse would remain empty. Each family's payoff is γ, even though the higher payoff β could have been achieved. Expressed in terms of our matrix, the Smiths and Greens end up in the lower right-hand quadrant, although they could have found themselves in the top left-hand one where both are better off.

This failure reflects the tension between individual and collective rationality that typifies situations referred to in game theory as prisoner's dilemmas. Game theory is that part of applied mathematics that deals with the analysis of strategic interactions, and it is used by economists, political scientists, sociologists, and biologists researching the emergence of cooperation. The logical structure of the common ownership system we have been considering corresponds to the logical structure of the prisoner's dilemma discussed in game theory. In a prisoner's dilemma, no matter what the other player is doing, cooperation results in a lower payoff compared to a strategy of "defection" (the game theorist's term for refusal to cooperate). Cooperation is therefore not chosen as a strategy.

In game theory, those combinations of actions which result from the strategic interaction between rational players are called equilibria. In an equilibrium, none of the players has an incentive to change his course of action on his own. Nevertheless, an equilibrium may lead to a situation in which players as a group unanimously want to change their behavior collectively. When that happens, it shows that the equilibrium is inefficient, as in the hypothetical system of common ownership described above. In that case, players as a group would like to achieve the greater efficiency of mutual cooperation, yet the equilibrium is established by the fact that, as individuals, they choose to shirk.

Repeated Games

So far, we have limited our thought experiment to a system of common ownership that exists only as a one-off interaction. This assumption excludes an essential aspect of reciprocity—namely, that it develops over time. People often want to reward the past social behavior of others, and often they want to earn a subsequent reward from others. Such considerations are important incentives for cooperation at the workplace and in neighborhoods. To identify common ownership's chances of survival, it is therefore necessary to expand our thought experiment.

Instead of assuming that the system of common ownership formed by the Smiths and Greens has a lifespan of just one period of interaction, we now assume that the interactions described above will be repeated for several such periods. Let's assume, for example, that the system lasts a full year, and that the families exchange keys to the sections of the warehouse at the end of each month during that time. Thus, at the end of every month, each family collects goods for its own consumption that have been produced by the other family. For the following month, the sections for depositing the goods are swapped, and at the end of that month, the keys are again exchanged—and so on, until the end of the last month of the year.

Such repeated interactions create a threat of retaliation or "tit-for-tat" response that can complement the positive appeal of cooperation. To be more precise, each family can decide to trust the other initially, and therefore put in the extra effort for the other during the first period of time. But its behavior in subsequent periods of interaction will depend on what the other family does. If the other family reneges on the agreement, cooperation will be ended.

The question is whether such a threat actually would motivate rational egoists to cooperate. As we have seen, to begin with, each family has an advantage if it does not put in the extra effort for the other, but the cessation of cooperation that would follow such shirking would leave the family worse off in the long run. Both families would therefore consider such a step carefully. The short-term exploitation of the other family's trust raises a family's well-being from β to α for the first month. But once retaliation sets in, that family's well-being decreases from β to γ. Whether or not it pays for the family to cooperate thus depends on the relative values of "$\alpha-\beta$" and "$\beta-\gamma$" and the length of the period of retaliation. The longer the other family extends this period, the less it pays to cheat on them.

The incentive for cooperative behavior is strongest if both families threaten to end cooperation for good should they ever detect that they have been defrauded. This threat says: "If you cheat on me once, it is all over!" In game theory, such forms of behavior are called trigger strategies. A player who uses a trigger strategy begins with cooperation and continues to cooperate as long as he is not being cheated. The first time he is exploited triggers him to shirk indefinitely. Obviously, if all players followed a trigger strategy, then we would always observe cooperation.

In a system of common ownership, could the adoption of trigger strategies be the result of rational reflection by members? If we assume that the actors involved are all aware of one another's reflections, this, surprisingly, leads to a negative result. Even if the trigger strategies are publicly announced before the interactions begin, and even if α–β is much smaller than β–γ (meaning that cheating brings only minor gains, but is severely punished), the system of common ownership would not pass the cooperation test!

To understand the reason, think about the situation the families are in at the beginning of the last month of the proposed system. Suppose the interaction lasts from January to December. If, at the beginning of December, a family decides to work only to meet its own needs, it does not need to fear retaliation from the other family, because their interactions will end on December 31. Thus, in December, neither of the families has a reason to put in any effort for the other one. Of course, we might imagine they would suffer pangs of conscience for cheating people who had always cooperated with them. But we have decided to exclude such possibilities from our considerations for the moment, because we want to examine whether social norms could sustain cooperative behavior among individuals who are interested only in their own material well-being. If we assume this, it is clear that each of the families would work only for itself in December, independent of what has happened in the previous months.

What does this mean for the decisions made in November? It turns out not to pay for the families to cooperate in November either. After all, if one of the families exerts in the extra effort in November, it will not be rewarded for it in December, as we have already established that both families will tend to only their own needs in the last month. Thus, the two families will cooperate neither in December nor in November. And, of course, the same consideration then applies to October, given that there is no chance of cooperation in November or December. And this line of reasoning proceeds until we are all the way back in January. Strange as it may seem, if families think ahead, they will rationally decide to shirk in every month.

A Never-Ending Story

There is something peculiar about the stylized common ownership we have looked at so far: it is temporally limited. The families know exactly when the last interaction will take place, and at that point it will be impossible to achieve any cooperation between the two families. This is the reason, ultimately, that cooperation fails. But how does this conclusion change if we assume that the system of common ownership stretches across innumerable generations, and is not subject to any explicit time limit?

Let us take another look at our hypothetical economy consisting of the Green and Smith families, but this time we will suppose that, with respect to planning their productive activity, each family confronts an infinite time horizon. This does not mean that the community lasts forever; inevitably, the interactions will have a final period. This period, however, cannot be determined by the actors in advance. In other words, the system of common ownership exists for an indefinite period of time. Within this framework, the trigger strategies described above could constitute an equilibrium outcome.

We will assume that one of the families tells the other that it will behave reciprocally, with a trigger strategy. The latter family now reflects on what to do in light of this information. Is it rational for it also to adopt a trigger strategy? If there is no other strategy that is more advantageous for the family, then, in game theorists' terms, this constitutes a "best response" by the second family to the trigger strategy of the first family. If that is the case, then the trigger strategy is also the best response for the first family to the trigger strategy adopted by the second family, because the decision-making problem it has to solve is identical. If strategies are the best responses to each other they form an equilibrium: none of the players has an incentive to deviate from his or her strategy, as long as the other player adheres to his or hers. If the trigger strategies of the two families produce an equilibrium and thus stabilize each other, there will be eternal cooperation even though the members of the families are all pure egoists.

Under certain conditions, trigger strategies produce an equilibrium. Let us assume the Green family uses a trigger strategy. If the Smith family responds with the same strategy, it will receive a payoff of β each month. Alternatively, the Smiths may eventually deviate and exploit the Green family. This would give the Smith family a payoff of α for one month, but they will only receive this high payoff for the month in which they cheated, because thereafter retaliation will set in, and in all subsequent periods the Greens will only work for the satisfaction of their own needs. In all subsequent periods, the Smith family will only achieve a payoff of γ instead of β.

In the final analysis, whether it pays for a family to deviate from the trigger strategy depends on three factors. First, the temptation to cheat will grow if payoff α is large compared to payoff β. Second, the temptation will shrink if payoff β is large compared to payoff γ. Third, the temptation will weaken the more the families factor the future into their calculations. This last point is easy to explain. Cheating has negative consequences for the one who decides to cheat only if the system of common ownership continues to exist and the decider is interested in the level of future payoffs—perhaps because his or her children and grandchildren will live in this community in the future. The more likely it is that the interactions will continue, and the more pronounced the altruism toward one's descendants, the more the sanctions and their consequences will be part of the calculations.

These three factors may come into play to varying degrees and, in particular combinations, they will ensure that neither of the two families wants to deviate from the trigger strategy. In that case, the strategies will produce an equilibrium.

Thus, we have a qualified, positive initial result. Even among purely rational human beings who think only of themselves and their families, and know nothing of morality or civic virtue, the problem of incentives within a system of common ownership can be solved under certain conditions. A central precondition is that the system of common ownership is temporally unlimited. If that is the case, the problem of incentives can be solved by using trigger strategies, as long as payoffs are comparatively high under mutual cooperation and individuals consider future developments to be important—because they are, for example, concerned for the well-being of their children.

Credible Threats

Let us assume that the factors mentioned above have produced a positive outcome. This would mean that any deviations from the trigger strategy would prove to be unrewarding, and so the founders of the system of common ownership would announce that their members would adhere to it. Members would not violate the norm of cooperation, out of fear of reprisals.

But what would happen in this community if, one day, the Green family found to its surprise that there were no products waiting for it in the warehouse? According to the trigger strategy that had been declared when the community was founded, the Greens would have to stop cooperating from this point onwards. Instead of achieving the level of wealth corresponding to β, they would from then on only achieve that corresponding to γ, because the Smith family would then also continue with their noncooperation. In such a situation, the Smiths might send the Greens a message like the following: "It is true that last month we did not provide you with goods. But the past is the past, and there is no point in quarrelling over it now. We have the whole future ahead of us. Forget about retaliation: that would only lead to a γ-level of wealth for everyone. Let us rather make a conscious decision to return to the previous trigger strategy, and we shall continue to achieve the β-level of wealth."

This actually sounds like a reasonable suggestion. If it were accepted, both families would be better off. But what would happen if such a reasonable suggestion were accepted? In that case, the deviators would never be punished. And if the families anticipate this outcome from the very beginning, then the trigger strategy is no longer credible. Exploitation would not trigger any sanctions, because the families would just renegotiate their relationship—and in light of that, they would lose any incentive to cooperate in the first place. It turns out, then, that trigger strategies are no protection against the possibility that a superior course of action than the agreed punishment is negotiated in cases of deviation.

Nevertheless, game theorists have developed a solution to this difficulty. The credibility problem in trigger strategies arises from the fact that the one who is meant to be the punishing party is at the same time also punished, because the other party ceases cooperation as well. This is what introduces the possibility of renegotiation, and makes the threat ultimately not binding. To formulate a binding threat, a punishment must be specified that, should it become necessary, will undoubtedly be carried out by the punishing party. The question, then, is whether there is such a punishment.

The answer provided by game theory is: "Yes, under certain circumstances."

Suppose a victim of cheating were to adopt the following course of action: "Stop cooperating until you have established that the cheater has again put in the effort for you." In other words: a family that cheats over a period of time will be exploited in return for a period of time, so as to earn a return to mutual cooperation. It must "show remorse," so to speak. If it doesn't, both families remain in dire conditions (S, S).

In contrast to trigger strategies, this threat is genuinely credible, because the punishing party achieves an α-level of wealth, instead of a β-level (as in the case of cooperation). The party therefore has a real incentive to carry out the punishment, rather than just to "forget" that it was cheated by the other party. A social norm that demands that a cheater "show remorse" may thus be able to support cooperation within a community.

Large Communities

What about the incentive to punish in a system of common ownership extending across an entire society—a system that takes in not just two but a large number of families? According to the norm just formulated, if even a single family in such a system did not deliver its target production, all other families would need to stop delivering goods to the communal warehouse until that deviator family had "shown remorse" and started to deliver the agreed amount of goods again. This is hardly, however, a reasonable course of action where the number of families is large and the division of labor is advanced to a point where the production of one family covers only a tiny fraction of total consumption. The situation is similar to the one we came across when criticizing trigger strategies: the families would find that they were better off if they turned a blind eye and simply continued cooperating. And in that case the deviating party would not be punished, because its level of provision would not decrease. If the families anticipate such amnesties, they will no longer have an incentive to make an effort for the community.

These considerations yield another important insight: It tends to be more difficult in larger schemes of common ownership to solve the cooperation problem. True, a large community may try to inflict targeted punishments by not allowing deviators access to the goods for consumption until they have shown remorse, for instance by working overtime for the others. As in the hypothetical case of the two families, this threat could be credible and could support cooperation. But such targeted punishments create a new problem: Who exercises the coercion that guarantees that cheaters do not gain access to the communal warehouses?

Such an exercise of coercion represents yet another problem of social cooperation. If the exclusion of the deviators is guaranteed, this helps to uphold cooperation throughout the whole community. But it is costly to keep the cheaters away from the warehouse, because someone must guard the entrance rather than enjoying their leisure time. Each member of the community would want someone to take on this task—as long as it were someone else.

There are two ways in which we might try to get out of this new dilemma. The first one is to deny that the dilemma would actually arise. We might argue that, in a technologically highly advanced system of common ownership, information technology—even robots—can be used to punish freeloaders. Machines might, for instance, check whether the agreed amount of goods has been delivered, and at that point confirm the validity of a swipe card that enables access to the warehouses.

This first response is not wholly convincing, however, because the information problem is more difficult than it appears at first glance. It is not just a matter of checking whether the agreed amount of goods has been delivered, but also of ascertaining whether an insufficient delivery was deliberate or not. This is a point that will be discussed in more detail in the following section. Here, let it suffice it to say that today's lie detectors do not solve the problem, and computers that can read our minds are a distant prospect indeed.

The second response would be, in effect, to delegate the power to restrict access to the warehouses to a state police, and thus to move away somewhat from the ideal of a free system of common ownership. But this proposed solution also has its problems. It is not enough to invoke coercion by the state to establish cooperation among egoists, because, in line with our assumptions, the individuals who would make the state function would themselves be egoists. Ultimately, then, the effectiveness of the state would rest on nothing but a social norm. The empirical evidence regarding the functioning of states and their civil servants provides a broad range of possibilities, from a strong rule of law (corresponding to high cooperation) right up to rampant corruption (corresponding to high shirking). Thus, the possibility of enforcing cooperation through the state only shifts our problem onto another level; it does not solve it.

Asymmetrical Information

As is becoming clear, cooperation within a system of common ownership depends on the information that is available for the purposes of mutual control among its members. To illustrate the part played by the distribution of information, let us return to our thought experiment.

Suppose that deliveries from the Green family have unexpectedly decreased in volume through no fault of its own—because of bad weather conditions affecting deliveries, or a large number of workers being off sick, for instance. Then, despite the Green family's having taken all reasonable precautions for avoiding such problems, the Smiths would be undersupplied at the end of the month. If the Smiths know that the lack of agricultural products is not the Greens' fault, then there should be no retribution; otherwise, punishments would in such cases be meted out to individuals who had acted in good faith and cooperated to the full extent they could. Problems in the supply chain that are no one's fault should therefore not lead to discontinued cooperation. The problem is that limited information can make it impossible to distinguish between those shortfalls that are no one's fault and those that result from intentional behavior.

If this information deficit were too great, it is possible that cooperation would break down. The Green family, in their role as producers, could exploit the fact that the Smiths were not able to ascertain the environmental conditions in which the Greens work, in order to save on their efforts for the Smiths. The Greens would explain the missing agricultural products for the Smiths with reference to adverse circumstances beyond their control. The Smiths would, in turn, have an incentive to behave opportunistically: Each time there was a lack of agricultural products, they might claim that they believed the Greens to be responsible so as to force them to show remorse—that is, to provide for the Smiths for a certain period without being provided for in return. Under these conditions, the system of common ownership would not be able to pass the cooperation test.

A system of common ownership should therefore try to establish as much transparency as possible to remove the asymmetry in the access to information, and thus to lower the risk that mutual distrust would build up and make individuals cease cooperating. This transparency in mutual control is easy to achieve if the community is small and its membership stable. In a large community in the twenty-first century, new information technologies would need to be developed and used for the close surveillance of the productive and consumption activities of members (including leisure activities). To be economically feasible, any system of common ownership would require transparency among its members. This is another important result of our thought experiment.

Let us at this point draw a preliminary conclusion regarding the extent to which social norms may function to support cooperation within a system of common ownership. It can at best be a cautiously optimistic one, because this mechanism can only work under very specific conditions—that is, in comparatively small communities in which all members know each other well and live together over long periods of time. Social norms, however, are not capable of supporting cooperative behavior among a large number of egoistic individuals who have little information about each other.

The literature on game theory has clearly demonstrated these conclusions with precision. They are borne out by numerous case studies of cooperation problems that resemble common ownership systems, such as, for instance, the exploitation of the oceans through overfishing and the use of common land and resources in agriculture.

INTERNALIZED VALUES: THE ACT OF GIVING OUT OF A SENSE OF DUTY

Next to charity and social norms, internalized values represent a third mechanism that may help an economic system based on common ownership pass the cooperation test. When looking at social norms, I have assumed not only that human beings are egoists, but also that they are materialists who are interested solely in their own material well-being—or, at the very most, that of their own offspring. The question of whether or not their action has value in itself does not influence how such human beings behave. These unscrupulous individuals would do anything to get rich at the expense of their fellow human beings, and it therefore comes as no surprise that a system of common ownership does not have much chance of success among such people.

In reality, however, the motivational forces governing human behavior are more complicated. The motivation to advance one's own prosperity is only one such force, and within a developed economy probably not even the central one. Often the nonmaterial value of actions is more important for actors than is the prospect of securing their own material well-being. Such nonmaterial, symbolic value may help to solve the problem of cooperation in a twenty-first-century common ownership system.

Human beings attribute value to certain forms of behavior as the result of reflection, discussion, education, training, indoctrination, tradition, imitation, and habituation. Values form especially during childhood and youth, and slowly take the shape of a relatively fixed individual system of values. But even at a more advanced age, someone might have a change of heart and modify his or her values—for instance, following a traumatic experience.

Value systems ultimately underlie one's sense of self-respect and the social respect one enjoys from others. Thus, the self-respect of individuals depends crucially on their ability to live in accordance with their values and ideals. Respect and acceptance require that one lead one's life in accordance with the values of others.

How might values help to solve the cooperation problem within a system of common ownership? Let us first look at the incentive effect of internalized values considered by themselves—that is, apart from the motivational effects of charity and reciprocity.

Value systems that emphasize honesty and fairness might lead individuals to act cooperatively. A particular social contract is in force in a community of common ownership according to which its members agree to work to the best of their ability to satisfy the needs of the polity. If they do not abide by it, they break their promise. For individuals who value honesty, dishonest behavior is bad in itself, and thus it gives them pangs of conscience. And fairness is a similar case. It is certainly fair to give to society if one is able to do so, and if the others who are able to do so give as well. Fairness, or justice, in the sense of Kant's categorical imperative, also dictates that every member of a community of common ownership behaves in cooperative fashion. If honesty and fairness have been internalized as values, and if self-respect and social acceptance are more important to the individual than any material gain he or she may achieve by abusing the system of common ownership, then the individual will abide by its rules and act cooperatively.

But note: The fact that individuals pay attention to the symbolic consequences of their actions can be good or bad for a system of common ownership, depending on the values. If, for instance, individuals attach importance to being considered wealthier than others, then these symbolic values undermine individuals' preparedness to act cooperatively. The question, therefore, is which conditions foster values that help to solve the cooperation problem in common ownership.

On the Stability of Successful Value Systems

The differences in ethics and customs across time and between different countries, as well as among different individuals living in the same society, bear witness to the diversity of possible value systems. Values emerge and are passed on; they change as a consequence of environmental influences and are subject to a lengthy process of cultural evolution. Whether or not value systems that promote common ownership prevail depends on this process of value transmission.

Values are more likely to become internalized if they can be justified to others, or if there are people who can and do justify them. Thus, public discourse is a central source of values because it serves to identify maxims for action that are considered reasonable from the perspective of the collective. To communicate honestly and to act fairly are precepts that are almost universally affirmed by the public. We may therefore expect that the public discourse will promote values that support cooperation within a system of common ownership.

The effects of public discourse may be limited, however, if words are not matched by deeds. Research into cultural evolution, following the theory of natural selection, has therefore proposed the hypothesis that values establish themselves through the success of those who embody them. This idea suggests that values are propagated by groups or individuals, and that they spread in accordance with the relative success of these groups or individuals. Those who are more successful than others are imitated, and thus their values are appropriated by others and gradually determine the character of a broader social environment and possibly even of society in general.

A crucial point revealed by this evolutionary approach is the significance of the level at which the process of cultural selection takes place. It makes a substantial difference whether the long-term selection of values depends on the relative success of specific individuals or of specific groups.

In order to recognize this fully, we must return again to the island of Utopia. Let us imagine that some of its fifty-four cities—each of which is a system of common ownership—are exclusively populated by moralists who attach importance to honesty and no importance to displaying a higher level of consumption than their fellow citizens. In the other cities, all inhabitants attach importance to higher levels of personal consumption than other citizens, and no importance to honesty. The latter are the cities of the materialists. The cities of moralists will achieve cooperation to a much greater extent than the cities of materialists, and the cities of the moralists will therefore flourish while the cities of the materialists will be poor. Gradually, the materialist cities will disappear, because their populations will flee poverty, or because these cities will try to adopt the value system of the successful cities of the moralists. The moralists' cities, by comparison, will thrive and have resources for expansion.

In this case, it is the comparison between groups that is decisive for cultural development, because the values are subject to group selection, and group selection promotes the value of honesty that characterizes the moralists' cities. The comparison of performance between the groups thus contributes to the dissemination of "good values."

But let us now look at a case in which the selection of values depends on the success of individuals. Imagine a city of moralists in which, at a certain point in time, there is perfect cooperation. Then, one day, a single family of materialists shows up. Perhaps they have immigrated, or perhaps a moralist family has simply changed its mind, for whatever reason. In any case, this family has decided to instill in its children a materialist attitude. They thus shirk work and get as many consumer goods from the public warehouses as they possibly can. In all this, the members of this family do not suffer guilty consciences. Quite the opposite: they are especially proud of their high standard of living compared to other families. They believe that they act intelligently, and that the others are stupid.

If, because of a dearth of information or because of coordination problems, these deviators are not punished, they will be materially much better off than any other family in the city. According to our selection hypothesis, this difference in wealth will, over time, entice other families to imitate the deviators. These families will give up their traditional values and bring up their children as materialists. The perfectly good value system will nevertheless begin, slowly but steadily, to crumble. The more that families adopt materialism and shirk their responsibilities, the less danger there is of being punished by those moralists that remain. In the end, the whole city will be materialist, thus noncooperative and poor. The attempt on the part of each individual family to be better off ultimately leads to the ruin of all families. The result is astonishing: The good value system is pushed out by the bad one. The system of common ownership collapses.

INTERACTION BETWEEN ALTRUISM,
SOCIAL NORMS, AND VALUES

A free common ownership system forgoes policing and money as instruments for disciplining producers and consumers. Cooperation is meant to be upheld by charity, social norms, and internalized values. Upon closer inspection, however, not one of these three driving forces, on its own, appears to be able to encourage the members of a community to engage in enduring cooperation. Beyond a tight circle of family and close friends, charity is too weak a force, social norms are fairly easy to circumvent, and moral values tend to be crowded out by material values. None of this bodes well for the prospect of society-wide common ownership's passing the cooperation test.

But charity, social norms, and internalized values are not isolated motivating forces; rather, there is a mutual influence among them. If we look at the effect of their simultaneous operation, we can be much more optimistic about the prospects for common ownership in the twenty-first century.

First, morality helps to support cooperation as a social norm. Someone who violates this norm is not only exposed to the risk of social punishment, but also feels morally bad. And a value can be attached to just punishments, as experimental game theory has unambiguously shown. In numerous laboratory experiments, participants were prepared to bear costs to punish the unfair behavior of others, even if they knew that this would not result in a higher payoff for them at a later stage.

Second, adherence to a norm of cooperation is likely to strengthen altruism in a society. Observing that fellow human beings act cooperatively can strengthen altruistic tendencies in the observer. As one benefits from a system of common ownership, a feeling of gratitude toward its members develops. One assumes benevolence on the part of others, and tends to respond to good intentions with good intentions. Thus, sympathy with the givers—that is, with the whole community—can grow.

Third, adherence to a social norm may promote the distribution of values like honesty and justice, which in turn motivate people to cooperate. If the majority attaches importance to honesty, then behaving dishonestly causes one to lose social esteem. The fear of such loss may impel materialists to act like moralists. If that happens, it would no longer make sense to cultivate a materialist attitude, only to defy it with one's own behavior. Rather, such individuals would have an incentive to adapt their value system so that they could be proud of their honest behavior. Thus, if materialist values disappear, the incentives to act cooperatively increase.

INTERPERSONAL RELATIONS AS
A DISCIPLINARY INSTRUMENT

Human beings encounter each other not only as consumers and producers, or as citizens and representatives of the state; they also interact socially as, for instance, neighbors, friends, fellow club members, and congregants in a faith. Such social interaction can also help to solve the problem of cooperation in a system of common ownership.

To understand this, consider the distinctive implications of social exchange. The members of a community of common ownership cannot get all the things they value from the public warehouses. Pleasantries or unfriendliness are experienced in the context of social interaction. As opposed to the general principles that apply to the collective warehouse, it is individuals who decide to whom they will send a Christmas card or an invitation to a party, and whom they will ask to join them for some activity. Friendships are not professional services that one can use according to one's own whim; they assume the mutual consent of the individuals involved. Individuals can therefore be excluded from enjoying friendship. And the same applies to loving relationships and to the founding of families.

Social exchange in a system of common ownership provides us with the possibility of social exclusion as a means against free-riding. As long as those violating the norm are only a small minority, it is not particularly costly for the other individuals to exclude them from their social life. This might even go as far as exerting pressure on individuals to avoid any social exchange with norm violators to avoid being excluded from the rest of the community themselves. This possibility also increases the chances of a twenty-first-century system of common ownership being able to pass the cooperation test.

THE FINAL CONCLUSION: A DIFFERENTIATED PICTURE

In capitalism, individuals act according to the maxim: "I give you this, if you give me that." In free common ownership, the maxim governing actions is: "I give this to us." The former affirms individual self-interest, the latter brotherhood. Most of us probably would prefer to be surrounded by people following the latter maxim. But is this possible, and if so, what conditions must be fulfilled to bring it about?

We looked at a hypothetical economy in which the community declares certain norms governing labor and consumption, and the members decide autonomously about their individual labor efforts and have access to public warehouses where they can freely help themselves to goods. In order for such a system to work, the individuals must decide, of their own volition, to put appropriate efforts into their labor and adequately to limit their consumption. Such behavior can, in principle, be brought about by various motivational factors: altruism, social pressure, and a feeling of duty. These driving forces might develop further within a system of common ownership compared to capitalism. Whether or not this would suffice, in the end, to achieve a lasting solution to the problem of cooperation remains an open question.

The pessimistic thought does not seem justified, however, that an economy based on common ownership must necessarily perish because of the lack of effort and the abuse it would give rise to. We can conceive of arrangements that appear to offer solutions to the cooperation problem. A promising system of common ownership in this regard may be characterized as follows.

It would be decidedly decentralized. Individuals would interact for the purposes of production and consumption in relatively small communities that were to a large extent autonomous. Rich communities would give away part of their production to poor communities. Every individual would spend the majority of his or her life in one and the same community. In each community everyone would know everyone else. This would create clarity, transparency, farsightedness, and social control.

The system of common ownership would feature a minimum level of public institutions for control and, where necessary, punishment.

There would be a computer-based information system to capture the productive and consumer activities of individuals in minute detail, with its findings accessible to everyone. Large-scale systematic abuse by individuals or groups would be punished by the public authorities.

The citizens would have deeply internalized the values of honesty and fairness, and their actions would be subject to superego governance. There would be a strong subjective identification with the polity. These values and this sense of identification would be vigorously promoted in education and culture.

These three conditions—the local rootedness of the individual, public control, and morality—could compensate for each other in different measure. A community might, for example, allow for greater geographical mobility by practicing stricter public control or having a stricter moral code.

Solving the cooperation problem would require us to strengthen conditions along all those three dimensions substantially compared to the situation at present. It goes without saying that such strengthening would imply significant disadvantages for people. Local rootedness implies sanctions for changing place of residence, and lesser geographical mobility means, in a certain respect, narrowing one's horizons. Social pressures often produce simpleminded conformity. Public control of labor and consumption means that legal rules, spyware, video cameras, searches, and punishment would become even more a part of everyday life. A strict morality can lead to intolerance toward oneself and others.

These costs must be compared to the prospective benefits deriving from the introduction of common ownership—that is, to material equality and security for everyone, less competitive attitudes, a diminished urge to acquire possessions, and more companionable relationships between people. The weighing of these costs and benefits is obviously highly subjective, and depends on one's value judgments.

Throughout these final reflections, the implicit assumption has been that, once the cooperation problem is solved, the level of material prosperity in the system of common ownership can become comparable to that of today's capitalism. We do not yet have any reason for making this assumption, however, because the level of prosperity is not only determined by the willingness to cooperate, but also by the degree of efficiency in the use of all economic resources—in other words, the allocation problem highlighted in the previous chapter.

We know that capitalism does not guarantee an optimal allocation of resources. In the next chapter, we will take a closer look at the kind of allocation to be expected in a system of common ownership.

4

LUXURY AND ANARCHISM

TODAY'S DIVERSITY IN TECHNOLOGICALLY sophisticated consumer goods goes way beyond anything imagined by science fiction authors of the past. Many inventions that just four decades ago astounded those following the exploits of the Starship *Enterprise* crew are now part of everyday life. People with average incomes today can afford things that fifty years ago were not even options for the rich: short vacations abroad, surfing the Internet, fresh strawberries in winter, and fresh oranges in the summer. Even the most idiosyncratic of preferences can be accommodated because products, however trivial their function, are available in innumerable variations. All in all, this seems to be a fabulous world of consumption.

Great German social scientists such as Theodor Adorno, Herbert Marcuse, and Erich Fromm, all of whom emigrated to the United States in the 1930s, wrote eloquent warnings about the consumer fetishism of our affluent society. They claimed that the external richness of capitalism was a sign of internal poverty. People's frustration with a lack of personal fulfilment in their work and in social interaction, they argued, expressed itself in an urge to amass possessions, and led to a frenzy of consumption.

Although this critique may in some ways remain persuasive today, it should not lead us to downplay the importance of consumption as a criterion in our search for an alternative to capitalism. For most people, consumption is highly important. It is no secret that the downfall of actually existing socialism in Eastern Europe was largely owing to people's desire for a level of consumption similar to that in the West.

Simply to demonize consumption is too facile. Of course, it is true that one may become a slave to one's impulses to consume; but many people learn to control themselves, and thus are able to exert some control over the bewitching world of consumption. A path of choice and self-control is surely superior to one based on the removal of choice. Having multiple options from which to choose and declining many of the things on offer is a sign of great personal freedom.

In a community of self-determining individuals, access to a broader range of products amounts to a greater freedom of choice, and this respects the diversity of personal needs and preferences. A broader range of options for consumption also creates more space for the development of personality. One need only think of the new opportunities that medical product improvements bring to those with disabilities and illnesses.

An alternative to capitalism should therefore also be able to offer a large range of consumer options. This range must include the freedom not to make use of whatever goods are on offer, and instead to opt for a simple life close to nature. At the same time, if an alternative to capitalism is to be taken seriously, it must appeal to people other than just the ascetics among us.

In Thomas More's time, the spectrum of available technologies and the range of products were comparatively limited. In his Utopia, he could therefore afford to ignore the question of how his allegedly exemplary economic system would have provided for a reasonable allocation of resources given a great variety of products. After the Industrial Revolution, by contrast, the critics of capitalism could no longer neglect this question of allocation. In this chapter, we shall begin discussing how different economic systems manage the allocation of resources. We will continue the discussion of general common ownership. And in our ongoing quest to envision a better world, we will scrutinize a design that prioritizes the question of the diversity of consumption.

KROPOTKIN'S ANARCHIST COMMUNISM

A hundred years ago, Pyotr Kropotkin, a Russian geographer born into an aristocratic family, was a leading light of anarchism. By nature, he was of a gentle and kind disposition. For defenders of a society-wide system of common ownership, his collection of writings, published towards the end of the nineteenth century under the title *The Conquest of Bread*, offers perhaps the best attempt at solving the allocation problem. Kropotkin's writings here amount to neither a philosophical treatise nor a utopian novel. They rather contain practical suggestions for the period immediately following a successful revolution.

Like More, Kropotkin wants to replace capitalism with an economic system based on common ownership. But his vision differs from More's in two important respects. First, the Russian anarchist does away with the state and its institutions altogether (there are, for instance, no philarchs) and thus, he also does without any of the regulatory functions commonly performed by a state. (The family does not figure centrally in Kropotkin's thought either.) Second, he describes in great detail how the provision of "luxury goods" should be organized in a system of common ownership. Such goods include not only extravagances like truffles and jewels, but any good that does not serve to satisfy primary needs such as eating and sleeping.

THE STATE AND THE HUMAN BEING

Like all anarchists, Kropotkin believed that authority, and in particular coercion by the state, is the ruination of the human. This thesis is based on the idea that a state's authority is grounded in a ruler's credible threat of violence against subjects. The threat has the purpose of preventing people from breaking the law; but anarchists believe threatening people has a far more significant effect: it saps their natural virtue as human beings, and ultimately destroys it.

This anarchist thesis may well contain a truth at its core. It is altogether possible that, under certain circumstances, coercion by the state gradually dissolves the motivation to act cooperatively. A law that prohibits and punishes is always a signal from the legislative authority to those subject to that law, and it may communicate several things at once. On the one hand, a legal prohibition may communicate something about the attractiveness of what is prohibited. If a ruler threatens punishment, the prohibited actions may become all the more interesting to the subjects. They might even suspect that the prohibition has no rational basis—because, if the action were so injurious, why would coercion be needed to stop it? As we all know, such thoughts occurred to Adam and Eve as a result of God's banning the fruit of a particular tree (and we still suffer the consequences). Thus, the exercise of authority may in fact motivate individuals to carry out the forbidden actions.

On the other hand, a law may convey a message to subjects about the kind of fellow human beings they are dealing with in their country. An ordinance of the state instructing subjects to act in a particular way may be interpreted as a lack of trust in the population on the part of the rulers. It might have the effect, then, of a warning that the population consists predominantly of "bad people" whose behavior needs controlling. With such a message, the state reduces individuals' willingness to act in cooperation with others, and invites suspicion toward one's fellow human beings. Here there is the possibility of a kind of self-fulfilling prophecy.

An experiment carried out in Israel in 1998 provides striking confirmation that the punishment of noncooperative behavior can sometimes be counterproductive. The experiment dealt not with serious violations of the law, but rather with the contravention of more customary rules of politeness—in this case, in day care centers in Haifa. Children at these day care centers were sometimes picked up late by their parents, which is a common enough occurrence all over the world, but which caused problems for the staff, who could not properly control their working hours. To solve the problem, some day care centers introduced a financial penalty for parents who were late picking up their children. In others, no change was introduced—that is, there was no penalty for lateness.

The results surprised even the experts. Lateness *increased* in the day care centers where financial penalties had been introduced, while in the others there was no change in behavior. A possible explanation is that the financial penalty eroded parents' motivation to conform to the rules of politeness. Even once the financial penalties were removed, those parents who had experienced the sanctions tended to be late more often than those who had not.

Experiments like this hint at the complex structure of human motivation, and show that, under certain conditions, penalties can have counterproductive effects. They do not, however, prove the thesis of the anarchists, which is that the authority of the state necessarily has deleterious effects on human nature.

The anarchist creed emerged and spread at a time when most states were nondemocratic, and the anarchists, seeing the faults of these states, ascribed them to states in general. In a democracy, however, as opposed to an authoritarian regime, legal commands and prohibitions are not expressions of the capricious will of a ruler, but are connected to the preferences of the citizens; thus, they can generally be justified. The previous chapter noted, for instance, that a system of common ownership would be bound to fail without at least a minimal level of state control preventing abuse. It is not clear why such justified legislation should be resisted.

In fact, empirical studies have established a positive correlation between the extent of direct democracy and the sense of citizenship among a populace. This is presumably because when the people subject to laws have directly consented to them, the laws are easier to justify. This suggests that the authority of the state does not erode empathy with others or the feeling of duty toward the polity as long as there is a general feeling that the legislation is democratically legitimate and its content is appropriate, so that the laws are observed by the majority.

THE PROVISION OF LUXURY GOODS

Kropotkin's description of a successful postrevolutionary economic system involves a distinction between two major sectors of production, one producing essential goods and another producing luxury goods. This distinction is reminiscent of that between agriculture and the crafts on Utopia, and it corresponds to the division between necessity and freedom.

According to Kropotkin, there is a duty to labor only with respect to essential goods. This is a moral duty, supported by a social norm. It is not a legal duty: the state does not prosecute idlers. Every able-bodied individual between twenty and forty-five or fifty should work in this sector for four or five hours each day. In all establishments, jobs are distributed in a balanced way such that all employees must do their share of the more unpleasant work. A rotational principle and technical adaptations are meant to overcome the division between manual and intellectual labor. Everyone may freely choose their workplaces, although Kropotkin does not give a precise explanation of the mechanism that guarantees the production of the required amount of each of the essential goods. Regarding the distribution of essential goods thus produced, it works just as More envisioned for Utopia: everything is shared by all, with all individuals helping themselves from the common stores according to their needs.

In Kropotkin's work, the diversity of consumption finds expression in the luxury goods sector. Laboring in this sector is entirely voluntary: there is no duty to do so. Those who are interested in consuming a particular kind of luxury good may freely agree, on their own initiative, to produce the desired good. This is the key respect in which Kropotkin goes beyond More. Kropotkin uses books as his example of a luxury good. People who like to read or write books will get together to print books. Within his system, individuals may join any number of associations to satisfy, in cooperation with others, their desires for certain products.

What is immediately attractive about this suggestion is that it relies on the formation of free associations among free people. Production is determined by neither profit seeking nor the authority of the state, but by the consumer demands of autonomous individuals. This system of associations thus offers an approach to the allocation of resources within an economy quite unlike anything that has been tried before.

In Kropotkin's vision, the population is provided with luxury goods by numerous independent associations, each formed spontaneously for its purpose. The members of each association also have the moral right to exclude other members if they do not cooperate. Exclusions take place in such a way that the excluded individual is given to understand the justification for his exclusion. If the individual does not come around to an acceptance of the judgment, then, according to Kropotkin, "sturdy members of the association"—as a kind of substitute for the state which Kropotkin does not want—will bring that individual to his senses, and will forbid him access.

Initially, each association keeps its products for itself, rather than freely giving them to the polity. Such an association can be compared to a small, independent system of common ownership in which individuals voluntarily contribute their labor and make collective decisions about the product of their labor, possibly through discussions with other associations. This implies that each association is given limited property rights over its production, although Kropotkin does not provide any precise details regarding these rights. We may expect that the products of an association are initially, or perhaps even exclusively, offered to its members. Kropotkin does not describe in any further detail how an association distributes its goods among its members. The crucial difference from the sector of essential goods is the following: instead of production for the whole of society, here we have production for the consumption needs of only those individuals who have come together to form a specific association.

THE ECONOMIC JUSTIFICATION FOR THE ASSOCIATIONS

Why does Kropotkin introduce these associations, and so deviate from the principle of generalized free giving?

One reason may be that the associations mitigate the problem of co-operation. In the case of luxury goods, compared to that of essential goods, there is a strong temptation for individuals in a scheme of common ownership not to follow the norms for consumption. Whereas the needs of individuals with regard to essential goods can be met with relative ease, in the case of luxury goods, the appetite knows no upper limit and some individuals would therefore take too many luxury goods from the common stores. An association, by contrast, creates a smaller, specialized community of common ownership with a better system of incentives; individuals who want to consume a particular luxury good must take part in the association that produces that good.

The problem of cooperation becomes easier to solve within an association, because its members share a preference and have come together to pursue a common interest. To this extent, they resemble each other. There is additionally the threat of "dismissal," because an association is allowed to exclude members who do not cooperate.

Another interpretation of Kropotkin's free associations is possible. They may be a reaction to the undeniable difficulties associated with making collective decisions about society-wide allocations of resources. If a scheme of common ownership concerns only essential goods, it might be relatively easy for citizens to agree on how the needs of individual households will be met by available resources, and relatively straightforward for them to establish norms for consumption. But in the case of luxury goods, identifying an appropriate level of provision is much more controversial, because tastes concerning luxury goods differ so greatly. The fact in itself that a sufficient number of people have formed an association for the production of a particular product should prove there is a corresponding social need for this product.

The institution of the voluntary association is an attempt by Kropotkin to meet the more sophisticated consumer wishes of people in a free and fraternal fashion. The members of an association voluntarily provide an input in labor to achieve a goal that they formulate together. This kind of free, bottom-up economic enterprise does not seem at all utopian. Today, the information platform Wikipedia, for instance, operates on such a basis. Indeed, we may observe such forms of self-organization in many cases where people come together in some joint effort. For instance, people take the initiative to decorate their homes with the help of a few friends or acquaintances; people pitch in and help when others move house. There are no payments for this kind of help. Rather, they are cases of "I'll scratch your back if you'll scratch mine"; one day your house gets decorated, another day mine does.

But is the system of associations really a feasible alternative solution to the allocation problem?

ASSOCIATIONS AND THE PRODUCTIVITY OF LABOR

Let us now attempt to implement the economic system suggested by Kropotkin as a thought experiment, to identify its consequences for the allocation of resources.

Imagine that the countries of the European Union suddenly put Kropotkin's ideas into practice. First, a clear line would need to be drawn between the goods and services to be produced and consumed by all (the essential goods), and those to be produced by associations for their respective members (the luxury goods). An obvious criterion for determining in which category a particular good belonged would be its distribution among the population. Goods that were used by almost all households—let's say by at least three-quarters of them—could be declared essential. Electricity and water, meat and pasta, detergents and toothpaste—all of which are used to satisfy universal basic needs—would then all fall into this category. Associations would produce all the other goods that are desired by the population. Examples might include running shoes, music concerts, computer games, and vacations to exotic places.

Looking more closely, however, at these basic needs for food, accommodation, household goods, personal hygiene, and more, it becomes clear that there are many different products that can satisfy them, and that people have varying preferences among these different products. Perhaps, then, just a basic model of the product should be socially produced, leaving any variations on it to be produced, or not, by voluntary associations. For example, a simple white toilet paper would, as an essential good, be provided by society for everyone, while the provision of a five-ply, decorated paper would be up to an association. You would find a simple toothbrush in the common stores, but to get one with an ergonomic handle and multicolored bristles, or an electric one, you would need to join an association.

Thus, in this economic system, individuals who wanted running shoes, an electric toothbrush, or five-ply toilet paper would need to join the corresponding associations and contribute to their production. If an adult, or one of his children, wanted to practice a certain sport, he would need to join the association set up to produce equipment for it. Perhaps people would also need to join the associations producing goods they expected to want in their old age, past the point where it would be reasonable to expect them to still be working.

For the sake of our thought experiment, let us assume a woman wanted to consume three hundred such luxury goods a year. If contributions to production had to correspond to levels of consumption, then she would need to contribute labor to all three hundred associations producing these goods. For each good, she should put in roughly the amount of work required to produce the good in the quantity she desired. Naturally, because differently skilled individuals work at different levels of productivity, the calculation of labor required of her would also need to take that into consideration.

We can see straightaway that this system would not be practical. In our thought experiment, any Europeans wanting to maintain their current levels of diversity in consumption would need to participate in as many production processes as there were luxury goods on their wish lists. The expenditure on commuting between home and the numerous places of production alone would be enormous. And the associations do not seem altogether feasible either. The continual rotation of members, some of them working at a particular place for only a day or less, would create considerable challenges for the organization of production.

Thinking through what it would mean to implement Kropotkin's design, one realizes that his economic system would have catastrophic consequences for the growth of productivity, which is driven by improvements in productive technologies. For this, specialists are needed—that is, people who have gained deep knowledge of the technological processes in a specific area of production. In Kropotkin's system, any such specialists would, in practice, consume almost nothing but essential goods, because they would not have time to work in dozens of different associations. Thus, hardly anyone would want to become a specialist. Yet, without experts, many high-quality forms of production could not be conducted at all. Technological progress would come to a standstill.

A DISTORTED STRUCTURE OF PRODUCTION

Let us imagine another situation, this time involving a group of people in Kropotkin's ideal world who want to play tennis. As tennis is not essential, rackets, tennis balls, and all other necessary equipment, including tennis courts and so forth, belong to the luxury goods sector. Thus, the tennis players form an association for their purpose of playing tennis. But what is the concrete task of such an association?

Such a tennis association is not to be confused with a tennis club that one might join. The task of this association is in the first instance to produce the goods necessary for the game, and then to make them available to its members. But the labor power of the tennis players is not sufficient for the production of tennis balls, because this requires special plants, machines, and other input factors. For the production of the felt, for instance, sheep wool, nylon, and cotton are needed. For the core, natural rubber, clay, quartz, sulphur, zinc oxide, and magnesium carbonate are used. If the players want pressurized balls, they also need the gas for the inflation of the rubber shell.

The specialized machines for the production of tennis balls, tennis rackets, and so forth are themselves not essential goods in Kropotkin's sense. As intermediary goods they do not serve the purpose of final consumption; thus, they are not to be found in the large common stores that are available to all. The same can be said of the specific raw materials and substances that are processed for the tennis industry. They do not belong to the essential goods that are produced by, and supplied for, all of society. This raises the question, therefore, of how our tennis players can get hold of the intermediary goods they need for the production of their equipment.

If no one else produces the required machines, then the members of the tennis association have no choice but to produce the machines themselves. And the same applies to all the other intermediary goods. The tennis players need the intermediary goods for the production of the machines that produce the tennis balls and other equipment. And so on, and so on. Thus, in principle, the tennis association would need to organize the entire vertical chain of production—from the raw materials to the end product—to realize its aim of making tennis-playing possible.

In Kropotkin's system, such vertical integration is necessary for all luxury goods. For any given luxury good—for instance, a smartphone—the corresponding association would need to be organized as a perfectly integrated production chain. This is a logical consequence of the principle that the production of any luxury good is to serve the needs of those participating in its production.

In most cases, complete vertical integration is not an efficient mode of producing goods. This is because, crucially, the typical intermediary good enters as one input factor into the production of multiple final products. Because of rising returns to scale in the production of intermediary goods, it is more efficient as a rule to produce them in relatively large quantities. Rather than having all the users of an intermediary good producing that good, it therefore makes sense to have a smaller number of providers satisfying the demand of the many users.

THE FUNDAMENTAL PROBLEM: AN INADEQUATE DIVISION OF LABOR

The example of the tennis association has more to teach us. The production of the tennis ball's rubber shell makes use of chemical processes that are designed and controlled by specialists. Trained chemists are needed. What if, however, the chemists living in our hypothetical society (assuming there are some) do not care to play tennis, and don't want to become members of the tennis association? As chemists are required to produce the balls, it will not be possible to manufacture them—and without tennis balls, no tennis! Unfortunately, if the chemists in Kropotkin's world are not passionate about the game, then no one will be able to play.

This absurd result follows from the rule that so-called luxury goods are to be produced exclusively for one's own enjoyment. This rule means that there can be no efficient division of labor.

This fundamental problem with Kropotkin's system may be illustrated with another thought experiment. Imagine that there are only two people, with different skills, living in Kropotkin's world. And let us assume that their need for essential goods is already met, and that they have skills necessary for the production of luxury goods. And let us further assume that these two individuals do not share the same tastes: any luxury good that interests one of them does not interest the other. In this situation, each individual would form a one-person association and would consume all that he or she produces.

Now, however, imagine that each of the individuals has only the skills needed to produce goods that are *liked by the other*. Under this condition, no one-person association would be formed at all, and no luxury goods would be consumed—and both individuals' skills would be useless, because they would not be used to produce value. This is obviously not efficient. It would be better if each individual produced something that was useful for the other, and that the goods were exchanged. That would make both individuals' skills valuable, whereas in the context of Kropotkin's system they would be wasted.

As a practical matter, the person who desires a particular thing the most is rarely the one who is best at producing it. And the groups who especially like to consume a thing are rarely the groups who can most efficiently produce it. For these reasons, a polity with a society-wide division of labor is able to generate more wealth for everyone than a polity in which individual groups of consumers cater to their own needs through their own production. But in Kropotkin's system of voluntary associations, the latter is just what happens: Production for one's own needs determines the allocation of resources. This is the fundamental reason why his system fails the allocation test.

The technical superiority of the division of labor over production for one's own needs is one of the central facts of economic history and the decisive factor behind the emergence of economics as a science. For the majority of homo sapiens' two-hundred-thousand-year history, there was very little improvement in levels of material well-being from one generation to the next. During these thousands of years, human beings gathered, hunted, and produced for consumption in small groups, and any division of labor existed only within these small groups. In our part of the world, the most recent period to see a regression to subsistence production was the early Middle Ages, when the European economy was made up of autonomous rural entities. Only with the development of larger towns and their markets, and the establishment of a monetary economy, did production for exchange take off once again. The exploitation of the advantages of the division of labor, and of the specialization that accompanied it, provided the basis for a long period of sustained technological progress and exponential economic growth from which we still benefit immensely today.

TWO UNHAPPY ENDINGS

It is doubtful that Kropotkin's suggestion for the provision of luxury goods could ever work. His voluntary associations, should they be able to form at all, would have a strong incentive to overcome the inefficiency of this system. Presumably, the associations would begin to exchange a part of their production for the products of other associations, to provide more to their members. Once bilateral exchanges had been established, there would soon be attempts at organizing multilateral exchanges between several associations, which would allow them to take advantage even further of the benefits of the division of labor. Individuals would have similar incentives. Instead of working in dozens of associations as unskilled laborers, they would divide tasks among themselves in small groups, and subsequently exchange their products. As a consequence, both associations and individuals would soon have a strong interest in introducing a generally accepted means of payment to facilitate multilateral exchanges. And once money and markets have been reintroduced, it is but a small step to the resurrection of a capitalist economic system.

Perhaps this final scenario is implicitly biased, however, toward a view of human beings as acting and thinking predominantly in an individualistic fashion. If we suppose a preponderance of more collectivistic motivations in human beings, then Kropotkin's anarchism might wind up in an altogether different scenario. To reduce the inefficiency of vertical integration, two associations that require the same intermediary good might join forces to produce this good for them both. The tennis association and the wool sweater association, for instance, may agree to breed sheep together so that they get the wool for both tennis balls and sweaters. This cooperation may lead to a desire on the part of both associations to merge, and thus to provide access to both consumption goods for their members, and at the same time to avoid the rotation of workers between the two chains of production. As these advantages grow with further agreements, the mergers would lead to increasingly large associations until, finally, all goods are produced by a single massive association. The rational control of such an all-encompassing association is what many socialists imagine under the term "planned economy."

THE STUFF OF SCIENCE FICTION

Despite its original ideas, Kropotkin's design does not represent an alternative economic system that would allow for the maintenance, let alone the further development, of the rich diversity of today's world of consumer goods. On the contrary, a drastic reduction in the division of labor would lead to a dramatic decline in wealth. There would probably be no luxuries. The only economic sector that might work is the general system of common ownership that provides individuals with the most essential goods and thus guarantees the minimum necessary for subsistence. There might also be some voluntary associations that did not require a pronounced division of labor, such as for staging theater performances, for instance, or playing chess.

Given the drastic reduction in the standard of living and in the utilization of technology this implies, people would have a strong incentive to reduce the misallocation of resources by way of a purposeful division of labor. This incentive might lead to the emergence of markets, or to the establishment of a central agency for the coordination of all processes of production and distribution. One can only imagine the conflict that would arise from maintaining such an inefficient scheme of common ownership, and defending it against attacks by counter-revolutionaries or new revolutionaries. The very thought of it is alarming.

Therefore, while Kropotkin's idea of a system of common ownership might be good raw material for a science fiction novel, we must conclude that it does not provide a serious alternative to the present system. The cooperation problem would not necessarily lead his community based on common ownership to fail; it is not ludicrous to suppose that, under the right conditions, people could be driven to cooperate economically by more noble motives than mere financial advantage or fear of the state. But his system is altogether incapable of providing a solution to the allocation problem—that is, a way of making rational use of society's resources for realizing technological possibilities and meeting the greater consumption needs of individuals. The demands of this requirement far outstrip the capacities of spontaneously self-organized free associations.

This conclusion raises the question of whether a centrally coordinated system of common ownership—that is, a planned economy—would be better able to pass the allocation test. The following chapter is dedicated to this question.

5

PLANNING

MIGHT IT BE POSSIBLE TO REPLACE capitalism with a system in which: 1) all means of production are common property; 2) the political system is democratic; 3) citizens' shared right to the ownership of the means of production is effectively transferred to the state, which then uses those means in the interest of the citizens and ensures a just distribution of the resulting aggregate output; and 4) citizens, through the state as their representative, control the allocation of all resources in the economy by means of a central plan?

Under capitalism, the coordination of economic processes happens mainly through the market system. In the alternative to be discussed in this chapter, central planning takes on this responsibility in place of the market. This solution was suggested as early as the nineteenth century by the followers of so-called "scientific socialism," who wanted to distance themselves explicitly from more romantic versions of socialism. For these "scientific" socialists, including Karl Marx, planning was the path to a more humane society. The central plan was considered to be the new institution that would finally allow humanity to become master of its own destiny. Instead of the anarchy of capitalism, with its cyclical crises and the impoverishment of the masses that went along with them, economic life was to be rationally controlled by a plan for the overall economy, a plan that would draw on all available knowledge from the sciences and technology. Following the victory of man over nature, the economy—and thus also most of social life—was to be ruled by man.

Indeed, the attraction of this promise was so strong that the planned economy was—unlike the systems conceived by Plato, More, and Kropotkin—put into practice. This experiment, which began with the Russian Revolution in 1917, is generally considered to have failed. At present, North Korea and Cuba are the only countries with planned economies. We can see the results. These economies have for a long time been in desperate conditions. Even among left-wing intellectuals, almost no one continues to countenance central planning.

And yet we cannot conclude merely from actually existing socialism's failure that a planned economy could not be an attractive economic system for our present times. First, the experiment of actually existing socialism was not a scientific test but an historical experience. And any such experience is sensitive to the technological, cultural, and geopolitical conditions under which it is carried out. Because the conditions existing then differ markedly from our own, the failure of that experiment does not prove that a planned economy could not function properly in the here and now. Second, the planned economy was tested in combination with a particular political system—namely, the so-called dictatorship of the proletariat. It was a system featuring no democratic control: power was in the hands of the ruling clique of a political party. By contrast, we want to look at a democratic system in which the level of citizen participation exceeds even that of today. Framed within democratic institutions, a planned economy might work considerably better than it did, for instance, under the rule of the SED in the German Democratic Republic. Third, a planned economy can operate on the basis of various sets of rules, and the set that was used in the Eastern bloc countries was certainly not the best of them. Mathematical economists have since developed optimized planning procedures which promise far better results.

For all these reasons, we should give the idea of a planned economy as a possible alternative system our serious consideration. Maybe Marx was right after all!

Here we will investigate the scope and feasibility of a planned economy in two steps. First, we will consider it in the abstract, focusing on the fundamental characteristics of a hypothetical optimally planned economy to draw conclusions about its possibilities and limitations.

Then, we will combine the insights thus gained with analysis of the experiences of planned economies in Eastern Europe.

PLANNING AS AN ALTERNATIVE TO THE MARKET

Let us set aside for now the sorry story of the Eastern bloc and begin at the level of theory, by outlining the fundamental characteristics of a planned economy. The ideal mode of operation of a pure planned economy may be sketched as follows. First, the government gathers extensive information about the production potential of the economy and about society members' needs. This gathering of information is concerned with not only the present, but also how production potential and needs can be expected to develop over several years to come. Then, the state makes decisions regarding the volume of production and the investment of all enterprises, and the distribution of all goods—both to private households for final consumption, and to enterprises for their ongoing production and the expansion of productive capacities. All those fit to work have a general duty to do so, and there are legal guidelines for determining the amount of labor people need to perform depending on the workplace and factoring in relevant personal characteristics, such as age and health. The distribution of consumer goods is determined by similarly detailed guidelines. Based on criteria such as age, sex, and place of residence, the state specifies the bundle of goods and services that an individual is to receive. Decisions of the state regarding the overall production and distribution of goods are summarized in the form of a coherent plan in which, for each good and service, the volume of production matches the volume of consumption. All enterprises and all distribution centers are legally bound to follow this plan.

The plan incorporates decisions that may or may not be the result of some process of democratic will formation. From this point on, let us assume a form of central planning that *is* democratically legitimized, since this is certainly desirable. The process might, for example, involve competing political parties presenting overall economic plans to voters that have different emphases—with some of their plans, perhaps, assigning more resources to the health sector, others favoring the energy sector, and still others, the protection of the environment. Whichever party wins an election takes on the responsibilities of government, and can be expected to put its plans into practice.

At the level of theory, there are three major differences between planned and market economies that are useful to keep in mind as we try to establish the prospects for a planned economy in the twenty-first century. First, an economic plan is a centralized mechanism for the co-ordination of economic activities, whereas the market is decentralized. Second, the allocation of resources under planned economies is done on administrative orders, whereas under market conditions it results from voluntary transactions; thus, a plan represents a hierarchical, vertical form of coordination, whereas the market is a horizontal form. Third, central planning aims at explicit coordination in advance, which is to say *ex ante*, whereas coordination in a market system takes place *ex post*, on the basis of the adaptive behavior of economic agents.

Although central planning is likely to appear alien to today's readers, it is a strikingly commonsense idea. It can be thought of as simply the economic functioning of a family, transposed onto society as a whole. In a sense, a family is a miniature planned economy, with a planned division of labor and distribution of the production yield among its members. Disregarding the "external trade" of this miniature economy, the allocation of resources within the family is rarely ever based on market transactions. Rather, an explicit coordination takes place: the adults agree on what is to be done for the good of the whole family, and on who gets what.

The idea of a planned economy is further made plausible by the ob-servation that large-scale capitalist corporations, with their strong in-ternal divisions of labor, often prevail in competition with smaller firms—and that resources within such corporations are allocated through a hierarchical structure that is similar to a planned economy. From this perspective, the idea of organizing the overall economy as if it were one gigantic corporation does not appear outlandish at all. One might even hope, in this way, to achieve for the overall economy the comparatively high efficiency in production that characterizes individual capitalist corporations.

We should be cautious not to overstretch the analogy with corporations, however, for two reasons. First, the aims of corporations are relatively clearly defined. The capitalists who own a corporation demand that its value be maximized; they want the corporation to achieve the maximum possible profit. By contrast, the citizens of a state have diverse interests. For a planned economy, then, it is much more difficult to reach decisions, and later on to evaluate and judge their consequences, than it is for a corporation. Second, although corporations are hierarchically organized, they make extensive use of financial incentives to achieve their goals. Corporations have "profit centers," profit sharing, performance-based pay schemes, and so forth. By contrast, money does not play any role in a pure planned economy, other than as a unit of account. A planned economy should, in principle, be able to do without material incentives, because part of its justification is the aim of replacing self-interest as individuals' main economic motivation with a nobler, socialist morality.

THE THESIS OF SUPERIORITY

The cardinal question is: plan or market? Interestingly, there is a logical argument that speaks in favor of a planned economy. Imagine an economy in which there are no markets, financial relations, or money, but in which all resources are used precisely as in an actually existing market economy. In this economy, enterprises produce and supply, and individuals work and consume, exactly as they do today. Such an economy, mirroring all real aspects of an actual economy, can in theory be established by a central plan containing all the necessary instructions for the economic behavior of the various enterprises and individuals. This only necessitates that the planners correctly assign the economic processes to the enterprises and individuals, and that they possess the authority to implement the plan. In such a planned economy, the real economic processes are not based on market transactions, but on orders. But the material consequences are identical.

What this thought experiment shows is that our polity could, in principle, fare as well under a planned economy as it does under today's economic system. If the planners were benevolent, and if the existing system were suboptimal, they could even achieve an allocation of resources for the polity that was superior to that achieved by the current system. They might improve on the results of a market economy by, for instance, not allowing unemployment, not allowing social inequalities to arise, or not allowing stultifying commercials to be shown.

AN AGNOSTIC INTERLUDE

This logical argument is based on the assumption that a planned economy and a market economy should be considered of equal worth if they correspond to the same real economy. But is this really the case? This perspective on things neglects the psychological dimension of economic activity. The motives that lead to a certain service's being rendered or received also play a role in the satisfaction of the people involved. And these motives differ strongly between a planned and a market economy.

A supporter of market economies may point to the fact that when services are provided through market transactions the one who provides the service receives something in return. The individuals involved are doing each other a favor. This mutual advantage makes it easier to understand the situation of the other person and promotes everyone's preparedness to adopt a common perspective. This mutuality has a positive effect on human relations. The provision of services in a planned economy, by contrast, is based on carrying out orders from the state. The relationship between provider and recipient lacks the sense of mutuality, and they can therefore not share the feeling of pursuing a common undertaking. Seen from this perspective, the psychological dimension of economic activity is more appealing in the case of a market economy.

A supporter of central planning, however, would stress entirely different aspects. He might point out that market negotiations mean that each side tries to get the better of the other, which leads to mutual distrust. In a planned economy, by contrast, the provision of services takes place within the context of a society-wide project in the interest of the common good. This motivates the individuals involved to help each other, as any help rendered does not benefit the private advantage of someone else. Especially when a central plan is democratically created, people feel that they are achieving something together.

As these opposing perspectives show, the attitudes and motivations of individuals in a market and a planned economy can differ widely even if the results achieved in terms of the real economy are the same. The two perspectives remind us, moreover, not to expect any consensus on which system should be valued more highly based on the human disposition it engenders.

THE PROBLEM OF INFORMATION IN PLANNED ECONOMIES

Perhaps it is best to put aside considerations of effects on fellow-feeling. We can find a clearer argument for rejecting the thesis that central planning is superior to a market economy. Specifically, we can note that the whole thesis rests on untenable assumptions regarding the planner.

First of all, who or what is the "planner"? The term refers to the institution that draws up the concrete plan on behalf of the citizens, and which makes it operational and controls its execution. Of course, a benevolent, all-powerful, and omniscient planner could bring about the best of all possible worlds through its edicts. But for our purposes, it is more interesting to find out what a polity may actually get from central planning if the planner is not fully benevolent, not all-powerful, and not fully knowledgeable of all the aspects important to the decisions to be made. This is much more plausible than any assumption of a perfect planner in the best of all possible worlds.

To elucidate the fundamental problem of information in a planned economy, let's begin by assuming that the planner is perfectly benevolent— meaning the planner sincerely acts in the interests of the polity—but lacks complete knowledge of the production possibilities of enterprises and of the preferences of private households. Without such knowledge, the planner cannot determine the optimal allocation of resources. On the production side, this lack of information concerns mainly quantitative values that represent technological relations. Making a sound plan requires information about the maximum output for a given product within a specific time frame, as determined by the technological possibilities of an assemblage of factors of production. A planner also needs to know which alternative assemblages of production factors would allow for the manufacture of the same amount of the product (at the same level of quality). The planner needs to know all this for multiple output levels and for all products in the economy. This information is necessary to calculate the point at which it might be beneficial, in order to achieve a particular production output, to shift production factors from one product, enterprise, or sector to another product, enterprise, or sector. On the consumption side, the planner also lacks direct access to the preferences of households. Yet any sound plan must recognize how households would choose among alternative consumption patterns if given the opportunity to do so, as well as how many of one kind of good they would be willing to do without to raise the consumption of some other good by a specific amount. This vast amount of information is necessary to plan optimally for the overall economy and the distribution of goods.

The information needed for central planning can be collected only at the level of individual producers and individual consumers. Ideally, the knowledge that producers and consumers acquire is passed on to the planner, so that the planner can work out the optimal plan on the basis of the information.

This way of proceeding faces two technical problems, however. First, the volume of information at the level of producers and consumers that is relevant for the construction of the plan is extremely large and complex. It is therefore not clear whether it can be communicated to the planner at all. In a distant future, there may be a technology available that allows us to read minds, and which can at regular intervals upload the totality of producers' and consumers' knowledge to the memory of a central computer, to which the planner has access. But no such technology will exist in the near future.

Second, the volume of information outstrips the computational capacities of the planner. To establish the optimal plan, he or she must solve an extremely complex mathematical maximization problem, one that is too complicated for today's computers.

At least at present, then, the idea of a planner who knows everything and commands an infinite computational capacity is a chimera. If we want to think seriously about the prospects of central planning, we should therefore assume that the planner can absorb and digest only a limited amount of information.

THE PLANNING PROCEDURE ACCORDING TO ARROW AND HURWICZ

Mathematical economists have by now developed methods by which a planner could establish an optimal plan for the overall economy in simple computational steps, even given a limited exchange of information between the planner and enterprises and households. All these "scientific utopias" are based on iterative procedures that are repeated in virtual form until a coherent and stable plan emerges. Only if such a virtual end point is reached do the real economic processes actually happen in accordance with the plan.

The most convincing idea for a planning procedure was suggested by the American economists Kenneth Arrow and Leonid Hurwicz in the 1960s. Their basic idea harks back to work the Polish economist Oskar Lange did some thirty years before that. Lange had been a big name in the international debate about socialism in the 1930s, in which many famous economists, such as Ludwig von Mises and Friedrich von Hayek, took part. After the Second World War, Lange served in political offices at the highest level in the People's Republic of Poland. Kenneth Arrow received the Nobel Memorial Prize in Economics in 1972; Leonid Hurwicz received the same in 2007. Arrow was the youngest economist so honored, and Hurwicz the oldest. Both exerted an enormous influence on the development of economic theory. Some economists say that, really, Arrow deserved two of the prizes.

The planning procedure suggested by Arrow and Hurwicz makes use of so-called shadow prices. These are fictional prices, whose sole function is to measure the relative scarcity of various resources and their social value in alternative uses, and not genuine prices, which, within a market economy, are one of the factors that determine the purchasing power of economic agents. The procedure begins with the planner's drawing up a complete list of such shadow prices, assigning one price for every good and for every type of labor performed. Next, the planner communicates to each enterprise the list of shadow prices relevant for it within a certain time frame—that is, the prices for its products and production factors, including the labor force the enterprise uses in production.

The next stage draws on the enterprises' own expertise. Each of them prepares a hypothetical production plan on the basis of the shadow prices. A production plan lists the amounts of the various products an enterprise intends to produce within the given time frame, as well as the amounts of the various input factors required for that production. It is the enterprise's task to select, out of all the technically possible production plans, the one that will lead to the highest hypothetical profit, given the shadow prices dictated by the planner. In other words, the enterprise identifies the program with the highest difference between the shadow value of produced goods and the shadow costs of the production factors used up in producing them.

Once all enterprises have submitted their production plans, the planner can easily calculate the enterprises' levels of hypothetical supply and hypothetical demand for each of the goods and services. The hypothetical supply of a particular good equals the sum of the amounts of that good that each of its producers has indicated. The hypothetical demand for a good is the sum of the amounts of it submitted by those enterprises that use it as a production factor.

It follows that, for those goods produced for final consumption, only the hypothetical supply can be calculated. According to the process outlined by Arrow and Hurwicz, the hypothetical demand of private households is determined by an algorithm. The hypothetical household-sector demand for a particular good is found by adding or subtracting a certain quantity that is proportional to the difference between the social value of that good and its shadow price, using a given amount (for instance, the amount consumed in the previous economic period) as the basis for the calculation. The social value of a good is, in turn, mathematically determined by the first derivative of the planner's objective function, which reflects the planner's view of the effect that the availability of consumer goods will have on social welfare. This objective function should represent a just balancing of the interests of various groups of the population, and possess clear democratic legitimation. If the social value of a good exceeds its shadow price, a proportional quantity is added to the assumed level of demand for it, and the hypothetical demand is thus greater than the assumed basis amount. If the social value is lower than the shadow price, a proportional quantity is subtracted and hypothetical demand is below the assumed basis amount.

This admittedly slightly artificial approach was chosen by Arrow and Hurwicz because they did not want to obligate every private household to draw up a hypothetical consumption plan, similar to the production plans drawn up by the enterprises. There is another alternative, however: the task could be carried out by means of a poll of households. The planner could give each of the households polled the list of shadow prices and a fictitious budget. The projected total sum of these budgets would have to correspond to the value of the enterprises' hypothetical supply to the household sector. Participants in the poll would then have to allocate their budgets to the various consumer goods according to their preferences, and they would then report to the planner the resulting hypothetical demands for the various goods. By projecting these values, the planner would then be able to calculate the overall hypothetical demand in the household sector.

In any case, once the information has been compiled about the responses of enterprises and households to the initial list of shadow prices, the planner is able to establish the hypothetical demand of the household sector and the hypothetical supply and demand of the enterprise sector. This yields, for each good, a hypothetical supply and demand for the overall economy.

It is highly unlikely at this point, however, that supply and demand actually match each other. More probable is that for some goods, supply exceeds demand, and for others, demand exceeds supply. The planner therefore revises the shadow prices according to the following rule: if demand for a specific good is greater than supply, raise the shadow price for that good slightly; if there is excess supply for a specific good, reduce the shadow price slightly. Larger discrepancies between supply and demand call for larger price changes. Similarly, the shadow prices of various kinds of labor are adapted by comparing the demand of enterprises and the size of the available labor force given the skills of the existing working population.

Now the procedure enters a second round. The revised list of shadow prices is again sent to the enterprises, and they use it to generate the new production plan that would maximize their shadow profits. Enterprises will tend to increase their supply of a product if the price for it has risen, and to reduce supply if it has fallen. With demand and input factors, of course, the opposite will be the case. The revised production plans are handed over to the planner, and become the basis of a revision of the hypothetical demand of the household sector.

If discrepancies between supply and demand continue to exist, the planning procedure goes into a third round. The planner once again changes the shadow prices, according to the same pattern as before, and the whole procedure is repeated until, at the end of the cycle, hypothetical supply matches hypothetical demand for each good. The production and consumption plans that make up this match are therefore coherent— that is, the economy can actually put them into practice. They are subsequently codified in the central plan and the plan is carried out.

Arrow and Hurwicz were able to prove that, under certain conditions, a central plan that results from their procedure is not only technically coherent, but also economically efficient—that is, without wasting any resources, it realizes the goals the planner set having evaluated the various groups' interests within the population. Thus, this planning procedure achieves optimal allocation of resources.

This is an extremely significant result. What it suggests is that a planned economy with decentralized information and a limited capacity for communicating and processing information can pass the allocation test.

OPEN QUESTIONS REGARDING THE UTOPIA OF ITERATIVE PLANNING

Unfortunately, Arrow and Hurwicz's procedure has not been tested so far, and nor has any other method for optimal iterative planning. This is not because of the mathematical challenge of the approach; some countries that have experimented with a planned economy have had excellent schools of mathematical economists who could easily have mastered these methods. Perhaps such planning procedures did not appeal to the political elites of these countries, who might have sensed a threat to their power. Any planning procedure using such a transparent set of rules would certainly reduce the scope for interventions by party bigwigs. It is also possible that these planning procedures were rejected on ideological grounds, because they make use of variables—such as profit, price, and supply and demand—that are associated with capitalism. Although the Italian economist Enrico Barone showed in 1908 that even in a planned economy such concepts are needed to make rational use of resources and avoid waste, this line of thought never got much traction among socialists. Socialist leaders would have had to explain, for instance, that not all profit was the same. The profit of a monopolist employer often reflects the exploitation of workers and of those consuming the products, while the profits of enterprises who face the challenges of highly competitive markets are first and foremost an indication of their efficiency.

Today, such ideological objections are of only secondary importance; most people could accept that the economic concepts associated with capitalism could also be useful in the coordination of a planned economy. But there are weightier reasons for the fact that procedures for optimal planning have not so far been tested. There are further questions we need to ask of such procedures, and these can be divided into three categories. The first category concerns the allocation problem; the second category concerns the cooperation problem; and the third category concerns both these problems at once. Taken together, these questions lead to serious doubts that a theoretically optimal planning procedure could work under contemporary conditions. Let us look at these problems in more detail.

Complexity

The first problem concerns the actual complexity of the planning procedure, which is likely to be of such a magnitude that we are unable to master it. The individual steps in the procedure are simple, but in the case of a developed economy they have to be applied to an extremely large number of goods. The reason for this is that technological progress continually produces new goods and innumerable variations of products; standardized products give way to products that are tailored to the wishes of diverse consumers. This applies to goods used by enterprises as intermediary goods just as much as to consumer goods. As a consequence, it is not really possible to determine the number of different goods that exist today. Even with state-of-the-art information technology, it would be a task of Herculean proportions to take account of each of these goods individually within the planning procedure.

To reduce the required amount of information, the planning procedure could combine a number of different goods into a class of goods. But this would produce brands that no one wants to consume, while for other brands the supply would be insufficient. It is not possible to say in general how detrimental this would be, as this depends on the extent of the discrepancy between supply and demand, as well as on the significance that people attach to their consumption.

Another approach would be to incorporate a proper market for consumer goods into the planning procedures. Households would receive a genuine monetary income for buying consumer goods. The planner would dictate prices and observe the available stocks in warehouses to see for which goods demand was higher than supply, and for which supply was higher than demand. The planner would then raise the price in the first case, and lower it in the second case, aiming at balancing out supply and demand.

Unfortunately, however, a genuine consumer market for private households does not fit in with the iterative planning procedure for enterprises. In the case of the latter, we have shadow prices and fictional production plans that are not put into practice before the procedure has established a correspondence between supply and demand for each good. A genuine consumer market, by contrast, operates with proper prices and quantities and informs the planner only ex post. To put it differently: to establish which goods are in excess, and which goods are experiencing shortages, the goods must have entered the market. The enterprises must therefore already have begun production—which they were supposed to do only at the conclusion of the iterative planning procedure.

Of course, each round of the procedure could immediately be put into practice, with enterprises trying to implement their production plans even before the planning procedure has come to a conclusion. But in this case, the prices being used by enterprises to attempt to maximize their profits would not be reliable indicators of the social values of the various goods, because supply and demand would differ. Enterprises would be left with products for which there was no demand, while not all goods for which there *was* demand would actually be available. These discrepancies between supply and consumption mean that the distribution of productive activities cannot be efficient. As it takes considerable time to set up a revised production plan, the allocation of resources would, for the most part, be inefficient. And from time to time, some of the framework conditions would change, too, so that the adaptation of the plan might go in the wrong direction. Additional damage would be caused by the fact that some decisions on production are irreversible, as for example when intermediary goods are used for building machinery that is specifically designed for the production of particular goods. In such cases, misplaced allocation on the basis of inaccurate prices would have long-term effects, because irreversible decisions—for instance, installations of new machinery—would influence the supply behavior of enterprises in future planning cycles.

It also not clear what an iterative planning procedure would need to look like to establish optimal investment and consumption for durable goods such as housing and cars. The procedure developed by Arrow and Hurwicz makes sense for production and consumption over the relatively short term, meaning perhaps a quarter or a year. But an attempt to use it for long-term planning would lead to extreme complexity. Strictly speaking, the planner would need to provide the enterprises and distribution centers with instructions for each good for each relevant point in time (for instance, for each quarter of a ten-year period), and for each potential future situation (anticipating, for instance, results in the area of research and development, the discovery of natural resources, climate change, the occurrence of natural disasters, or the development of prices on the global market). With this approach, this would be necessary because the value of a good for producers and consumers depends not only on its technical features, but also on the point in time at which it is available and on the external conditions at that moment. In the case of durable goods, such as machinery, the hypothetical demand can only be established if shadow prices are time-specific as well as situation-specific.

Take as an example a pharmaceutical enterprise that has the option of building a manufacturing plant specifically designed for production of drug X. The profitability of this investment depends on the shadow price for X over the period during which the plant produces the drug. The price of X will be high if, in the meantime, no better drug is synthesized and prepared for production, but it will be low if a new, better drug appears. The planner therefore needs to tell the enterprise the shadow prices for X across the various time periods and possible situations if the enterprise is to be able to maximize its hypothetically expected profit within a given time horizon.

A pragmatic solution for making central decisions on investments might be to distinguish between short-term adaptations of production and long-term projects. Decisions could be made about the former on the basis of a slightly extended iterative planning procedure, as described above. Decisions concerning the latter, by contrast, could be made in the context of strategic planning that established the long-term structural development of the economy as well as the level of investment for the economy as a whole. An example of such strategic planning will be presented in the next chapter. Nevertheless, this approach, too, raises numerous questions to which planning theorists have so far not been able to provide satisfactory answers. It is, for instance, not clear where the dividing line between the two types of investment should be drawn. And there is also the question of the coherence between short-term and long-term planning, given that the effects of the short-term plans need to fit with the long-term plan.

The Threat of Manipulation

The second serious criticism leveled at all iterative planning procedures concerns the cooperation expected from individual agents.

Clearly, to begin with, what is needed is the cooperation of individuals in their roles as employees and consumers. A pure planned economy has neither a labor market nor a market for consumer goods. The individuals are supposed to inform the planner truthfully about facts about themselves insofar as these are relevant to labor and consumption, so that the planner can determine the optimal distribution of tasks and goods. Once the plan has been determined, all individuals are supposed to stick to it. As there are no financial incentives, the question of motivation arises: Why would individuals cooperate honestly with the planner? But this question is more or less the same as the one we came across in our discussion of common ownership. And since we discussed it in detail there, we do not need to go into it again.

The cooperation problem for iterative planning procedures also concerns the enterprises. Within the framework of the planning procedure described above, there is a strong temptation for enterprises not to adhere to the rule of profit maximization and to hand over incorrect production plans, because in this economic system there is no genuine profit for the enterprises—money serves only as a unit of account, and does not give anyone a claim to resources. As the enterprises' profits are fictional, they do not provide an incentive. Under these circumstances, an enterprise would be tempted to lie to the planner and present a production plan that would be particularly easy for their workforce to carry out. While the implementation of a production plan is comparatively easy to control, it is difficult for the state to check the accuracy of the data used for the construction of a profit-maximizing production plan. If similar enterprises were to present production plans that differed widely, this would indicate that the planner had been lied to. But even if the production plans were uniform, the planner could not be certain that they were also efficient, because the enterprises might have simply colluded in drawing up their plans. And if the enterprises distorted their production plans in this way, there could be no efficient central plan.

Because the accuracy of the information cannot be checked, and because there is no incentive to be truthful, this system can work only if the sense of duty to tell the planner the truth is strong enough to keep the enterprises on the straight and narrow. A healthy skepticism is warranted at this point. The situation we want—for everyone to act honestly and provide the correct information—seems a very fragile one. As in the case of the value systems we discussed in Chapter 4, there is reason to fear that in the long term, individual transgressions will lead to a general deterioration of those values that could, in principle, support cooperation.

Weak Innovation

The third question about the centrally planned utopia is how such a system would produce the innovations that are necessary to increase an economy's long-term productivity and diversity of products. As we shall see, this question entails an allocation as well as cooperation problem.

One problem is that the planner faces an overwhelming information problem when it comes to establishing the overall available resources for research and development, as well as their distribution among the various enterprises, research institutes, and individual projects. Decisions on research and development resemble those on investments, because they bind resources to particular projects over a period of time and produce only long-term, and uncertain, gains. As explained above, we do not know what a theoretically efficient and practicable planning procedure for investments would look like.

Another problem is that in a planned economy enterprises have no financial incentives to be innovative. Innovation means structural change, and that often comes with inconvenience, such as having to learn new ways of working, making changes to the workplace, and instructing suppliers and customers. It is also questionable whether the workforce's own motivation would be strong enough to maximize the potential for innovation. Perhaps, instead, employees would keep bright ideas and innovations to themselves and would never make them known to the planner.

This does not mean that central planning is always inferior to capitalism when it comes to innovation. Here we should make two distinctions, one between radical and additional innovation, and another between the initial introduction of an innovation and its subsequent diffusion throughout the economy.

Capitalism is probably better suited to small innovations which spread across a broad range of enterprises, because under capitalism, competition forces enterprises to adapt quickly to the "best practice" in their sectors.

In the case of the quick distribution of radical innovations across the overall economy, by contrast, we might expect that central planning is more efficient, because there are no patents to act as obstacles.

But such radical innovations must first be made. When we look at the history of capitalism, we find that the majority of radical innovations came about due to the assertiveness of individual entrepreneurs. Private property, credit markets, open access to markets, and market testing provide an institutional framework for probing the intuitions and idiosyncratic ideas of innovators. The planning utopia we are considering here cannot avail itself of this tried and tested model for generating innovation.

Most importantly, what the pure planned economy lacks is the maverick individualist, as there is no space for private enterprise. In a planned economy, potential innovators are not allowed to introduce innovations on their own initiative and at their own risk. An innovation can only be implemented if it is part of the overall plan. And if the plan is to be democratically legitimated, this means that an innovator would need to seek the democratic approval of his idea. It is difficult to imagine that under these conditions innovations would proliferate as they have done under capitalism.

PRELIMINARY CONCLUSION

We have seen that even the best models of the planned economy raise serious questions. Despite the sophisticated design of the planning procedure, central planning turns out, upon closer scrutiny, to be an extremely complex task, and thus difficult to implement. It is susceptible to problems arising from asymmetric information and would most likely engender only a weak dynamic of innovation.

Let us nevertheless ask: What could a planned economy for a future United States of Europe look like?

Maybe like this. The European planning commission would use an iterative planning procedure similar to that of Arrow and Hurwicz, but limited in scope to a comparatively small number of aggregate goods categories. The people would prepare themselves for a markedly reduced diversity of products. This disadvantage would be compensated for by an emphasis on democratic participation in the planning process, including the determination of norms regulating work and consumption. All economic processes would be agreed by democratic bodies and would be closely monitored by the state, using the most advanced information technologies. All individuals would be asked to participate in multiple democratic committees to work out declarations, resolutions, and statutes. The enterprises would prize, above all else, codetermination and overcoming the division of intellectual and manual labor. The society overall would be characterized by the priority of politics, and thus would reward those inclined towards politics.

Because the rhythm of innovation would slow down, the level of prosperity would lag behind that of the rest of the developed capitalist world. Technological progress would follow a different path than under capitalism, because it would no longer be guided by the pursuit of profit, but by the processes of democratic will formation. The main focus of investment, for instance, might shift toward environmental technologies.

The majority of European voters would want to see an equalization of living standards within the population. But because the overall level of prosperity would be lower than in the richest capitalist countries, many highly qualified individuals and those with entrepreneurial talent would emigrate. The divergence from the economies of China and North America would thus only increase. The public mood would turn ever more against the egoists turning their backs on the United States of Europe, and a national debate would develop about if and how such emigration could be stopped. The specter of a new wall is haunting Europe.

CENTRAL PLANNING IN REALITY

The planned economy implemented in the Soviet Union and in Eastern Europe differed in three important respects from the utopia (or dystopia?) of planning described so far. First, the plans did not correspond to a democratic will. They expressed the goals of a government that in most cases did not enjoy the support of large parts of the population. Second, the plans were created in a top-down fashion through numerous negotiations between different hierarchical levels. At the top of this hierarchy stood the governmental cabinet of a communist party. Then followed, in descending order, the ministries for the various sectors, the production associations, individual enterprises, groups of workers, and individual workers. In the process of drawing up the plan, individual groups within this hierarchy were clearly seeking to advance their own particular interests. The honest communication of information to create an efficient central plan was not the priority. Third, as opposed to a pure planned economy, labor power was sold for a wage on a labor market, and, correspondingly, the people received a part of their provisions on a market for consumer goods. The system did not do without money as an incentive, and the communist ideal of distribution according to need was postponed indefinitely into the future. But income inequality stayed within relatively narrow limits. Of more importance was the inequality that resulted from the many privileges enjoyed by party members and bureaucrats.

The planned economy developed into a functioning economic system first under Stalin in the Soviet Union at the end of the 1920s, and then shortly after the end of the Second World War in some European countries that had been occupied by the Red Army. The majority of countries who introduced central planning had underdeveloped economies in which most people worked in agriculture. Their populations were poorly educated and trained, and they had little capital. These countries were also unable to draw on long traditions of democratic self-government, as those in Western Europe could. Some had not even had the experience of being states under the rule of law. Lacking in them was a lively civil society, with its clubs, political parties, and multifarious associations, which is the fertile ground for a dynamic economy. Moreover, the planned economies of the Eastern bloc used a significant part of their resources, including the most qualified individuals, for military and "intelligence" purposes in the context of the Cold War—a conflict in which they were confronting an obviously better equipped enemy. Towards the end of the 1980s and beginning of the 1990s, actually existing socialism collapsed.

What were the fundamental principles underlying the Soviet-type economic system? The yearly plan determined economic activity at the operational level. After initial negotiations with the ministerial offices, and prior to any decisions having been taken, each enterprise received hundreds or thousands of indicators—figures the enterprise had to meet in the course of the planning period. These included figures for the output of products as well as the intermediary goods to be received from other enterprises. The plan determined the number of employees and their levels of qualification, as well as the total wages to be paid by the enterprise. The plan further contained financial figures for costs, profits, and borrowings, as well as the volume of investment and selected innovation targets.

Certain planning targets were generally considered to be priorities and, under certain circumstances, meeting or exceeding these targets was explicitly rewarded by the party hierarchy in the form of material or symbolic advantages.

Unlike an ideal planned economy, the central plans were not coherent in themselves, were modified several times during their execution, and were ultimately never fulfilled. And money and markets did end up playing a role in the Soviet economic system. Employees received monetary remuneration for their work, and could use this money to buy commodities. The state exercised a monopoly power over the labor market (on the demand side), as well as over the market for consumer goods (on the supply side). Individuals could only escape these monopolies by creating shadow economies or by participating in the few sectors of the economy in which limited private initiative was permitted. For the official markets, the planners fixed the wages and the prices for consumer goods, guided not just by considerations of relative scarcity, but also by political aims. Compared to capitalist economies, the wage gap was narrow and everyday consumer goods rather cheap. Apart from provision through markets, administrative rationing played an important role. Some goods and services were organized for employees by their enterprises.

While prices and money income were important to private individuals, they were of only secondary interest to most enterprises and ministries. As opposed to market economies, money did not play an active role within the enterprise sector. Enterprises' decisions on production were not guided by prices, and prices had scarcely any influence on the structure of production. The enterprises were, in fact, not subjected to strict budgetary constraints and thus relieved of the responsibility for economic accounting, and of the ultimate threat of bankruptcy. The only purpose of prices was to represent the flow of resources in a universal currency. Only in those branches of the economy that engaged in foreign trade with capitalist countries (and which thus provided welcome foreign currency) were decisions guided by prices. These prices were those of the world market.

COOPERATION PROBLEMS

In this economic system, the problem of cooperation was magnified by the political leadership's lack of democratic legitimacy. Those governing the country tried to consolidate their domination by influencing public opinion, by means of their monopoly on the media. The population had to be convinced that the party alone knew the truth, and was on its way to fulfill its historical mission in the service of humanity. Any event of importance had to be reported against this backdrop. But this attempt at indoctrination failed, and soon the saviors of mankind were unmasked as narrow-minded liars. The dishonesty of the elite had an impact on people's attitudes. It damaged trust in general, and thus eroded the willingness to cooperate that is so essential to successful planning of an economy.

The diverging interests of the various economic actors and the limited knowledge about subordinate units within the planning structure resulted in all sorts of misconduct. Individual actors sought to improve their own situation at the expense of those of others. As far as their dealings with the superior ministry were concerned, the enterprises tried to receive the maximum level of input factors, along with a production target that was as low as possible. As the profitability of the enterprise was immaterial, this was a rational strategy for trying successfully to implement the plan—and the career of the manager of the enterprise depended on implementing it. As a result, an important part of the available human resources was spent on just negotiating the plan, rather than on optimizing the production process.

In the course of drawing up and carrying out the plan, enterprises were always requesting more natural resources, intermediary products, workers, and investment goods. They routinely underestimated their resources to their higher-ups while secretly building up reserves, in case planning targets were raised. Even when targets could easily have been exceeded, the enterprises did not exceed them, for fear that in the following year the ministry would order them to achieve still higher production targets, or assign them fewer resources.

ALLOCATION PROBLEMS

As all enterprises tried to extract as many resources from the rest of the economy as possible, and at the same time ignore requests from others, their demands always exceeded what they received. There was a chronic shortage of intermediary goods, especially spare parts, qualified labor, and machines. At the same time, these shortages caused the enterprises to hoard even more resources—a vicious circle. Thus, this shortage economy was accompanied by spare capacity; machines stood idle and workers had nothing to do despite the general dearth of goods.

Continual shortages of goods, deliveries that were expected in accordance with the plan but that never arrived, and the absence of a free market as an alternative all led enterprises and ministries to try to protect themselves against these uncertainties by becoming as autonomous as possible—that is, by producing for themselves the input factors they needed. Unfortunately, this made the organization of production extremely cumbersome, while inhibiting efficiency gains that could have been achieved through the division of labor across the entire economy.

The continuous absorption of labor power by the enterprises did put an end to the misery of unemployment. This was certainly a significant achievement of the countries of actually existing socialism, and it set them apart from capitalist countries. But the removal of the threat of redundancy also produced some problematic effects with respect to labor discipline. What's more, the wage gap was small and important consumer goods were rationed. All this weakened the incentive to work. As a result, workers were absent for long periods and changed jobs frequently, and there was a good deal of theft from workplaces. Attempts at strengthening the motivation of the workers with moral appeals and by instilling social norms, as in the case of the Stakhanovite movement, ultimately failed. This, however, should not come as a surprise given the leadership's lack of democratic legitimacy. All in all, the working population of these countries was characterized by a pronounced passivity.

The intensity of work often varied markedly. Periods of more or less enforced idleness due to broken machinery, missing spare parts, or absent specialist workers, were followed by periods of hectic activity when the economic system was suddenly put on a sort of war footing, and tasked by the party with mobilizing all its resources to achieve some important goal of historical significance.

The state monopoly on the production and distribution of consumer goods, the lack of democratic accountability for the planner, the artificially low prices, and the fact that considerations of profitability did not play any role led to an insufficient level of provision of goods and to goods being of a relatively poor quality. Where capitalist countries were characterized by buyer markets, the economies of the Eastern Bloc were seller markets—the seller always had the upper hand. Thus, households would try to improve their living conditions by buying on the black market and participating in the shadow economy. These parallel activities weakened the allocation of resources in the official sector even further—for instance, because of workers who stayed home from work to decorate their apartments, or who stole tools. These conditions contributed to the fact that even those true believers who had initially acted in accordance with all of the official rules gradually became cynical and disillusioned, and eventually lost faith in socialism.

EXTENSIVE GROWTH BUT NOT INTENSIVE GROWTH

Given all these systemic failures and in light of the dismal historic precedent, it is perhaps surprising that, in fact, the planned economies managed to grow quickly for several decades—very quickly, actually. In the 1960s, there were still several Western experts who were convinced that the Soviet Union was set to overtake the United States in terms of per-capita income within a generation. And, indeed, until the mid-1970s the annual real rate of growth of gross domestic product (GDP) per capita was usually higher in the USSR than it was in the United States. Even when looking at the overall period between 1950 and 1989, the USSR has a slightly higher average rate of growth than the United States. More recent empirical work has shown that the rate of long-term growth in the countries of actually existing socialism was not much different from the rate of growth in comparable market economies. Among developing economies, growth was slightly better in planned economies than in comparable market economies; among richer economies, it was slightly worse.

What were the reasons for this? Soviet-type economies were, initially, able to produce substantial "extensive growth." This means that resources that had previously lain idle, or had not been used very productively, could be mobilized, and with their help, fairly simple production chains could be replicated and extended. This strategy allowed planners to modernize large parts of the economy. Large numbers of workers were shifted from traditionally organized agriculture into modern industry. The percentage of women in the workforce was raised substantially. The level of education improved dramatically across the whole population. With the help of concentrated efforts in a few key sectors and the construction of a comprehensive infrastructure, it was possible to overcome problems of coordination that often prevent the development of modern sectors in developing market economies. The USSR was thus able to resist military attack by Nazi fascism and ultimately able to defeat Hitler's Germany, thanks to the rapid creation of a strong heavy industry and modern infrastructure.

This rapid growth, however, was bound up with the technological conditions of the first decades and the initially backward economic structure. In Marx's terminology, the development of the productive forces was eventually fettered by the Soviet-style relations of production, which became a rigid obstacle to their further development. This meant that once the reserves of mobilization had been exhausted, the phase of "extensive growth" came to an end. From this point onwards, the planned economies would have had to move on to a phase of "intensive growth," based on innovations and enduring increases in productivity. But they were unable to do this. The economies of the Eastern bloc proved incapable of keeping up with the West in an age of product flexibility and customized production. Their central planning mechanism was neither able to generate the necessary technological progress, nor able to assimilate it from outside, to achieve an acceptable level of economic development.

THE FAILURE OF REFORM

As early as the 1950s, it was clear to some economists and politicians in the socialist countries that Soviet-style planned economies were not sustainable in the long term, and that ways to reform them had to be found. The most comprehensive attempt in this direction was made by Hungary with the introduction of the so-called New Economic Mechanism on January 1, 1968. On that day, Hungary abolished the entire system of annual planning. Formally, state-owned enterprises became independent and were allowed to determine their short-term production program for themselves. The enterprises were supposed to follow the dictates of the market rather than those of the planner, motivated by the prospect of retaining a share of the profits that were made.

But old habits persisted under the new system. In a relatively small economy like Hungary's, in which production in the state sector is strongly concentrated in a small number of large enterprises, the state bureaucracy did not need an explicit plan to steer the economy. Thus, actual economic processes continued to reflect bureaucratic priorities rather than needs expressed in the market. The ministerial bureaucracy now negotiated with individual enterprises about prices, taxes, subventions, credits, and investments. And it had a significant hand in determining the structure of economic sectors by regularly saving existing enterprises from bankruptcy and regulating the entry of competitors into their industries.

Under the new mechanism, the decisions of the bureaucracy were still decisive for how enterprises and their workforces fared. Governmental support was more important than success on the market. It was therefore the enterprises' main goal to negotiate bureaucratic interventions that were as advantageous as possible. While under the old planning system the enterprises had demanded more real resources and lower production targets from their ministry, they now asked for more advantageous price formations, higher subventions, and cheaper credit. The disciplinary effect of the market test thus was not felt. State interventions and the erection of barriers to market entry and exit nipped competition in the bud. In slightly different forms, the phenomenon of insatiable enterprise demand continued to manifest itself, and buyers' markets remained the exception rather than the rule.

Nevertheless, there were some improvements for consumers under this new "goulash socialism." But they did not result from the abolition of the central plan for state-owned enterprises. For one thing, the Hungarian reforms allowed the nonstate sector to expand considerably. Small private enterprises and cooperatives thus seized the opportunity to improve the provision of goods and services for the population. For another, under Hungarian Prime Minister Kadar, a new political style developed that was more tolerant and attached greater importance to the material concerns of the population.

WE CANNOT PLAN ON PLANNING

The planned economies of actually existing socialism failed when it came to the product differentiation that was made possible by the revolution in microelectronics. While in the West, technological change continuously enriched the world of production and consumption, and the speed with which new products and production methods were introduced kept accelerating, the East increasingly lagged behind. The planned economies of actually existing socialism turned out not to be suited either for producing innovation, or for taking up and implementing technological progress originating from elsewhere.

The planned economies of actually existing socialism were not pure planned economies, because the workers sold their labor for a wage and used the money to buy goods for their subsistence. The procedures used in formulating the plan and for monitoring its success were altogether inadequate. The whole economic system ultimately lacked democratic legitimacy.

In theory, we could today aim for an entirely different planned economy, one that is embedded in democratic institutions and is guided by coherent procedures. But even with the best planning procedures theoretically available, a planned economy would not be an attractive alternative to the present system.

All planning procedures that have been suggested so far are afflicted by problems concerning the collection and processing of the information that is necessary for an efficient planning of the allocation of resources. First, overwhelming complexity is the problem. The diversity of consumer needs and of technological developments represents a huge challenge for the creation of an efficient plan. Second, planning procedures suffer from the fact that, at the lower end of the hierarchy, there are no incentives for faithfully passing on the requisite information. Essentially, such an economic system depends on each individual possessing an exceptional sense of duty. But a system that only works with exceptional individuals only works in exceptional cases.

6

SELF-MANAGEMENT

WE ARE NOW AT THE HALFWAY point of our journey. Let us take a short look back at the path we have traveled so far.

We were looking for a promising alternative to capitalism, defined as a system that combines market exchanges and private property. What we demand of such an alternative is that it passes the cooperation test and the allocation test. Along the way, we visited systems of common ownership and planned economies, both of which eschew markets and private property, but we reached the conclusion that these do not amount to promising alternatives to today's system. We could not rule out that they would be incapable of solving the problem of cooperation, and it is certain they would fail to solve the allocation problem.

Where do we head next?

One thing appears incontrovertible: We must retain one of the two components of capitalism—namely, the market. The market is the only institution we have that is able to solve the allocation problem in complex economies. If an alternative to capitalism is to solve the allocation problem, then the market is, at present at least, indispensable.

Our onward journey will therefore lead us to economic systems that combine the market with noncapitalist institutions. The indispensability of the market does not say anything yet about the role of private property within the economic system, and it also leaves open the question of how large a share of the resources is to be distributed via markets. In other words, the concepts of the market and of capitalism are distinct: To concede the indispensability of the market is not to give up on our search for a better economic system.

Before moving on, it will be useful to identify the economic advantages of markets explicitly. These advantages are often overlooked, and not only by the critics of capitalism.

WHY MARKETS?

Markets can encourage economic efficiency and frugality, and they can bring about valuable innovations and coherence within complex economies. They are therefore extremely helpful in solving the cooperation and allocation problems that economic systems face. How do markets manage to do all this?

Markets reveal what individuals really want, and they motivate individuals to be careful with their resources. In a market context, prices migrate toward the level at which supply and demand are in equilibrium. Because prices reflect the overall behavior of all sellers and buyers, they are a reliable signal of the social value of the various goods and services. They guide the decisions of producers, who try to produce more of those goods with rising prices, and hence rising value contributions to society. Producers also try to save on any production factors that are becoming more expensive. This is a good thing, because production factors become more expensive when demand is high for them from other producers; and this high demand, in turn, derives from the increase in profits these producers can achieve with the use of these factors. At the same time, market prices guide the decisions of consumers. People consume less of what becomes more expensive, which means lower consumption of goods which require more resources to produce. Conversely, they consume more of a good if its price drops— that is, if society is able to produce it at a lower cost.

The information on the relative scarcity of resources, which a central planner must try to extract from individual producers and consumers, flows out all by itself from a market, in the form of prices. This easily accessible information guides the production and consumption decisions of all economic agents. The result is that resources are made available to those producers who can make the most productive use of them, and to those consumers who are prepared to pay the highest price for them. Thus, a relatively efficient allocation of resources emerges from innumerable independent decisions.

The market system also serves to promote useful innovation, because it provides incentives for individuals and enterprises to earn money by innovating. Such innovations always entail costs and their results are always unpredictable. The market mainly rewards individuals and enterprises whose innovations respond to real needs in society. There is thus an incentive to think very carefully about which innovations are really worthwhile. This applies just as much to the opening of a snack bar as it does to the launch of a revolutionary technological product. A supplier can be successful only if it manages to produce something that is valuable to others. In effect, buyers collectively select, through the things they purchase, who gets to be a producer and who does not. Established enterprises can be voted out and new enterprises with better ideas can prevail. The market rewards useful innovations and punishes useless ones; it thus dispenses with the latter and allows society to benefit from the former.

The beauty of markets—if they function properly—is their pluralism, and the fact that they do not involve concentrations of economic power. The challenge for the design of a promising economic system in the twenty-first century is to find an institutional arrangement that allows the full effects of these key advantages to be felt, but that keeps the negative effects of markets—wastefulness, inequality, the stultifying effects on personal development—to a minimum.

THE SYSTEM OF SELF-MANAGEMENT

The market can be combined with public ownership of firms, democracy in the workplace, and the central planning of strategic investment. Thus, we can imagine a mixed system in which infrastructure and the structural development of the economy, education, and the health system are subject to national planning, while the majority of goods and services are provided through self-managed enterprises and cooperatives operating in free markets. Let us call this a system of self-management. Such a system promises to combine the advantages of the market when it comes to specialization, flexibility, and diversity with the social advantages of planning and collective property. The system of self-management is the subject of this chapter.

Since the beginnings of the labor movement in the nineteenth century, the idea of producers managing themselves has informed visions of future socialist societies. The idea of self-management competed with the idea of planning, and managed to win over those socialists who were skeptical of authority and bureaucracy and had some sympathy for moderate versions of anarchism. Today, self-management is still an important point of reference for some left-wing intellectuals considering alternatives to capitalism. It is also a widespread idea among those who are partial to cooperatives. These people are by no means all socialists; there is a strong Catholic tradition, for instance, of supporting cooperatives. Some grassroots trade union organizations are also sympathetic to the idea of self-management.

Economists, especially some working during the 1970s and 1980s, have suggested various designs for economic systems based on self-management. Rather than focus on the design of one particular economist, however, we will consider here a model that integrates the most interesting elements of various designs. This is an economic system consisting of four fundamental elements. First, the means of production are, formally, the property of the state—but in contrast to planned economies, a considerable part of these property rights are transferred to the workforce that makes use of the means of production. Second, the decision-making process within enterprises is based on self-management by those employed in them. Third, the supply of goods and services to households and enterprises is mainly provided by markets. Fourth, a central plan determines the volume of overall investment within the economy, as well as the distribution of the overall investment among economic sectors and regions.

Under this economic system, the impact of the central plan is much more attenuated than in a planned economy, because at the micro level of individuals and single enterprises, the coordination of economic activity is fundamentally organized through myriad decentralized market transactions. In the system of self-management, the planner is responsible for only the macroeconomic steering and long-term development of the economy. This frees the planner from the nitty-gritty work of determining production processes in detail, and so avoids the complex procedures that raised so many problems and questions in the previous chapter.

Since the planner is responsible to citizens, the investment rate for the overall economy and its structural development is subject to the will of the electorate, whereas individuals and enterprises retain control over concrete decisions about consumption and production. In this respect, this system clearly offers more individual freedom than a planned economy. Freedom of work and freedom of consumption are enshrined, at least formally, in capitalist democracies; but self-management turns out to be superior to capitalism in this regard, insofar as it avoids concentrating wealth in the hands of a few and offers workers more opportunity to make autonomous decisions about their own activities within firms.

In short, the system of self-management promises to combine the collective rationality of planning with the flexibility of markets and the autonomy of works councils. This makes it a potentially attractive alternative to capitalism, including to the social market economy—arguably the most successful version of capitalism so far.

Self-management is not only a possible economic system for the future; it is also an empirical reality of which people have had some experience. Shortly after the end of the Second World War, the former Yugoslavia initially introduced a Soviet-style planned economy. Because the desired economic effects of this system failed to materialize, the Yugoslavian government under Marshal Tito introduced a new system in January 1953 that corresponded in its essential aspects to the economic system just sketched. It was based on collective ownership, planning, markets, and self-management. The fundamental traits of this system remained in place relatively unchanged until the early 1960s. The results it yielded were disappointing, however. When far-reaching reforms became necessary, Yugoslavia continued to experiment with new forms of self-management, but never managed to find a satisfactory solution.

The former Yugoslavia was not a democratic country and was seriously handicapped by a history of violent political conflict. With enormous economic and cultural discrepancies between its regions, it was not entirely well-suited for experiments with new kinds of economic systems. Thus, the fact that self-management failed there and then does not mean it could not be successful today. As we did with the idea of a planned economy, we will need to identify the fundamental characteristics of self-management as a system to develop an opinion about its capacity to function under today's conditions.

THE CENTRAL PLANNING OF INVESTMENTS

In a system of self-management, the planner determines the annual volume of investment for the whole economy, and decides on the distribution of this investment across all sectors and regions. This plan should be the output of a process of democratic will formation. The central planning of investments may have three important advantages compared to the determination of investment under capitalism. First, the polity may be able to get a grip on macroeconomic stability, or at least bring about a better management of the general economic cycle. Under capitalism, private investment is mainly responsible for cycles of boom and bust. Investment behavior is highly volatile because it depends on capitalists' profit expectations. Keynes memorably described the psychology behind capitalist investments, calling the decisions "the result of animal spirits." If the overall level of investment was instead under government control, it might stabilize macroeconomic activity.

Second, central management of investment would allow for a wide range of consequences of such investment—beyond the simple expectation of profitability—to be taken into consideration. This is economically warranted especially if the social value of an investment diverges significantly from the expected private profit of an investor. Unlike a capitalist investor, a central planner might, for instance, take the long-term effects of investments on the environment and on global climate change into account. The planner could also take into consideration that large investment projects have an influence on the population's preferences regarding their place of residence, and thus select investments that support a sustainable geographical distribution of the population.

Third, the central planning of investment could avoid the kinds of structural impasse that arise from the coordination problems inherent in developing two or more business sectors simultaneously. Such structural impasses are well-known from the history of industrialization. For instance, no heavy industry enterprise will invest in a country in which the supply of electricity may be insufficient, because such industries depend on large quantities of it. But if there is no heavy industry, then the electricity suppliers have no reason to create the required capacities, because they have to calculate their investment decisions on the basis of a relatively low level of demand. The country becomes stuck in a development trap, because the two types of investors are unable to coordinate their actions. Such interdependence between two or more business sectors is by no means only a phenomenon of past industrialization. New technologies frequently raise questions of coordination, as for instance in the case of personal computers and the provision of broadband connections. Central management of investment by a planner would take such mutual dependencies into account and avoid structural impasses.

A core question for the economic system of self-management concerns how, exactly, the central investment plan is to be implemented. How can the common will of the polity embodied in the plan be reconciled with the independence of the self-managed firms?

The most convincing suggestion for a solution to this problem comes again from the Polish economist Oskar Lange, whom we met in the previous chapter as one of the pioneers of iterative planning procedures. According to Lange, the government should regulate the volume of investment made by enterprises by granting credit. The overall economy is divided up by the planner into S number of sectors and R number of regions. Each enterprise belongs only to one sector and one region. Thus, there are altogether $S \times R$ possible combinations of sectors and regions, and to each such combination belongs a group of enterprises. The task of the planner is to make sure that over a particular period of time there is a certain democratically decided volume of credit available for each group of enterprises. To achieve this, the planner makes use of the connection between the enterprises' propensity to invest and the rate of interest. Enterprises invest more when the cost of financing investment drops—that is, when the interest rate decreases.

Lange suggests a setup by which credit can be granted to enterprises only by a state bank, or by a number of state banks. For each group of enterprises, the planner decides on a specific rate of interest at which they may borrow money from the banks to finance investments.

At the micro level, the enterprises devise their own investment projects, while the state banks decide on the credit to be granted and control the finance that is made available. Leaving aside the unlikely case in which the enterprises are financially powerful enough to fund all their investments exclusively through retained profits, their investment volume will be determined by the credit they are granted.

The rate of interest at which an enterprise borrows money from the bank influences its willingness to invest. The lower the rate of interest, the more attractive an investment is for the enterprise. The planner alters the rate of interest for each group of enterprises until the overall demand for credit from all enterprises in the group corresponds to the level at which the planner's intended volume of investment is likely to be realized. As part of this process, the planner has to estimate the proportion of investment that will be financed by the enterprises' retained profits. Given the state's control over the banking sector, and assuming mandatory financial disclosure on the part of the enterprises, this should not be difficult to estimate. In this way, the planner can realize its aims relatively easily without having to undermine the autonomy of the enterprises.

ECONOMIC DEMOCRACY

After central management of investment, the second characteristic element of this economic system is the democratization of the workplace. Self-management means that authority within enterprises rests with the entire workforce. The workers are subordinated neither to a capitalist nor to a bureaucrat, but decide for themselves about the details of their productive activities and about how the output of their production should be used.

The workers of a self-administered enterprise form a long-lasting community, with all members enjoying equal rights in directing the enterprise. There are different ways in which the workers' collective might make decisions. In smaller enterprises, it could be that many of them are made at general meetings and thus according to principles of basic democracy. In larger enterprises, perhaps only important strategic questions would be taken up in general meetings. As a rule, the workforce elects a workers' council and delegates to it far-reaching decision-making powers.

The election of the workers' council is of central importance for self-management because the council possesses powers that are similar to those of a capitalist joint-stock company's supervisory board. However, the election of a workers' council is, for the most part at least, based on the principle of "one man, one vote." (Voters' rights could be made dependent on level of employment: a part-time worker, for instance, could be given one vote, but full-time workers two.) The workers' council in turn elects an executive board whose members are charged with managing the enterprise.

A self-administered enterprise makes autonomous decisions on all market transactions, including new investments, the use of new production methods, and the marketing of new products. It decides on redundancies and on new recruitment, on the speed of assembly lines, and on the organization of labor. The enterprise determines the level of specialization for each job. Its members can either specialize in one task to be performed, or decide in favor of a rotational principle that has each member alternately performing manual and intellectual labor.

A self-managed enterprise autonomously decides how its post-tax income is to be used. In particular, this means it determines the income of its members. The income of the enterprise may also be used for funding social projects, such as a canteen or childcare facilities for the workers and their families. Part of the income is retained by the enterprise and used for productive investment.

How does a self-managed enterprise determine how much to pay its members? This is an important question, because the rules for such payments influence income distribution across the whole society. It is possible to conceive of a wide range of rules. One possibility is for each worker of an enterprise to receive the same income. In this case, there are no hourly wages and pay does not depend on either the quantity or the quality of the work performed. Alternatively, an enterprise might measure individual members' working hours and pay them accordingly. Another option is to establish hourly wages corresponding to workers' qualification levels and to the tasks required. It is also conceivable that an enterprise might refer to market rates for labor, perhaps in neighboring capitalist countries, to set its hourly wages. This would result in payments to workers that combined individual market-based wages with shares of profits. The profit shares might be the same for every worker. Alternatively, an enterprise might use different criteria for distributing profits, perhaps based on the merits and needs of individual workers, as established in public discussions at regular general meetings.

In any case, payments are an internal affair to be decided collectively by the members of an enterprise. Typically, the larger part of an enterprise's workforce is made up of workers with relatively low qualifications. Workforces deciding on the basis of majority voting therefore tend to be in favor of an equalization of incomes. In effect, this means that workers with different qualifications receive roughly the same remuneration for working the same hours.

Enterprises are in competition with each other, however, for the recruitment of the most productive laborers. A perfectly egalitarian enterprise therefore finds it difficult to employ and retain highly qualified workers if other enterprises adopt a system of differential payments according to workers' qualifications. Self-administered enterprises in that case have to pay unequal incomes to remain competitive.

Because all enterprises' products ultimately have to be sold in competitive markets, and because more productive workers have stronger bargaining positions, it is reasonable to expect that workers' payments will be based on their productivity. The better qualified among them will receive higher incomes, which means some income inequality. But compared to income gaps under capitalism, these inequalities are likely narrower. Some evidence for this can be drawn from actual experiences of cooperatives and firms with some worker representation or strong union influence over wage policy. Such institutions undeniably lead to flatter wage structures in companies—and presumably the institution of self-management only strengthens this tendency. Further, the members of a self-managed business enjoy shares of its profits, and these can be expected to be distributed in relatively equal fashion. This also contributes to a relatively small income gap among members of the company.

The value this economic system places on the democratization of the workplace stems from a central criticism commonly leveled against capitalism. Self-management allows everyone involved in the production process to articulate their ideas and suggestions about the organization of work, the distribution of profits, and the strategic development of the business, and it allows them to influence decision making on equal footing with all other workers. Ideally, this framework affords individuals a better understanding of their work and leads to more independent behavior and a more consciously controlled life.

Nevertheless, the democratization of enterprises also has its downsides. There is a trade-off between democratic participation in decision making and an enterprise's capacity to react quickly and flexibly on the basis of decisions taken by its board. The more perfectly democratic the business, the more difficulty it will have reaching decisions. Too much democracy at the workplace can also have negative effects on workers: Individuals may become frustrated and weary having to participate in frequent, lengthy processes of collective decision making.

To introduce a system of self-management, we would need to answer difficult questions: Should the legislator be entitled to impose a certain type of democratic decision making on all enterprises? Would having such uniformity be a good idea? Should the legislator prescribe a detailed charter for all self-managed firms, perhaps depending on the size of their workforce? Or should the firms independently draw up their own assignments of participation rights and duties? Allowing the free stipulation of those rights and duties, and thus of the extent to which the workplace is democratized, has the advantage of allowing experimentation with different rules for worker involvement, and means that individuals can choose their workplace depending on the level of participation they desire. The risk, however, is that people who have been socialized under capitalism will assign a relatively low value to workplace democracy, and will forgo worker control—particularly if a hierarchical decision-making structure in a firm is able to achieve higher incomes.

FIRST CRITICISM: UNFAIR INCOME DISTRIBUTION

The system of self-management appears at first glance to capture the best aspects of both planned and market economies. Closer inspection, however, reveals a series of faults in the design. While each fault by itself may not be particularly serious, they combine to make self-management significantly less attractive.

One of the defects concerns precisely what critics of capitalism decry about the current system—namely, its lack of distributive justice. In a system of self-management, the problem is not the distribution between capitalists and laborers (for capitalists do not exist within this system), but between workers in different enterprises.

An important principle of justice is that like cases should be treated alike. Imagine two twins who have so far lived similar lives and now do the same job in two different enterprises. If both of them invest the same effort, it would seem fair that they receive the same income. Uneven incomes would be unfair. A crucial disadvantage of the system of self-management is that it is extremely susceptible to precisely such violations of horizontal justice.

Planned and market economies suffer less from this problem. Both probably treat our twins alike. In a pure planned economy, the planner determines the consumption norms for all workers in all enterprises. A sufficiently well informed planner can take care of horizontal justice and make sure the twins receive the same provision. In a market economy, meanwhile, wages are determined by the labor market, which also tends to establish horizontal justice. Laborers avoid enterprises that are paying less than other enterprises for the same jobs. Labor market forces thus tend to equalize the twins' wages. In a system of self-management, by contrast, there are three reasons to worry that the income distribution among similar workers in different enterprises will be unfair.

The first problem concerns the capital stock of the enterprises. Imagine that all capitalist enterprises become self-managing enterprises overnight. Naturally, there are huge differences in value between their facilities, machines, and administrative buildings. Some workers therefore become members of enterprises with a great deal of capital, others of enterprises with a great deal less. To avoid a situation where the former workers simply pocket their windfalls in the form of higher remuneration, the state asks all self-managed enterprises to pay a price for their inherited capital goods, as well as for patents and brand names.

In principle, each enterprise makes a payment to the government that corresponds to the value of the inherited capital assets. Instead of a one-off payment, this can also be arranged in the form of annual payments, much like interest payments. The problem is that, upon the introduction of self-management, it is likely very difficult to determine the value of the inherited assets correctly. There are often no market prices for equipment, because they are goods that are specific to the enterprise. If recent market prices can be identified, it is necessary to take into account that these were formed under capitalist conditions, and the value of the same asset might be dramatically higher or lower in the system of self-management. The value of a luxury brand, for instance, might turn out to be much lower if, under the new system, luxury is so derided that luxury articles have to be sold much more cheaply.

It is likely, then, that the state is not able to identify the initial capital value of an enterprise. The price for the inherited capital stock therefore has to be determined jointly by a government agency and the workers' council. The result depends on the latter's negotiation skills and political contacts. In the overwhelming majority of cases, therefore, the prices paid by enterprises diverge from the real value of their initial capital assets; and this might establish enduring differences in the incomes of different enterprises' members.

The workers of an enterprise whose initial capital stock has been under-valued receive a higher income for the same labor than the workers of an enterprise whose initial capital stock has been overvalued, because the former do not pay enough to the government. It is difficult, however, to correct for this unfair treatment retrospectively, because the government is unable to determine whether differences in income were caused by mistakes in the evaluation of the initial assets or by later intervening factors, such as differing efforts exerted by the workers to make their firm more profitable.

The second factor leading to unequal pay for the same work has to do with how investment is managed under this system, as described above. Because interest rates are made to vary according to regions and economic sectors, the workers of enterprises that can borrow from state banks at low interest rates receive a higher net income than workers of enterprises that face higher borrowing costs. This follows from the fact that workers share in the profits of their own enterprises, and these profits rise when the interest on debt falls. In this case, too, a violation of horizontal justice is the consequence.

Finally, undeserved differences in income result from random fluctuations in enterprises' profits. That is, these profits are dependent upon uncertain sales and price conditions. While in the case of capitalism the owner of an enterprise absorbs most of these fluctuations, in the system of self-management the whole workforce bears this risk. Under capitalism, the remuneration of the workers takes the form of a fixed wage that is agreed ex ante, while the owner's profit is uncertain. In a system of self-management, by contrast, workers' pay contains an element that depends on the profits, which depend in turn on the vicissitudes of the market. Workers who happen to be members of enterprises that strike it lucky on the market therefore earn more than workers whose enterprises lose out through sheer bad luck.

SECOND CRITICISM: UNCERTAIN INCOMES

Tying personal income to profits not only leads to inequality. It also means that workers bear a great deal of risk, since their disposable income is directly affected by profit fluctuations. This constitutes a further deficiency of the system of self-management.

The allocation of risk in a capitalist market economy is more efficient than in a self-management system, because individuals can choose whether they want to be self-employed or work as regular employees. If they have access to sufficient capital, those more willing to take risks can start businesses. Their income will therefore be less certain than those more risk-averse individuals who opt for regular employment and fixed incomes. Individuals who have accrued some savings can also invest their money in portfolios made up of stocks from enterprises across diverse economic sectors and regions. If a portfolio is carefully assembled, the investment risk is diminished. In a self-managed economy, by contrast, a worker-saver implicitly puts all his money into one "stock"— namely, the share of the profits generated by the enterprise where he works. Thus, far from being well diversified, investment risk is dangerously concentrated. An individual who loses her job loses her labor income and capital income—that is, her right to a share of the profits. Within a self-managed economy, therefore, individuals are subject to maximum income risk.

Inevitably, given the dependence of workers' incomes on all the chance factors that affect a company's profits, there are sometimes calls for the government to step in and intervene—especially as the state formally owns all the enterprises. To the extent the government heeds these calls, however, it imperils the entire economic system. The threat here is the complete erosion of market discipline, as happened in Hungary after the reforms of 1968. The prospect of explicit subsidies and hidden aid causes enterprises to concentrate their efforts on establishing privileged relationships with politicians and bureaucrats instead of focusing on cost-cutting or raising the quality of their products.

THIRD CRITICISM: MISDIRECTED STRUCTURAL TRANSFORMATIONS

A capitalist enterprise has an incentive to produce more if the market price for the good it supplies goes up, because by doing so it can increase its profits. And if the enterprise expects the price rise to continue for some time, it recruits additional employees. The opposite is the case if the price sinks over a certain period of time: it is then no longer profitable to maintain the previous level of employment. The redistribution of the workforce within the economy that results from overall product price changes corresponds to the changing needs of society. If the market price of a product rises, this is a sign that this product has become more valuable for society. Consumers are willing to pay more money for it. A falling price, by contrast, indicates that the need for a product is diminishing. In sum, this means that the redistribution of labor from products with falling prices to products with rising prices corresponds to the changing desires of consumers.

Under conditions of self-management, by contrast, price changes may be followed by paradoxical reactions from the enterprises: price rises may lead a self-managed enterprise to reduce the level of employment, while price drops may lead it to increase employment! In 1958, the U.S. economist Ben Ward was the first to point out this surprising flaw in self-management, having discovered it through mathematical simulations. The clear implication is that a market consisting exclusively of self-managed enterprises does not respond in the right way to changes in social needs. This defect essentially results from the rational self-interest of the self-managed enterprise's workforce.

The core of Ward's analysis can be stated simply. A self-managed enterprise acts in the interest of the individuals who are its members at a certain point in time. Its decisions, including decisions about hiring, are therefore guided mainly by expectations about how alternative moves would affect members' incomes. New members are recruited only if their joining will improve the incumbent members' financial position.

If the enterprise is able to sell its products at higher prices, its existing members stand to profit; assuming their number is held constant, their per-capita income will rise. Taking the same logic a step further, members' incomes also grow if their numbers are reduced, so that each has a bigger slice of the extra profits from rising prices. Thus, there may be an inclination towards reducing the membership, perhaps by opting not to replace workers who leave the enterprise for age-related or other reasons. Rising prices could in this way be followed by a reduction of the employment level in the enterprise.

If prices fall, however, there is less profit to distribute, and the disincentive to recruit new members therefore loses force. Given the lower amounts involved, existing members are less reluctant to share profits with new colleagues. In a situation of falling prices, it is more important to have new colleagues helping to bear the fixed costs of the enterprise. Each enterprise must cover the costs of the capital goods it uses, such as interest on credit and payments to the state for inherited capital equipment. These costs are the same regardless of the number of members in the enterprise. If the number of members rises, the costs are distributed more widely and, other things being equal, the old members' per-capita income rises. A fall in prices can thus lead to recruitment of additional members.

Ward's discovery revealed a remarkable defect in the system of self-management—namely, a behavioral pattern that is rational from the perspective of an individual firm's workforce, but absurd when viewed from the perspective of the overall economy. In the system of self-management, if the social value of a good drops (as indicated by its price), the level of employment in that sector and the volume of production of that good rises—and if there is an increase in social value, by contrast, production drops. This is paradoxical and, as a consequence, the distribution of resources in such an economy would be inefficient.

Interestingly, symptoms of the very kind of group egoism Ward highlights can be detected in successful cooperatives in our own economic system. Instead of raising the number of members, they show a tendency to bring additional workers on as wage laborers. Further growth often precipitates a legal transformation from a cooperative into a corporation, and thus an abandonment of the principles of self-management.

The Basque conglomerate Mondragón, which comprises several cooperatives, some of which date back to the 1950s, provides a good example of the uneasy relationship cooperatives have with market success. Its cooperatives' market success led to a remarkable expansion in the mid-1990s, but the new branches were, at the base of things, barely distinguishable from capitalist enterprises. Recent figures show that less than half the workers at Mondragón are actually members of a cooperative. The majority are regular wage laborers without significant chances ever to become cooperative members.

FOURTH CRITICISM: INSTABILITY AND UNEMPLOYMENT

These peculiar reactions to price changes can lead to instability in markets and increased unemployment—phenomena which were, indeed, typical of the Yugoslavian economy.

As an illustration of this problem, imagine an economy with only two economic sectors, and made up wholly of self-managed enterprises. Each enterprise is active in just one of the sectors. Now imagine that demand for one sector's products is decreasing, while demand for the other sector's products is increasing.

The enterprises in the sector with sinking prices try to increase their membership, to shift part of their fixed costs onto the new members. Although they offer lower incomes than the enterprises in the other sector, they are able to recruit new members, because people without a job prefer employment to unemployment. As the volume of manpower expands in all the enterprises in this sector, the sector's output rises. For this increased output to be sold, the price of the product has to fall further.

There is thus a cumulative reduction of the price and an expansion of employment that, ultimately, some enterprises are not able to survive. With falling prices, enterprise members also see their per-capita income fall, and beyond a certain point they no longer see a reason to continue working there. Some enterprises therefore close, and the whole sector abruptly shrinks. This adaptive process plays out through unnecessarily costly fluctuations: first, employment rises, then it suddenly falls.

Meanwhile, in the other economic sector, which is experiencing growing demand, the adaptive process is also unnecessarily costly. Here, enterprise members have no incentive to take on people looking for work and let them profit from rising prices. To the contrary, members even try, wherever possible, to do without replacing any workers who happen to depart. These enterprises have an interest in increasing their output only if this can be done with the existing workforce—perhaps by having people put in overtime, or by replacing old machines with new ones to increase labor productivity. The enterprises of this sector have no incentive to create new production facilities, even if these could produce a surplus, since the surplus would need to be shared with the new members. Say, for example, an enterprise with a hundred members has optimized its facility and generates a financial surplus. It could replicate that facility elsewhere and take on a hundred new members to operate it. While the enterprise's surplus would double, the per-capita income of the old members would remain unchanged. For the members of the already existing enterprise, the investments would therefore not be worth the effort.

The behavior of these individual enterprises raises the question of how a high rate of unemployment could be avoided under a system of self-management. One obvious notion is to declare a right to labor, so that enterprises were forced to accept anyone who wanted to become a member. This idea finds expression in works by Eugen Dühring and Theodor Hertzka, two nineteenth-century intellectuals who demanded a universal right to free access to the means of production. Their thinking was that, if self-managed enterprises were not allowed to exclude anyone who wanted to become a member, there would be no involuntary unemployment. Workers' freedom of movement would also lead to the abolition of income differences between enterprises, as workers would flow to those that were doing well, participate in their profits, and thus bring about an equalization of incomes across all enterprises.

Unfortunately, such a right to labor would have catastrophic consequences for productivity. Enterprises would have no incentive to become more profitable, because each improvement in income level would be absorbed by the arrival of new members. Further, the permanently changing workforce would make the daily organization of the production process much more difficult, a problem similar to that facing Kropotkin's associations for the production of luxury goods.

A promising strategy might be the creation of new self-managed enterprises by citizens, civil society organizations and—most importantly—the government. There could be a public office for the statistical identification of sectors in which incomes were high and rising, which would then lead to the foundation of new enterprises in these sectors (while taking into account variations in the supply of workers' qualifications and regional specificities). The government could, in this way, promote structural developments that fit better the evolution of social needs. This selective creation of new enterprises would reduce unemployment and income inequality. If the government were at the same time to implement active employment policies that supported the professional and regional mobility of the people, the problem of unemployment could be moderated even further.

On paper, this looks promising. In practice, the project of the targeted creation of new enterprises would probably ask too much of the state and other actors involved. To decide what exactly these new enterprises are meant to produce, they would need to have precise knowledge of market conditions and of the available production factors. It is unlikely that government officials and normal citizens would possess such knowledge. Civil servants would, at the very least, need to work very closely with the banks, which are in a privileged position to oversee the evolution of economic conditions. And, indeed, it is the banks that, upon closer scrutiny, turn out to be the hidden protagonists in the system of self-management. They would end up exerting far more power than one might expect at first. The next—and final!—criticism will highlight the central role played by banks within this economic system.

FIFTH CRITICISM: MISGUIDED INVESTMENT DECISIONS

In this economic system, efficient investments are expected to result when central planning of the investment structure is combined with enterprise-level determination of investment projects. A closer look at this system, however, reveals various problems that could be tackled only by exceptional regulatory efforts and with the help of banks that were loyal to the state.

The central plan is supposed to be executed by setting different interest rates for different enterprises' borrowing, according to their varying economic sectors and regions. Note, however, that different interest rates create possibilities for arbitrage. Two enterprises facing different interest rates have the incentive to devise an arrangement whereby the enterprise whose rate is lower takes out a loan with a state bank that covers the credit needs of both. By providing cheaper credit to the enterprise whose rate is higher, the two enterprises undermine the central planning of investment. Lending between enterprises must therefore be categorically prohibited, or must only be permissible to the extent that it is necessary for trade between suppliers and their customers.

To avoid other possibilities for arbitrage that would undermine the central plan, any loan from an enterprise to a private person, especially to a member of the enterprise, must also be prohibited. Robust state control of self-managed enterprises would be necessary to enforce these prohibitions. This control function could be delegated to the banks that lend money to enterprises, but this raises the question of whether the banks would actually perform this function, or whether they in turn would rather collaborate furtively with the self-managed enterprises.

This same mechanism of using different interest rates to direct investment also threatens to pervert selection principles within a group of enterprises—meaning, among enterprises that fall into the same category based on their economic branch and geographical region. Imagine such a group that, according to the planner, intends to invest too much. The planner raises the interest rate for this group. This reduces its demand for credit, and credit is eventually granted at a higher interest rate that would achieve the planning target. The increase of the interest rate, in fact, brings about a self-selection among the investment projects. Some are shelved because they are no longer worthwhile from the viewpoint of their proposer. Unfortunately, though, it may happen that the projects that make it through are not the ones with highest economic returns, but those with the highest risk. Given a high rate of interest, enterprises may embark on projects that present high likelihood of incurring losses and low likelihood of making very large profits. In the unlikely event of success, the enterprise repays the credit and its members earn a lot of money. If, however, the project fails, the members of the enterprise can expect that the government will bail it out or that they will be able to join another enterprise, keeping their personal situation more or less as it is. Thus, the interest rate mechanism may lead to the selection of the wrong investment projects: Comparatively safe projects promising an average profit are not financed, while resources flow toward high-risk ventures that produce, on average, meager returns. Avoiding such selections would, again, imply banks' strict control over investment projects.

Self-management may contain an even greater danger for enterprises' investment behavior. The members of an enterprise profit from an investment only as long as they work there. Investments that mostly raise profits in the distant future are of little interest to them, because they may no longer be members of the enterprise when such profits materialize. Enterprises therefore have a strong inclination toward short-term investments—and the older the workforce, the stronger this inclination is. If members close to retirement constitute a large proportion and dominate the workers' council, the incentive for investment is particularly weak. The workers' council may decide to cut expenditures for servicing facilities and machinery. It might even sell off part of the enterprise's equipment, to achieve higher payouts for members before they leave. Such decisions can spell the collapse of otherwise healthy enterprises.

The state therefore needs to introduce special regulations to try to prevent these developments. But this is easier said than done. Enterprises might, for instance, be obligated to maintain a balanced age structure within their workforce. If an enterprise is in decline, however, it makes little sense to compel it to take on new, young members. The age structure of enterprises further depends on general demographic developments. And if the population overall is aging, then the proportion of older employees will generally grow in all enterprises.

Another stipulation of the state might be that enterprises must maintain reserves that can be used only for investment. But how large should these reserves be? Surely the answer must take into account the financial situation of the particular enterprise, as it cannot build up reserves if it makes losses. Yet it is also true that an enterprise can misrepresent its financial situation. The state could also prohibit any part of an enterprise's physical capital from being sold without explicit authorization.

But this is costly and probably ineffectual, because the authority lacks the knowledge to make well-founded decisions.

All of these suggestions imply drastic interferences in the autonomy of enterprises, are associated with substantial bureaucratic efforts, and offer little hope of dealing justly with every individual case. It seems obvious that a government would opt for the simplest solution—namely, delegating control to the state banks.

State-owned banks would therefore play a central role in this alternative economic system. It is likely that the polity would ultimately allow for an exception to the principle of self-management and install representatives of the banks, endowed with special authority, on every workers' council, to control the use of publicly owned productive capital. The number of enterprises would be kept relatively low so as to render control easier. This, however, would increase the danger of monopolies and intensify the problem of unemployment, leading in turn to yet more need for regulation.

The representatives of the state-owned banks would thus participate in the strategic management of the production enterprises, but would—in contravention of the spirit of self-management—not be fully democratically controlled. And as a part of the state, they would be burdened with tasks that go far beyond the usual business of a bank. The vague definition of the scope of their responsibility, the lack of transparency in their dealings, and most importantly their power to distribute cash on a large scale would quickly pique the interest of politicians. The upshot would surely be the formation of personal ties between politicians and the directors of the state-owned banks whom they appoint, and therefore a great concentration of power in the hands of a small elite. Examples of corruption in publicly owned banks in our own capitalist economies give us little reason for optimism in this regard.

MOVING ON FROM SELF-MANAGEMENT

The economic system of self-management is characterized by four elements: public ownership of the means of production, central planning of investments, markets for goods, and self-management by workers.

We embarked on this chapter hoping that this system would avoid the defects of capitalism and of Soviet-style planned economies. But self-management turns out to have its own serious defects. It entails an unfair distribution of workers' income, and makes income subject to large, unpredictable fluctuations. Involuntary unemployment cannot be avoided. The allocation of production factors is not responsive to changing social needs, and the investments made by enterprises are inefficient. There are simply too many defects here for us to hope that a self-managed economy can function smoothly.

It seems clear that it would not take long before a government overseeing such a malfunctioning system would be forced to intervene with ad hoc measures to counteract the consequences of these defects. There is therefore a serious risk that the system of self-management would ultimately degenerate into a kind of cronyism, in which the personal relationships among politicians, bankers, and the leaders of a few large-scale firms' works councils become decisive in the workings of the economy.

Yet surely we do not want to abolish the social market economy only to end up with a new kind of feudal system. In the following two chapters, our search for an alternative economic system will therefore do away with two elements: the central planning of investment and the self-management of enterprises. These institutions are, after all, only means to achieving greater ends. The central planning of investment aims at macroeconomic stabilization and the management of structural developments. The self-management of enterprises is intended to allow workers to control their own activity. Both are important ends, but they can also be achieved by different means—the first, by monetary and fiscal policy and industrial and regional policy, and the second, by instituting codetermination and the manifold legislation that protects workers against employer abuses.

All these instruments are at the disposal of market socialism as an alternative economic system.

7

MARKETS AND SOCIALISM

MARKET SOCIALISM IS A MARKET economy without capitalists. The state owns the means of production. Enterprises are directed by managers and participate autonomously in markets. The profits they generate contribute to the state's revenues, and they can be used in any way the polity desires. An obvious way of using them is as a social dividend for all citizens—a transfer payment from the government made regularly to everyone.

The proponents of market socialism are socialists with a liberal streak, who are convinced that socialist aims are easier to achieve by means of markets than they are by central planning. Part of their liberal vision of socialism involves a strengthening of democracy in the workplace in the form of codetermination rights for the workforce. Unlike in the system of self-management, however, the managers of enterprises in market socialism are in the first instance responsible to the state.

In the history of the socialist movement, the ideas of market socialists have so far not exactly enjoyed universal acclaim. They were scathingly criticized by Marxists, especially in Germany. The dissemination of market socialist ideas in Germany was not helped by the fact that this economic system was associated with the name of Eugen Dühring, a man briefly mentioned in the previous chapter. Dühring became famous because of a popular text by Friedrich Engels, the title of which speaks for itself: "Anti-Dühring." After that, the ideas of market socialism retreated into the background. Nevertheless, they influenced some important liberal thinkers—those who were generally attracted to the pluralism and individual freedom provided by markets, but who were dismayed by capitalism's lack of equal opportunities and tendency to form monopolies.

When the Eastern bloc collapsed at the end of the 1980s, the ideas of market socialism experienced a short-lived revival. When it came to the question of how to organize society following the fall of the planned economy, the supporters of market socialism saw a chance to put their ideas to the test. The fact that enterprises were already in public hands helped; the ownership structure would not need to be changed. In academic circles, there was even support from renowned economists in the neoclassical "mainstream." But those who would have been directly affected by such a system did not want any further experiments. They only wanted—at last—the economic model already tested in the West. No experiments took place.

The transformation of the planned economy in China took a different course, and it led to the emergence of a new industrial superpower. The shift in economic policies, which started as early as 1978, did not aim to bring about any predetermined economic model, but rather to achieve some concrete results. The main goals were the modernization of the economy and the alleviation of poverty. To this end, individuals and organizations were given relatively free rein to seek better ways to satisfy the needs of the population outside the constraints of the planned economy. This led to a great deal of experimentation with markets, which actually initiated rapid economic growth. It would be wrong, however, to claim that the Chinese were thereby experimenting with market socialism. In the first phase of the reforms, up until the beginning of the 1990s, they had a two-tier economic system in which central planning existed alongside markets. At that point, the planning system was abolished and a "socialist market economy" was declared. But this was not market socialism. Rather, publicly owned enterprises, most of which were the property of local authorities and institutions, were privatized, and this gradually led to the formation of a new class of Chinese capitalists. The existence of a financial elite, and the dictatorship of a political party whose leadership partly overlaps with this elite speak of an economic system that profoundly differs from the one market socialists aim at.

WHY MARKET SOCIALISM?

The market socialism we are interested in is a market economy without capitalists, which is accompanied by a democratic process based on the broadest possible political participation. The first question, then, is this: Why should we get rid of the capitalists only to leave the rest of the economic system fundamentally unchanged? The proponents of market socialism emphasize four reasons.

A More Equal Distribution of Economic Wealth

Market socialism leads to a more equal distribution of income, because corporate profits are used to benefit all citizens rather than simply contribute to the wealth of a small minority of rich people.

The redistribution of corporate profits also has effects on the labor market that further increase equality. Because of the social dividend, all employees have an income at their disposal that does not depend on their selling their labor power. This especially improves the situation of those on low incomes. It becomes easier for less qualified workers to reject work that would exhaust them physically or psychologically. Thus, their position in pay negotiations improves, and the dispersion of wages becomes narrower than it is today.

The high earnings of top-flight lawyers, notaries, medical doctors, artists, and architects, as well as other self-employed individuals, diminish. Today, the most well-off members of these professions often work in the service of wealthy firm owners. They earn exceptional incomes because their clients are rich enough to foot astronomical bills. Under market socialism, they continue to work for those clients with the most money, but these clients have less money at their disposal compared to today. Thus, the gap narrows between the top flight and those with average incomes.

Fewer Resources Wasted in Battles over Distribution

The reduction in inequality may free up resources that are wasted in conflicts over distribution for use in different areas. An example here is the conflict between the wealthy and the tax authorities, and everything that goes along with it: the training and salaries of tax advisors and tax investigators; the creation and maintenance of securities accounts, shell companies, and foundations in tax havens; the acquisition of CDs with secret tax information by governments; and all the computers, administrative buildings, and personnel involved in this conflict. Some of these resources are freed up under market socialism, because there are fewer superrich seeking to conceal their income from the taxman. A similar point can be made for those human and material resources that are today used by the financial elite for costly divorce proceedings or for protecting themselves against thieves and kidnappers. Instead of being wasted in battles over distribution, these resources can be used in ways that benefit all of society.

Better Political Decisions

Under conditions of market socialism, money has less influence on politics. Without the capitalist concentration of wealth, it is easier to avoid a situation where large parts of the media landscape are controlled by a few individuals. There is no powerful class making substantial profits through neocolonial wars. And there are no billionaires buying their way into leading political offices as part of their own personal "reality shows." The quality of political decisions improves, as they are no longer driven by special interests.

Meaningful Work and Consumption

Under market socialism, there is far more democratization of production. Employees receive more rights to codetermination, and there are no capitalists trying to undermine the rights of employees or to sabotage unions.

Thanks to the social dividend, there is less of a need for individuals to base their choice of profession and workplace on financial considerations. Other factors, such as the quality of the work itself, the degree of self-determination, the existence of democratic structures at the workplace, and relationships among colleagues play a more prominent role.

Without the spectacle of the conspicuous consumption of those at the top, people attach less importance to their own consumption. They are less interested in appearances and develop a more sober and less impulsive attitude toward consumption. In both their values and their behavior, the simple goal of "having money" or "making money"—without consideration being given to the "how"—plays a much diminished role.

THE AIM OF MARKET SOCIALIST ENTERPRISES

But to provide us with these supposed advantages, market socialism must be adequate as an economic system—that is, it must pass the cooperation and allocation tests. As a standard of measurement for these tests we take the performance of our economic system today. We have already performed these tests for other alternative economic systems; it is easier to perform them for market socialism. This is because the "only" difference from the current system relates to the ownership of enterprises: the social market economy has private property, whereas market socialism has public property.

The behavior of its publicly owned enterprises is therefore crucial to the economic viability of market socialism. Which criteria do they apply in making their decisions? And do the enterprises behave as desired? We will take some time to discuss these questions in this chapter.

Recall one of the central conclusions from the previous chapter, on self-management: the market system will not produce an efficient allocation of resources if each enterprise tries to maximize the income of its own employees. But if they are left to their own devices, without any legal constraints being put in place, enterprises under market socialism will also surely aim to maximize the income of their own employees. Although market socialist enterprises are managed by directors, rather than by workers' councils, they are still under pressure from their work-forces to promote workers' personal interests—assuming the state has not prescribed some other target for the enterprise. The managers there-fore set the wages and salaries at such a level that the state cannot make any return on the invested capital. We thus end up with the same self-interested enterprises we found in the system of self-management, and thus with the same problems of short-term investment and mass unemployment.

The state should therefore set clear targets for enterprises. The en-terprises should maximize the difference between the value of goods produced and the value of the production factors used—that is, their profit—to make sure that they act efficiently. That is how economic surplus will also be maximized. Therefore the polity should charge market socialist enterprises with achieving the highest possible profit.

The target should not simply be the profits for the next quarter, how-ever, because this tempts them to make shortsighted decisions. Rather, in this context the aim of profit maximization entails maximizing the present value of earned profits across the entire life of the enterprise. This present value is the right criterion not only because in the long run it provides the state with the highest possible income (which, in turn, gets passed on to the citizens). More importantly, it promises to help the economic system as a whole solve the allocation problem.

It may sound like a paradox to say that, to achieve a socially desir-able result, each enterprise should think only of its own profits. But as Adam Smith, the founding figure of economics, explained as early as the eighteenth century, in the context of competitive markets, the aim of maximizing individual profit can lead to benefits for society as a whole. As his famous metaphor has it, the greed of the producers is re-strained and put in the service of the consumer by the "invisible hand" of market competition. To increase their profits, enterprises must either produce more cheaply or improve the quality of their products. And in the final analysis, it is consumers who benefit from these efforts, in the form of lower prices for better quality products.

Under conditions of market socialism one cannot speak of greedy producers, because their profits are passed on to the state, and so to everyone. Nevertheless, Smith may be basically right about the consequences of the pursuit of profit in market socialism.

EFFICIENCY AND THE PURSUIT OF PROFIT

Over the last one hundred and fifty years, economists have given the metaphor of the invisible hand a more precise formulation and analyzed it in almost every possible detail. Their research has led to a fundamental confirmation of the efficiency of markets as a mechanism for coordinating complex economies. Still, the limits of the invisible hand have also been charted and systematically presented as a theory of market failures. This theory thus identifies economic situations in which a polity cannot simply rely on the pursuit of profit by enterprises to produce the desired result.

According to the theory of market failures, the pursuit of maximum profit does not lead to an efficient working of the market if there is an absence of competition among suppliers, if externalities are significant, or if information is asymmetrical.

The first case concerns the intensity of competition. Under a monopoly, or when there are agreements between enterprises forming a cartel, the disciplining effect of competition is absent, and the pursuit of maximum profit by producers leads to an inefficient result. Monopolists bring about an artificial scarcity of their products through exorbitant prices. Instead of thinking about innovation, they use outdated methods and delay the renewal of their product range. Thus, without vigorous competition, the enterprises' maximization of profit takes place at the expense of the rest of society.

For example, in the utility sector (providing gas, water, refuse collection, and so forth), where the coexistence of competing suppliers would be expensive or even impossible, the government should therefore intervene and not rely on suppliers driven by the profit motive. In industries where barriers to entry are high and the market is dominated by just a handful of enterprises, the government should encourage competition through policies such as the prohibition of price fixing.

The second case in which the pursuit of profit leads to an inefficient allocation of resources concerns the so-called externalities of production and consumption. A classic example is the emission of pollutants during the production process. From the perspective of economics, an efficient use of environmental goods requires the balancing of the advantages of a better environment and the costs of reducing the emissions. As a profit-maximizing enterprise has little incentive to bring about reductions in the pollutant emissions, the result of the operation of the market is inefficient.

The government has various tools at its disposal to make profit-maximizing enterprises pay for the consequences of such externalities, and so to remove the inefficiency. In the case of environmental pollution, for example, a tax on the emitted pollutants can motivate enterprises to make their production more environment-friendly.

The third category of market failure arises when profit-maximization occurs in situations where the quality of the traded goods and services is insufficiently transparent. The mechanism of the invisible hand can function only if buyers know what they are actually buying. Otherwise, sellers will try to exploit the ignorance of the buyers to sell them bad quality products, or products they do not actually need. Think, for instance, of the lack of transparency in many financial products, such as private pension schemes, that are bought by households with little financial knowledge.

Such an informational asymmetry between buyer and seller may undermine trust and cause massive misallocations. The danger is probably greatest in the case of medical treatments, where the asymmetry is so vast that the suppliers (medical doctors) may determine the demand (of the patients) more or less by themselves. It is no surprise, then, that we rarely find a completely laissez-faire provision of health care.

The potential for problematic uses of information advantages by greedy suppliers can provide an economic justification for state intervention in other areas, too—for instance, in the educational, insurance, and credit sectors. The possibility of such uses is, further, the reason we need workers' and consumer protection.

Monopolies, externalities, and asymmetric information would also occur in the system of market socialism. They justify not only regulatory state intervention in the form of the prohibition of cartels, environmental taxation, and so forth, but also the existence of public and private nonprofit organizations that supply various goods and services. In the case of asymmetrical information, for instance, the fact that the supplier is not animated by the profit motive may instill confidence in customers, because it means that the supplier has less incentive to cheat or defraud. The resulting credibility explains why nonprofit organizations are often to be found providing, for instance, health care and childcare.

A plurality of suppliers is advantageous not only from the point of view of the consumer, but also from that of the employee. A profit-maximizing enterprise tends to subordinate its internal organization and customer relations to this aim. Many people do not like to work for such enterprises, and nonprofit organizations can offer jobs in which the needs of customers, rather than the returns to the enterprise, take center stage.

MARKET SOCIALISM VERSUS SOCIAL MARKET ECONOMY

If the enterprises in a market socialist economy would indeed maximize their profits, they would be as efficient as their counterparts in a capitalist economy. We would therefore have an attractive alternative to a social market economy, because market socialism, by comparison, has the advantage of eliminating the diverse negative consequences of income concentration in the hands of a few.

It is far from certain, however, that the assumption made above is correct. Capitalists pocket the profits of their enterprises, and it is therefore clear that they have a reason to want to maximize them. But the management of a market socialist enterprise does not gain anything from high profits, because these are transferred to the state. Of course, the state could ask the management to make a sworn declaration that it would try to maximize the enterprise's profits, but it would be impossible to ascertain whether the management actually did so or not. This is essentially the same information problem that we came across in the enterprises in Arrow and Hurwicz's iterative planning procedure. Whether market socialism is a viable alternative or not ultimately depends on whether there is a solution to this problem.

The fundamental question of profit maximization in a market socialist economy cannot simply be answered by pointing to the sense of duty felt by the managers cum civil servants in charge of the enterprises. We cannot rely on a sense of duty alone. Given the nature of human beings, we need suitable incentives to motivate the managers in a market socialist economy to maximize profits.

At this point, one may object that actually existing capitalist economies face the same difficulty, because many large private enterprises are not managed by their owners, but by paid executives. Would it not be possible, then, to deploy the incentives that capitalists use to motivate their managers under market socialism, as well?

OWNERSHIP AND CONTROL IN A CAPITALIST ECONOMY

These incentives will be described in more detail in a moment. But first, it is important to emphasize that even in contemporary capitalism many enterprises are still managed by their owners, who thus have an immediate personal interest in profit maximization. Manager-led enterprises compete with owner-led enterprises, and this competition has a disciplining effect on the former. If competition is sufficiently intense, a manager-led enterprise cannot afford to ask for higher prices, or to offer less quality products, than its owner-led competitors. Such an enterprise is soon driven out of the market, as it loses customers. Thus, competition ultimately forces enterprises that are not led by their owners either to go bankrupt or to seek to maximize their profits as avidly as the owner-led enterprises.

In some sectors, however, there are no owner-led enterprises to put pressure on the managers of other enterprises. One reason may be that firms need to be of a certain size to be able to exploit technically feasible economies of scale. Or there may be barriers to entry in markets because of patents. But despite there being relatively few external pressures, managers usually do what they are charged to do by owners—namely, try to achieve the highest possible profit for their enterprise. The question is: Why?

HOW MANAGERS ARE DISCIPLINED

Capitalists who do not manage their enterprises themselves use four main tools to motivate managers to maximize profits. The first is the labor market for executives. Senior managers who abuse their executive power to enrich themselves and their allies at the expense of the enterprise run the risk of being found out and having to leave their posts with tarnished reputations. The labor market provides an important reason to act loyally towards the owners, especially for younger executives.

A second tool is performance-based pay. Instead of a fixed salary, managers receive remuneration that is dependent on some measure of success. Thus, they may be paid bonuses for reaching agreed targets. Carefully selected performance criteria can act as effective incentives.

Third, monitoring by creditors, especially by an enterprise's main bank, plays an important role. If a bank has made a large loan to an enterprise, it wants to keep track of managers' performance so that it may intervene in good time if they act in ways that jeopardize repayment. Although the creditor's aim is not the same as the owner's, this monitoring can be helpful in avoiding any abuse of power by management.

The fourth mechanism for disciplining management is the stock market. In general, share prices mirror stock market investors' expectations regarding companies' returns. Under ideal conditions, share prices correspond to market expectations concerning the present value of future payments resulting from the corresponding part ownership of a company. If a company's managers embark upon business projects that increase its expected future profits, its share price will rise, because stock market participants will expect higher returns and will thus be eager to buy more share. If, however, the price of a share declines relative to the market, this is a signal that the management has opted for unprofitable projects and is thus running an inadequate business model. The owners of the firm can then hold the managers to account.

Thus, the stock market helps to discipline managers by providing up-to-the-minute signals about their performance. This informational content of stock prices explains why the payment of managers is often tied to the stock market's valuation of their firm. Companies often offer stock-option plans that allow managers to earn substantial amounts of money if their shares rise.

If management performs weakly, it may also risk a hostile takeover in the stock market. This means that external investors, or "corporate raiders," buy shares of the company until they hold a majority at share-holder meetings. As the new owners are in control of the firm, they can then fire the old managers and hire new ones who will increase the firm's profitability. Although such hostile takeovers are rare, a fear of them may lead executives to be more determined in their efforts at maximizing the value of their company, since a higher value is reflected in higher share prices, making the execution of a hostile takeover more difficult.

THE STOCK MARKET'S CENTRAL ROLE

Are the incentives provided by capitalists in a social market economy also available to the state under a system of market socialism? Although there is only one employer—the state—a labor market for executives nevertheless also exists under market socialism. Performance-based pay can also be offered to the managers of market socialist enterprises. And creditors can likewise perform monitoring functions. Thus, it seems the only one of the four incentives not available in a market socialist economy is the stock market. Three out of four isn't bad—but is it enough?

Unfortunately, no. The missing incentive, the stock market, is urgently needed for the other three to function well. This is one of the central insights produced by the field of "corporate governance" research in recent years.

It may not seem immediately obvious that the stock market should have such a crucial role. Certainly, critics of capitalism usually take a pretty dim view of the stock market. This thesis therefore requires a convincing justification.

To begin with, one might think it is relatively easy to monitor management. All owners need to do is to check the level of profits. Owners who are not involved in the daily running of their businesses, such as, for instance, the state under market socialism, could therefore make the payment of managers dependent on the financial success of an enterprise.

Yet this is highly problematic. Current profits depend crucially on investment decisions that were taken by management a long time ago. Thus, today's profits depend on whether in the past the management adopted the right business model, employed the right personnel, and made the right investments in, for example, research and development. These managerial decisions are reflected in an enterprise's profits with a delay of several years. Current profits also depend on accidental factors, such as the global economic cycle. It follows that annual profits are not a good indicator of the quality of management in that same year, but rather a noisy signal indicating the quality of management in the past.

If an owner measured the quality of his managers in terms of current profits, the managers would have an incentive to develop strategies for raising short-term profits at the expense of long-term profits. They would, for instance, fail to make reasonable investments whose benefits would only become apparent after a long delay. Of course, one might in principle continue to pay managers dependent on the profits of the enterprise even after they left the enterprise. Managers would then take the long-term effects of their leadership into account. But some of them might die in the meantime, or might perhaps reason that having a lot of money in old age is not that important, as consumption opportunities diminish. The enterprise might also go bankrupt, or even snub former managers by intentionally reporting lower profits for some time after they have left.

Similar shortcomings attach to other indicators, such as, for instance, market share or increases in turnover. They also do not reliably reflect the quality of the existing management, and are therefore not suitable for producing the desired incentives.

Thus, without a well-functioning stock market, it is almost impossible that owners could readily evaluate the quality of management.

And this means that, without such a stock market, it is not possible to develop models for remuneration that create optimal incentives. The same applies to reputation as an incentive. Even with a functioning stock market, this is a rather vague standard. But without a functioning stock market, reputations build up only slowly and therefore tend to have little influence on managers' behavior.

The monitoring of managers by creditors might, in principle, help to promote the long-term performance of manager-led firms. In countries like Japan and Germany, the control of enterprises by their main banks played a central role until roughly the early 1990s. A main bank organizes the majority of the financing needed by an enterprise, and accompanies it for the long term, ideally for its entire existence. In such a setup, the bank has an interest in monitoring management to reduce the risk of a credit default. If there are signs of such a risk, it can intervene. If it sees grave mistakes being made, it may even convince the owners of the enterprise to replace top management, to allow the enterprise to be brought back on course.

But this mechanism of control is also fragile, because banks have their own serious problems with governance. There are various reasons why the executives of a bank might turn a blind eye and grant the loans demanded by an enterprise without paying close enough attention to risks. At best, in such cases, enterprise managers intend to use the credit to expand the business, which improves their personal prestige but diminishes the profitability of the business. At worst, bad investments lead to heavy losses, which ultimately also affect the bank.

Japan provides a cautionary example of the insufficiency of the control offered by main banks. The overgenerous financing of enterprises in the second half of the 1980s caused a major banking crisis in the 1990s, which affects Japan's economy to the present day. In economic circles, these are referred to as Japan's two lost decades.

We thus arrive at the key role played by the stock market, not only because of the signaling function of stock prices and the threat of hostile takeovers, but also because it increases the effectiveness of the other three mechanisms—that is, incentive pay, labor markets for managers, and the role of creditor banks. The remuneration of managers can be tied to stock prices, and their developments inform the markets and the creditors about the quality of their work.

The stock market is not a perfect source of information, however. It is susceptible to speculative bubbles and can be manipulated with the help of insider knowledge. The scandals in which managers of publicly-quoted companies are regularly involved bear witness to this. The neoliberal claim that stock prices always and everywhere reflect the fundamental value of a firm is therefore more an article of faith than a scientific truth.

The signals the market sends regarding the quality of management are imprecise and difficult to read. If the price of a share changes, it is necessary to isolate what part of the change is caused by the management, rather than by sector-specific or stock-market-specific factors. In general, the reliability of the stock market grows with its size and liquidity. But even then, the market should be subject to regulations that increase its transparency and ensure that misconduct is penalized. Given sufficient liquidity and proper regulation, a stock market can contribute substantially to management discipline in large-scale enterprises, and thus to the creation of wealth.

IMPLICATIONS FOR MARKET SOCIALISM

It would certainly not suffice if the managers of market socialist enterprises had to swear an oath of profit maximization, and then relied on their consciences. There would have to be suitable material incentives, as well. But to let managers have a share of current profits would be counterproductive. It would lead to shortsighted behavior and "creative accounting." The labor market for executives is also not very promising as a remedy, because in a market socialist economy executives would be employed by other managers or by government civil servants—that is, by individuals who have no genuine interest in the profit maximization of enterprises either. What remains as a solution is control by state banks; but here, too, we should be skeptical. The susceptibility of this approach to the emergence of corruption involving politicians and banks was already mentioned in the previous chapter.

For all these reasons, our concluding judgment on the traditional model of market socialism must be pessimistic. The risk is too high that such an economic system would produce the cronyism and stagnation we know too well from the hybrid systems in Hungary and Yugoslavia before the turning point of 1989.

SHAREHOLDER SOCIALISM

AS WE HAVE SEEN, the traditional model of market socialism lacks actors who could successfully encourage managers of firms to achieve economic efficiency—that is, actors who could perform the task that in the current system is performed by capitalists. This is a grave defect that makes it significantly less attractive. But the traditional design is not the last word on market socialism. There are other models, and they were designed specifically to solve this problem of incentives. They are all based on the counterintuitive idea that a stock market can exist alongside public ownership of firms and, by encouraging managers in market socialist economies to maximize the profits of their firms, can contribute to the reduction of overall economic waste.

On the next leg of our journey, we shall therefore visit three economic systems that belong to the species of *shareholder socialism*. In each of these systems, the market socialist firms are listed companies to which the general norms of stock corporation law apply. In the first of these systems, the state merely owns a majority of the capital of each firm—for example, 75 percent. In the second system, private ownership of shares is abolished altogether, and numerous municipalities and communities who trade on the stock market are entrusted with the share capital. In the third system, all shares are ultimately owned by individuals, but the corresponding property rights are restricted on the basis of egalitarian principles that make the emergence of capitalist dynasties impossible.

If a "socialized stock market" works well, then the other tools for disciplining state managers—reputation, incentive pay, and monitoring by creditors—also work well, because, as we may conclude from our reflections so far, an intelligently regulated stock market generates valuable signals indicating the quality of the current management of enterprises. Ultimately, enterprises then base their decisions on "shareholder value"—with, in the case of market socialism, the whole polity's being a "shareholder"—and they thus produce efficiently.

Shareholder socialism possesses yet another advantage over both traditional market socialism and the system of self-management—namely, that it allows firms to spread their business risk. A firm bears less risk if it is financed through issuing shares, because equity owners participate not only in the firm's profits but also in its losses. Should a firm find itself temporarily in difficulties, it need not pay dividends to shareholders. Contrast this with loans, which demand fixed repayments regardless of a firm's situation. It is thus possible to avoid cases in which, from one day to the next, wages need to be cut and working hours extended to cover payments to creditors.

The three versions of shareholder socialism outlined in this chapter also allow for small private enterprises, but these will be discussed only in the last part of the chapter. First, we shall concentrate on the actual market socialist sector of these economic systems.

FIRST VERSION: X% MARKET SOCIALISM

The simplest method for generating useful stock market signals in a market socialist economy is the partial privatization of the firms in the state-owned sector. Thus, we may imagine a version of shareholder socialism in which x percent of the capital stock of each enterprise is owned by the state. The shares corresponding to this percentage are not traded on the market, but are held by the government. The remaining shares are traded on a free market. The figure for x—that is, the proportion of the capital stock that is state-owned—lies somewhere between 51 and 99, so that the state retains the majority of votes at the shareholder meetings of each enterprise, and exerts control.

The proportion of shares held by the state should remain the same across time and for all enterprises. It therefore makes sense to fix the figure for x explicitly in the constitution. The constitution may, for instance, stipulate that 75 percent of the capital stock of each listed company must be publicly owned. Actors in the stock market then own the remaining 25 percent.

The investors trading at the stock market consist of individuals, firms, banks, foundations, and pension funds. As in contemporary capitalism, they buy and sell shares to achieve the highest possible expected return. The evolution of the various stock prices therefore mirrors the market expectations regarding the future profits of the various firms. This information can be used by the state as the main shareholder to discipline the behavior of the firms' managers—for example, through the mechanism of stock option plans.

This version of market socialism deviates from the traditional model insofar as part of the enterprises' profits end up with private investors. This is the price to be paid for being able to guarantee the efficiency of the production sector. However, the private investors are barred from exerting control over the enterprises, because the state retains the majority of votes at shareholder meetings. It is therefore unlikely that a capitalist class will form that could, through its economic power, dominate the political decision-making process.

When an enterprise issues new shares for the purpose of financing investment, it must adhere to the x percent rule to make sure that the proportion of state property remains the same. Thus, if a hundred new shares are issued to increase capital, only twenty-five of these are offered on the free market, while seventy-five are bought by the state at market value. As this way of proceeding puts pressure on the public budget, the issuing of larger amounts of shares must be subject to prior approval by a state authority. The x percent rule should also apply when the capital stock is reduced by the repurchase of shares by firms.

In this economic system, new enterprises can be established by the state and by existing market socialist enterprises. Enterprises founded by the state are listed on the stock market within a certain period of time. At that point, the state must sell 100 minus x percent of the shares to comply with the constitutionally embedded rule. If an enterprise is founded by another market socialist enterprise, the x percent condition is already met, insofar as the parent company is x percent owned by the state. In that case, it is not necessary that the new enterprise be listed.

State Ownership and Political Interventionism

Having the state own part of the capital stock of enterprises is not really a new phenomenon. Think of the German companies Volkswagen and Deutsche Telekom, to name just two. The truth is that sometimes state involvement has worked, and sometimes it has not. Typically it has not when governments imposed business decisions on management and misused enterprises under their control for party-political ends.

A striking example of the dangers of state involvement in firms' management is the former industrial holding IRI in Italy. This huge state-owned conglomerate positively contributed to the development of the nation's heavy industry and helped to reconstruct Italy after the war. But subsequently, IRI was abused by the political parties in government to please their clients, on the pretext of pursuing developmental policies for the southern regions of Italy. Bad investments accumulated, and financial losses and state subsidies rose astronomically. The Italian taxpayer had to foot the bill for IRI over a long period of time, until the state holding gradually dissolved as a consequence of pressure from the European Commission.

Finland, by contrast, provides an interesting counterexample. In the same period of time in which IRI gradually disappeared, the Finnish state successfully controlled about a fifth of the country's manufacturing sector. State-owned enterprises made profits and contributed to the technological modernization of the country. Some Finnish industries to the present day are world leaders when it comes to innovation and productivity. The reasons behind the privatization of most Finnish state-owned enterprises over the past twenty years have been political rather than economic.

Examples such as IRI suggest that the x percent version of stock market socialism entails significant risk of political interventionism, because in this economic system the government is the main shareholder of all big firms. Governments would be the source of plausible-sounding entreaties to their firms—"Please, do something about unemployment," or for the environment, for equal opportunities, for technological development, or for any number of other concerns—that would lead them to deviate from their business goals.

Political interventions in the affairs of firms are problematic not only because such noble words are often cloaks for politicians' selfish motives. Even when interventions are based on the purest of intentions, the polity often does not benefit because politicians, as a rule, do not really know how a particular firm can best serve society.

If political interventions are not prevented in this economic system, the result is confused chains of mutual commitment between individual politicians and managers, and these ultimately suffocate the workings of the market. Managers no longer feel responsible for proper economic accounting, and they subordinate business decisions to the aim of maintaining good relationships with politicians.

An Independent Institution as Collective Shareholder

The x percent version of market socialism should therefore have a public institution in the form of a collective investor who represents the interests of the polity and protects enterprises against the government's constant temptation to intervene in their business. Let's call this institution a *federal shareholder*. The federal shareholder acts as a trustee for the public capital invested in enterprises. The central task of this institution, carried out by its employees in accordance with its shareholder rights, is to make sure that the capital invested by the state achieves the highest possible returns over the long term. Thus, the sole purpose of this public agency (which is the main shareholder of all big firms), is to seek the maximization of the collective "shareholder value." This clearly formulated aim is its mission.

Sitting as they do on the boards of directors, representatives of the federal shareholder are in position to hire and fire the top managers of enterprises, to be involved in the design of their compensation packages, to give advice to them about the strategic orientation of the enterprise, and generally to make sure that firms in public ownership are managed so as best to maximize profits.

The success of this institution is measured in terms of the contribution that market socialist enterprises make to the government budget, because the more profitable the enterprises are, the greater the amount of money that flows from them into public coffers. The whole polity benefits from this, as it means that taxes can be lowered, while public transfer payments (as well as the quality of infrastructure, education, and health provision) can be raised.

The federal shareholder should take long-term profit from the invested capital as the benchmark. This institution is therefore kept free of short-term political motives, and its independence is guaranteed by the constitution. Its management is not recruited from political parties, but made up of independent experts who are committed to the public good. Like Germany's central bank or federal audit court, this institution is essentially independent from the government; like them, it has a clearly defined task. The mission of the German central bank upon its inception was to guarantee the stability of the general price level. (Today, this is the responsibility of the European Central Bank.) In the case of the federal shareholder, the task is the maximization of collective "shareholder value." One can also conceive of this task in terms of a target return that can be newly established every few years by parliament or through a referendum.

As this institution acts in the name of the broad collective interest, it maintains a high level of transparency. Every interested citizen has access to the information that is necessary to judge its performance. The competition authorities, consumer organizations, and trade unions are all able to keep a very close eye on the work of the representatives of the federal shareholder to prevent a situation in which the maximization of profits is achieved at the expense of consumers and employees. Hence, they are granted far-reaching information rights.

How large an institution is the federal shareholder? In a country such as Germany, there are today about 750 listed enterprises. But many large-scale enterprises are at present not joint-stock companies. Thus, assuming the number of listed enterprises doubles under market socialism, the institution needs enough personnel to be represented on 1,500 supervisory boards. If the federal shareholder is represented on each board with three members, and each of them is a member of three different boards, then the federal shareholder needs 1,500 employees to cover all supervisory boards of listed enterprises.

Such an institution also requires sufficiently qualified personnel for finding independent solutions to the problems it encounters. It therefore needs a center of excellence for all important questions of corporate governance, investment decision making, financing, and risk analysis. It must be able to offer its employees a professional perspective and instill a sense of belonging and of the importance of the common good in them. The recruitment of staff must be transparent and follow criteria that are clear and, as far as possible, objective.

Another question concerns the constitution of the institution's executive board. The board members must be independent not only of the government, but also of the enterprises. One possibility is to apply rules similar to the ones used in the case of central banks. However, the experience of recent years shows that they need to be very strict to make revolving doors—that is, personnel movements between the public authority and private business—more difficult, by imposing sufficiently long interim periods between holding different posts. The government appoints the president of the institution, but he or she remains in office for a relatively long period of time. A removal from office is only possible in extreme cases, and must be confirmed by parliament. The parliament has the right to nominate, for instance, half of the institution's board members.

Critical Appraisal

As private ownership of shares is permitted within certain limits, x percent market socialism features a stock market that can be used to steer the behavior of managers towards profit maximization. Nevertheless, the majority of shares are in the possession of a single institution. This has two problematic consequences.

The first is that there can be no hostile takeovers of badly managed enterprises, because the federal shareholder is always the majority shareholder. As we saw in the previous chapter, just the threat of a hostile takeover, with the likely subsequent replacement of top-tier management, can be an efficient way of encouraging management discipline. In this system, this tool does not exist, because the replacement of bad managers can only be initiated by the state institution.

The second problem—the real Achilles' heel of this system—is the concentration of power in the government that may follow if politicians gain control over the federal shareholder, the institution in charge of the state-owned firms. As the resulting power is vast, so is the temptation to capture this institution. A government may therefore try to abolish the law guaranteeing the independence of the federal shareholder, or it may try to undermine it in practice.

This risk highlights the necessity of strengthening the position of private investors. These investors have an immediate interest in the profitability of those enterprises in which they hold shares, but due to their diversified share portfolio they have only a weak incentive to perform the necessary monitoring role. It is therefore exceedingly important that the polity supports organizations that help private shareholders articulate their interests and, if necessary, fight for them.

The suitability of this version of market socialism depends on country-specific factors that make political abuse more or less likely. A strong civil society, free and independent media, and intense competition between political parties can help to make it less so. An established tradition of the rule of law is also helpful. If the top positions of state institutions are filled with competent individuals who have integrity, they are less likely to come under the sway of intellectual fashions and political mantras being invoked by government members trying to subordinate the federal shareholder and its companies to their aims.

Although the presence or absence of these beneficial factors is not immutable, they can be changed only relatively slowly. In some countries, there may be only very weak expressions of them, and it may therefore be too politically risky to introduce this first version of shareholder socialism. In these countries, the power that results from public ownership of the means of production must be decentralized. One option is to return to the venerable tradition of local self-management—an option we will explore next.

SECOND VERSION: MUNICIPAL MARKET SOCIALISM

The design of *municipal market socialism* can be found in the work of U.S. political scientist and economist Leland Stauber. The core of the economic system he suggests is a stock market in which the shares of all large-scale firms operating in competitive product markets are traded. As opposed to the first version of shareholder socialism, however, the public institutions in charge of those firms are the local jurisdictions. Individual ownership of shares is not permitted in this system. People who want to save must do so with savings accounts, government bonds, and the like.

In the system of municipal market socialism, every local jurisdiction is the sole owner of an investment trust that administers the share capital of the municipality. Several smaller communities may join together for this purpose. The local investment trusts trade with shares and distribute the associated returns to the jurisdictions to which they belong. Enterprises are set up as joint-stock companies whose shares are mainly held by the local investment trusts in the form of their own investment funds. Enterprises and banks (who are also joint-stock companies) can also own the shares of other enterprises and banks, as is the case today. But ultimately all enterprises are owned by the local jurisdictions through their investment trusts.

It is worth noting that, in this economic system, the local investment trusts are not instruments for regional planning. Rather, their sole task is the generation of capital income from firm ownership. This corresponds to the brief of the federal shareholder in the first version of shareholder socialism.

Having a large number of profit-maximizing investment trusts creates a competitive stock market in which stock prices signal the efficiency of the corresponding enterprises. The local investment trusts exercise the control rights associated with their ownership of shares, and receive their dividends. This is meant to provide the investment trusts with the incentives and the instruments they need to encourage the managers of enterprises to maximize profits.

The fund managers of the local investment trusts are recruited on the job market and may receive pay tied to the performance of their funds. The fundamental rules they must follow are laid down in law. This law ensures the necessary independence of the investment trusts from local government. All investment trusts are controlled by external auditors, appointed by a national regulatory body. The auditors certify that the activities of the local investment trusts conform to the formal rules dictated by national legislation.

Mandatory disclosure forces the local investment trusts to be transparent, so that the residents of a municipality get as precise as possible a picture of how their investment trust works. An independent national regulatory body records the performance of all local investment trusts, conducts comparative studies, and publishes the collected data, as well as the results of its analyses. This helps each municipality's residents judge the quality of the management of funds in their own trust. It may be that municipalities remunerate their funds managers using the method of yardstick competition. That is, managers receive bonuses for above-average fund performance; if performance is below average, their salaries are reduced. The regulatory body produces a guide for the regulation of local investment funds and advises the municipalities.

All dividends and, where applicable, income from interest received by a local investment trust is passed on to the community. Trusts receive income from interest if they are allowed to buy bonds issued by enterprises. They are prohibited, however, from purchasing bonds issued by regional authorities; otherwise, the temptation might be too great for those authorities to misuse their investment trusts to help them pursue unsustainable fiscal policies.

The municipalities have fundamental decision-making authority over the use of the interest income and dividends they receive from the investment trusts, and they make their decisions democratically. Such income may, for instance, be used to reduce local taxation or to improve local infrastructure, it may be passed on to the residents as a local social dividend, or it may be used to increase the capital assets of the investment trust. As one possible scenario for the introduction of this economic system, perhaps all municipalities receive from the federal government the same amount of money for each resident to buy shares. At regular intervals, the federal government may decide to increase the investment funds of the municipalities to satisfy the rising demand for equity capital from the firm sector. This increase is financed through federal taxation, and the grant to each municipality is proportional to the size of its population. The individual communities may also decide to improve the financial endowment of their investment trust by means of additional revenues derived from higher local taxes or lower local expenditures. This may be desirable if shares are seen as particularly lucrative forms of investment. A further possibility to satisfy the rising demand for equity capital from the firm sector is to allow the investment trusts to borrow money for the purchase of shares from commercial banks and other investors.

Due to the decentralization of public ownership, this version of market socialism is better suited for implementation at the European level, or even at the global level. Note, for example, that it avoids disputes between nations over the filling of posts in a central authority.

Regulation of the Municipal Investment Trusts

In this economic system, the local municipalities bear a great responsibility for the allocation of resources. Two questions arise at this point: What we should make of this increased importance of the communities? And are they actually able to fulfill this function?

On the one hand, this system can draw on traditions of local self-management and local-level democratic involvement that are still very much alive in some countries. In Europe, where this tradition is strong, the introduction of municipal market socialism could lead to a renaissance of citizens' initiatives and local democracy.

On the other hand, the communities' desire to shape things implies the danger of political interference in the participant enterprises' decisions. A local government might, for instance, order an enterprise controlled by its investment trust to buy machines from a local producer, even though their quality is bad or they are overpriced. A local government might also force an enterprise it controls to invest in the community, even though an investment outside the community promises significantly higher returns. It is therefore anything but certain that the municipal investment trusts would perform the capitalist class function of encouraging enterprises to maximize their value. The danger of undue political influence appears even greater if we remind ourselves that, among local politicians, there are frequently individuals who have private economic interests in the municipality's decisions—perhaps because they are involved in the real estate market, for example. Such entanglements, together with the possibility of administering a considerable amount of money, could lead to cronyism.

If it is to work, municipal market socialism therefore needs rules to put up barriers to the exertion of political influence and to induce the local investment trusts to strive for the maximization of their financial performance over the long term.

Past experience with so-called sovereign wealth funds suggest the kinds of rules needed. Today, many states of the world have sovereign wealth funds that oversee the short-term administration of enormous volumes of financial assets. Some of these funds have achieved considerable returns over the past decades—Singapore's is a good example. And some of them have been not only financially successful but also transparent, and therefore amenable to democratic control. This is particularly true of Norway's. Sovereign wealth funds in today's states are comparable to the local investment trusts we are imagining in the municipalities of the market socialism. The shape of the rights and duties of local investment trusts in municipal market socialism can therefore be based on the regulation of the sovereign wealth funds under capitalism.

Further rules, more specific to municipal market socialism, are also needed. What if, for example, local enterprises that are inefficiently managed exert pressure on local government to receive financial aid from the municipal investment trust? The prohibition of direct subsidies is not enough, because such help can be covert. An unprofitable enterprise might, for instance, repeatedly get its municipality to buy new shares in it. Such an enterprise could operate at a loss without ever officially receiving subsidies.

The risk of local politicians' abusing their authority could be mitigated, however, by various generally binding rules. Stauber, the inventor of this economic system, suggests three such rules. The first is that *none of the municipal investment trusts may own shares of local enterprises*—that is, of enterprises whose activities have a focal point in the trust's municipality. Note that this rule does not apply to local utilities providing essential services, because (as discussed in the previous chapter) these are regulated by different means, due to their lack of competition.

Under this rule, an enterprise might count as "local" if it employs more than a certain proportion of the population or contributes more than a certain percentage to overall value-added in the municipality. The prohibition on owning shares of local enterprises should also apply to bonds issued by these enterprises.

This rule requires a further specification, however. As in the other versions of shareholder socialism, in this model, too, enterprises may be active in the stock market. This leads to ownership chains that create indirect relations between local investment trusts and enterprises. To avoid a situation in which enterprises circumvent the above-mentioned rule by taking indirect ownership of local enterprises, mutual stockholdings between enterprises must be taken into consideration. Otherwise, a local government can buy the majority of shares of an enterprise from another municipality, which, in turn, buys shares of an enterprise from its own municipality. With the help of today's information technology, it is possible to monitor such cross-shareholdings. Share transactions can't be allowed to remain anonymous, however, and therefore a centralized stock market is needed in which the shares held by each market participant are visible at every point in time. For the bonds issued by enterprises, similar arrangements must be made if they are to be part of the investment trusts' portfolios. And it is particularly important to take the effects of the combination of share and bond ownership into account. This makes it possible to prevent, for example, municipality A's owning an enterprise located in municipality B, which in turn buys bonds of an enterprise located in municipality A that would not otherwise be able to finance itself on the capital market.

If the regulator takes the municipalities' indirect ownership into account, a complete prohibition of the ownership of local enterprises may turn out to be a substantial drag on the stock market's workings. Given widely dispersed shareholdings and cross-shareholdings, a local enterprise may find it hard to buy any shares at all without its municipality's becoming an owner via some chain or other. It therefore makes sense to limit the ownership of local enterprises, without prohibiting it altogether.

There must also be limitations on the ownership of nonlocal enterprises, because even if the investment trusts do not provide equity capital, there is still potential for political abuse to the advantage of local enterprises. Imagine, for example, that municipality A's investment trust gains control of an enterprise in municipality B which engages in trade relations with a municipality A enterprise. Municipality A's investment trust could use its power of control to gain an advantage for its own municipality's enterprise; it might, for example, compel the management of the municipality B enterprise to buy from the municipality A enterprise at too high a price, or sell to it at too low a price.

For all these reasons, it is economically unwarranted for single municipalities to have exclusive control over market socialist enterprises. To rule out this possibility, a municipality's maximum ownership of an enterprise's capital equity should be legally restricted. This brings us to Stauber's second rule: *No municipality may directly or indirectly own more than six or seven percent of an enterprise.* The corollary is that every enterprise has at least fifteen owners. Since no single owner holds an absolute majority of the capital, the other shareholders can be relied upon to protest any abuse of power aimed at benefiting a specific municipality.

This prohibition also makes sense because it helps to avoid another kind of hidden subsidy for local enterprises. According to the first rule, an investment trust may not purchase shares in local enterprises. This rule can be circumvented, however, if two municipalities, each with one unprofitable enterprise in its district, agree to buy the shares of each other's unprofitable enterprises. Doing so allows them to give both local enterprises hidden subsidies. Although this kind of agreement is illegal, it is probably difficult to provide legally watertight proof that the law has been violated. But if a municipality's ownership of shares is restricted to six or seven percent of an enterprise's capital, then the volume of a possible subsidy is limited and such agreements become less lucrative. Of course, agreements between three or four municipalities could result in larger financial injections for the enterprises, but it is much more difficult to keep such agreements secret. Municipalities may still agree to subsidize their enterprises through the mutual purchase of bonds (if it is permitted for local investment trusts to invest in bonds). The restrictions on ownership should therefore be extended to include bonds issued by enterprises.

Another problem results if municipalities try to use up their assets held in shares without due consideration for the next generation of the population. If local governments are allowed to turn a municipality's assets into liquidity, they can very quickly have a lot of money at their disposal. It may be tempting for local politicians to develop strategies for directing this money into their own pockets and the pockets of those under their patronage. A municipality with a relatively small population might also think about dividing up the windfall among the residents and then vacating the impoverished municipality to move to a more prosperous one.

To avoid such forms of opportunistic behavior, the investment trusts, as a matter of principle, may not pass on the proceeds from the sale of shares to the budget of the municipality. This is the third rule suggested by Stauber: *The investment trusts must reinvest the proceeds from the sale of shares in the stock market.* The proceeds from sales of bonds and other financial securities must also promptly be reinvested.

This third prohibition, however, can be circumvented if a municipality invests its wealth in the shares of an enterprise that turns all its assets into liquidity within a short space of time, and thus distributes artificially high dividends. With a nod to the old Grimm's fairy tale about the "Gold-Ass"—the donkey that turns what it eats into gold droppings—let's give this kind of enterprise a name. It is a short-lived gold-ass. While its market value continuously declines, its shareholders receive huge dividends. Thus, a municipality that owns only short-lived gold-asses reduces its share assets to zero within a short space of time, but up to that point receives a lot of money. If the municipality keeps this strategy well hidden, it may even successfully insist that the central government bail it out—something the central government will do if it erroneously ascribes the loss of capital to stock market volatility, failing to see that the local government had a hand in it.

We will return to the subject of gold-ass enterprises in detail when we come to the third version of shareholder socialism, because the problems they create are more acute in that context. Here, it suffices to mention three simple measures that help defuse the dangers under municipal market socialism.

First, gold-ass strategies can be explicitly prohibited by laws spelling out penalties to deter them. Second, the federal government can resolutely commit itself to a policy of not bailing out municipalities who have been economically imprudent with their assets. This requires an insolvency law for local jurisdictions. Third, the government can introduce progressive taxation for per-capita dividends within the municipalities, placing higher tax burdens on very high payouts. This has the effect of markedly reducing the payoff of a gold-ass strategy.

The problem of short-lived gold-asses can be immediately defused if each investment trust represents a group of individuals with different interests. As a rule, some residents will be strictly in favor of keeping assets within the municipality and using them for long-term profitable investment in the stock market. These are the individuals who expect their families to remain permanent residents of the municipality and are therefore interested in its long-term prosperity. Such people are often politically active at the local level, and they are therefore well informed about the investment strategies of the trusts. If the investment trust attempts to buy a gold-ass enterprise, they ask the national regulatory body to investigate the investment trust.

The rule that dictates that no municipality may be the sole owner of an enterprise is also helpful here. To transform an enterprise into a gold-ass, the investment trust of a municipality needs to reach an agreement not only with the managers of the enterprise but also with the other shareholders. Given a maximum of six percent share ownership, there are at least seventeen shareholders. Keeping such an agreement secret is very difficult.

Inequality of Social Dividends

In a system of municipal market socialism, the dividend incomes enjoyed by populations of different municipalities often diverge. Some investment trusts are more successful in their stock market decisions than others, and their local governments are able to provide higher social dividends. This inequality represents a thoroughly desirable incentive for municipalities to invest their share capital as profitably as possible. Compared to the traditional model of market socialism, however, the income distribution is less equal. Although this is a disadvantage, it is not really a serious objection to the model. There are at least three reasons for this.

First, the traditional model of market socialism is not an attractive model for more general reasons. The municipal version of shareholder socialism must rather be compared to the version of *x percent market socialism*, where 100 minus *x* represents the proportion of share capital that is privately owned, and where the distribution of dividends is therefore also unequal. It is not possible to tell in general which version of market socialism results in the more unequal distribution of dividends.

Second, we must take into consideration that the income from dividends represents only a part of the income from capital, which, in turn, represents about a third of national income. In addition to a social dividend, individuals receive income from labor, and income from interest, that results from market transactions and is usually unequally distributed. There are also public transfer payments, such as old-age pensions and unemployment benefits, which may also differ from individual to individual. A small inequality in the distribution of dividends therefore has an even smaller effect on overall income inequality.

Third, the fact that individuals may freely choose their places of residence further weakens the influence that inequality among municipalities has on inequality among individuals. When the per-capita income in two municipalities seriously diverges, some individuals leave the poor municipality and move to the richer one, to raise their standard of living. As a result, the richer municipality's social dividend goes down and the poorer municipality's social dividend goes up. Thus, freedom of movement counteracts income disparities among regions.

THIRD VERSION: COUPON MARKET SOCIALISM

Yale University economist John Roemer has suggested an alternative form of market socialism that includes individual ownership of shares. Compared to the first two versions of shareholder socialism, this form significantly reduces the risk that the state will exert political influence over enterprises' decisions. It also allows citizens to choose share portfolios that suit their individual needs. Because the functioning of this ingenious system is conditional on the introduction of a parallel currency for stock markets—coupons—this is *coupon market socialism*.

Once again, we see here an economic system with a core of listed en-terprises that have the legal form of joint-stock companies. There are additionally numerous investment trusts created and controlled by the state. These own the shares of the listed enterprises and offer them to the citizens in the form of mutual funds. The shares of the mutual funds are owned by individuals and traded in coupons on an official market for securities. The ownership rights of individuals are restricted in such a way that the emergence of capitalist dynasties is prevented.

Coupons as the Currency of the Capital Market

In this version of shareholder socialism, each citizen receives an iden-tical sum from the government once he or she reaches a certain age— perhaps eighteen. This sum is denominated in coupons, not in euros or dollars—that is, not in the currency used for all other market trans-actions. The individuals may not change these coupons into other cur-rencies. They represent an initial capital endowment with which each individual buys shares in mutual funds. As there are hundreds of invest-ment trusts, each of which administers several mutual funds, each person can choose among numerous investment opportunities. If someone buys shares in a fund, he or she is then entitled to a proportional share of the dividends paid out by that fund. While the shares are priced in coupons, their owners receive their share of the dividends as ordi-nary money—that is, dollars or euros. They can then spend this money freely.

Coupons can be used only for the purchase of shares. And the shares, in turn, can be sold only for coupons. Shares of the various funds are traded on a state-regulated financial market in accordance with their market prices. Individuals invest in coupons, and so can enterprises, banks, foundations, and pension funds. Individuals can stockpile cou-pons in accounts, but they can neither exchange them against another currency nor give them away to other individuals or organizations. The fact that these assets are fixed in coupons means that each individual has a lifelong investment income, the value of which depends on the ac-quired shares' performance. Individuals therefore have an incentive to look out for the mutual funds that offer the best combination of returns and risks. Adventurous investors try to gather and analyze information to play the market, while risk-averse investors just invest their assets in funds that experience market-average performance.

The investment trusts that administer the mutual funds buy shares in enterprises using the coupons they have received from individuals in exchange for shares in the mutual funds. These shares, in turn, entitle their owners (that is, the mutual funds) to the dividends paid out by the enterprises (in euros, or whatever currency). The investment trusts, as the holders of shares, also exercise the control rights laid down by law for joint-stock companies.

For the enterprises, the coupon stock market is a source of finance— just like today's stock market. They turn to the stock market and try to convince investors of the soundness of the business projects they want to undertake. Coupons acquired through stock sales are exchanged by enterprises for ordinary currency at the central bank using an official exchange rate, and this money can then be spent on their investment projects—for example, building new production plants or investing in research and development. Enterprises are also permitted to exchange ordinary money for coupons at the central bank—for example, if they wish to buy back their shares.

Thus, coupons as a parallel currency are used on two securities markets. They are used on the market for trading shares of mutual funds, where the actors are state-owned investment trusts (to begin with, as sellers) and individuals (to begin with, as buyers). They are also used to carry out transactions on the stock market. On the latter market, enterprises, investment trusts, banks, and other institutional investors are the traders.

Because all individuals initially receive the same amount of coupons, everyone in principle has the same entitlement to the profits of market socialist enterprises. Across the years of their lives, however, their shares of profits become unequal, because they all invest their initial capital in whatever ways they like. In the end, some individuals make more out of it, and others less, despite the fact that they set out from the same position.

For this form of equal opportunity to be realized, it must be true that coupons or shares cannot be passed on to heirs or freely given away.

Upon someone's death, all shares and noninvested coupons of the deceased become the property of the state. The state then sells these shares and uses the revenue in coupons to finance the initial coupon endowments of individuals turning eighteen in that particular year.

The fundamental idea of this economic system is therefore easy to summarize. The polity, in the last instance, entrusts the administration of the capital stock to the entire citizenry. The individuals have a personal interest in administering the capital entrusted to them as profitably as possible, because they receive the returns from their investments. At the end of their lives, individuals return the potentially increased capital to the polity, and a new generation is entrusted with its administration.

Regulation of the Investment Trusts

The investment trusts form a central part of this system. They are set up by the state, but they are legally independent bodies and they compete over the administration of individuals' coupon assets. As they are major shareholders, they have representatives on the supervisory boards of market socialist enterprises. Like the corresponding institutions in the two other versions of shareholder socialism, the investment trusts are also embedded in an institutional framework that provides sensible incentives.

A well-respected, independent regulatory agency is tasked with monitoring the activities of the investment trusts. It creates the transparency in the coupon-denominated financial markets that is necessary for an efficient management of assets. The performance of the mutual funds is communicated to investors perspicuously, enabling them to make informed decisions. Bad funds are not selected and go to the wall; good funds grow. The regulatory agency in particular supervises the selection and pay of the fund managers, and sees to it that they are given the right kinds of incentives. Fund managers participate in the success of their funds. This provides them with incentives to make use of their control rights as shareholders—that is, to ensure the enterprises in which they hold shares are as profitable as possible. The regulatory agency stipulates mechanisms for the remuneration of fund managers that encourage them to maximize the overall market values of the mutual funds they work for.

How to Deal with the Gold-Asses

Let us imagine an older man with children who has accrued substantial assets in coupons through successful investments. If it is permissible, he likes to give those coupons as presents to his children; and even more, he likes to exchange them for money and bequeath the money to the children. The polity has good reasons for not allowing this. The man originally received the coupons as a gift from the state and thereby implicitly entered into a generational contract that stipulates that he, toward the end of his life, must return the coupons to the state. Alternatively, let us imagine a woman who wants to make a major purchase, perhaps of a new house. She also, of course, has a strong interest in exchanging her coupon assets for, say, euros. Perhaps that would mean she could buy a more beautiful house. In these and similar situations, we can expect some individuals to try to find strategies for turning coupon assets into money without breaking the law. One such strategy makes use of enterprises that offer themselves for use as "short-lived gold-asses."

The individual applying this strategy invests his coupon assets in a mutual fund made up of shares of enterprises that pay out disproportionately high dividends within short periods of time. These enterprises raise a lot of cash—perhaps by issuing new shares or by selling productive assets—and then report artificially high profits in their accounts, which they pass on to shareholders as dividends. In the most extreme form, this strategy is pursued to the point that the market value of the enterprise is zero, or even negative. By investing in such a fund of gold-ass enterprises, the individual has, in fact, found a way to exchange coupons for money. Thus, at the end of his life, he leaves to the polity shares in funds that are worthless. In essence, he raises his personal consumption, or that of his heirs, at the expense of fellow citizens.

Several measures might be put in place to keep people from pursuing this strategy. One of them is a law making the transformation of an enterprise into a short-lived gold-ass a punishable offense, and making the managers responsible for it personally liable. Stock corporation law and accounting rules can be adapted to make it difficult to hide gold-ass strategies. There can be strict limitations on payouts of capital reserves as dividends, for instance.

There can also be rules forbidding investment trusts to fill mutual funds intentionally with the shares of gold-ass enterprises. The monitoring of this prohibition becomes the remit of the national regulatory agency. This authority can recognize early whether a fund has become specialized in gold-ass enterprises by monitoring dividends paid out and share prices. High payouts happening in periods of low capitalization levels are indicators that an attempt at liquidation is being made. Investment trusts that want to offer the shares of gold-ass enterprises are compelled to communicate to potential customers that a particular investment fund consists of such enterprises. The information contained in these communications must be conveyed to a regulator that really deserves the name. Where there is justified suspicion of a secret liquidation attempt, the regulatory body immediately orders an investigation. Investment trusts that provide gold-ass funds lose their business licenses, and their managers, as well as the managers of gold-ass enterprises, are subject to criminal prosecution, as is the case with tax evasion.

If these measures are not sufficient, a prohibition can be placed—as in the case of municipal market socialism—on exclusive control of enterprises. The legislature may, for instance, prohibit a single investment trust—directly, or through ownership chains and cross-shareholdings—from owning more than twenty percent of an enterprise's capital. If an investment trust is the sole owner of an enterprise, it is relatively easy for it to persuade the executives of that enterprise (perhaps by offering them substantial pay raises) to transform it into a gold-ass. But where the owners number five or more, such a strategy is considerably more difficult to pursue. More parties involved make it more likely that one of them will not agree with the strategy, or that, even if all parties agree, someone will make a mistake that leads to the strategy's being detected.

Finally, the allure of gold-ass enterprises can be diminished through tax policy. Prohibitively high tax rates can be applied to any payouts of dividends that are very high in relation to the market value of the shares. At the same time, the threshold for tax-free dividends can be made high enough that investors have incentives to look out for lucrative mutual funds.

SHAREHOLDER SOCIALISM AND
THE GLOBAL CAPITAL MARKET

Finding ways to discipline the behavior of managers is one necessity to support the economic viability of these three versions of shareholder socialism—but not the only challenge. Assuming the system is not introduced on a global scale, there is also the question of its compatibility with a global capitalist market. Can the international division of labor we witness today be continued under it?

If, for instance, the European Union (EU) introduces shareholder socialism, and all other countries remain capitalist, the economic relationships between the EU and the rest of the world might remain more or less unchanged after the transitional period. This applies in particular to foreign trade. The consequences for migration will be slightly more complicated, because the entitlement to social dividends for people who emigrate or immigrate needs to be addressed. But that does not pose any fundamental problems. The only area in which the coexistence of different economic systems raises very difficult questions is in international capital movements.

Today, international capital movements are largely unrestricted. This freedom, however, carries with it the risk that capitalists will regain control over large-scale enterprises under conditions of market socialism. A rich resident of a market socialist country—the chair of a market socialist enterprise, for example—could transfer financial assets abroad, and then use them on the international capital market to gain control of a home-country enterprise, and perhaps the very enterprise of which that person is chair. Or a foreign investor could take control of a market-socialist enterprise. After enough such moves, the old capitalist order could become reestablished. To prevent this, the government at home can cut the country off from all international capital flows. But this way of responding has its own problems. First, it means that some private individuals and enterprises in the country are no longer able to buy the portfolios that are optimal for them, because such optimal portfolios contain foreign financial securities. Second, portfolio investments from the rest of the world could actually intensify the competition on the domestic stock market, thus improving its usefulness as a steering mechanism. And third, foreign direct investment is often associated with the spread of new technologies that, in turn, promote the growth of domestic productivity.

A better option than blocking access to the international capital market is allowing capital flows in both directions, but setting an upper limit to foreign ownership of domestic enterprises. A relatively low limit—perhaps ten percent, including indirect holdings—can guarantee that individual large-scale enterprises in the market socialist country are not dominated by capitalists. This measure is relatively easy to implement in all three versions of shareholder socialism.

In the system we're calling x percent market socialism, foreign investors are allowed on the domestic market without any specific restrictions. The shares acquired by them are added to the 100 minus x percent of shares traded on the market, and thus the share of an enterprise's capital that is controlled from abroad is never more than 100 minus x percent.

In the system of municipal market socialism, this rule can be applied on the basis of the information about the portfolios of the local investment trusts, especially since direct and indirect ownership is already monitored for other reasons. This monitoring provides sufficient data to quantify how much of a specific enterprise is owned by the municipalities overall. If foreign investors are allowed free access to the domestic stock market, the proportion of foreign ownership is equal to the proportion not owned by the totality of municipalities. Thus, this informational system tells us how much of each enterprise is in foreign hands. The national regulatory body can then establish whether the foreign ownership of a given enterprise exceeds the limit set by the legislator. Wherever the proportion of foreign ownership is too high, the last foreign buyers are compelled to sell their shares to domestic municipalities within a certain period of time, so that the relationship between domestic and foreign ownership remains within legal limits.

The system of coupon market socialism probably requires stricter controls on capital movements. Perhaps an authority issues licenses, after an examination, to foreign investors, giving them the right to buy stipulated amounts of coupons from the domestic central bank, and to exchange them for money, so they can be active on the domestic stock market. These foreign investors commit themselves not to execute orders for resident individuals. For each enterprise, the proportion of its shares owned by foreigners is not allowed to exceed a certain amount. The regulatory agency can use its information system on shares held directly and indirectly by domestic shareholders to audit this.

In all three versions, the limit on foreign ownership should be substantially less than 50 percent. This restriction has an impact on foreign direct investment—that is, it affects the decisions made by foreign multinational corporations regarding the creation of production facilities in the market socialist country. There are two reasons for this. First, the minority interest means that the foreign investor cannot exercise exclusive control. Thus there is a risk that the enterprise will be managed against his or her interests, perhaps competing with the investing multinational in other foreign markets, for example. Second, the foreign corporation does not receive even half the profits generated by an investment project. If the market socialist country is in competition with capitalist countries, a profit-oriented investor will consider choosing another location. Capitalist foreign countries can also retaliate and introduce similar rules, prohibiting majority positions of their enterprises from being held by the enterprises of the market socialist country.

INNOVATION AND MARKET SOCIALISM

This brings us to the last topic of this chapter: the capacity of shareholder socialism to generate enough innovation. This capacity plays a central role in economic growth, because growth comes from the continual qualitative improvement of products and production methods, as well as from the introduction of novel offerings. Growth is driven by a cumulative process of innumerable successful innovations. Over time, economic growth can truly transform people's living conditions. During the past sixty years, for example, real per-capita income in the Federal Republic of Germany has risen by a factor of five. Is market socialism able to retain capitalism's innovative dynamism, while also achieving more growth?

Shareholder socialism creates structural incentives that promise to encourage managers of public enterprises to pursue profit maximization. We may therefore expect large-scale enterprises under shareholder socialism to be no less inclined toward innovation than their counterparts under capitalism. And, as in contemporary capitalist societies, there are also research centers and universities contributing to innovation, especially in the area of basic or "blue-sky" research.

Nevertheless, one actor who is central to the process of innovation is missing from the traditional design of market socialism: the individual entrepreneur.

In the history of capitalism, a kind of division of labor exists between small-scale and large-scale enterprises as far as innovation is concerned. Individual entrepreneurs are more likely to be the protagonists in the introductions of radically new innovations, while large-scale enterprises specialize in extending these innovations to broader sets of industries and in generating smaller innovations that improve upon them.

It is easy to understand why there is such a division of labor. Large-scale enterprises, whether public or private, are hierarchically structured organizations that work according to bureaucratic rules. This also holds true for their large research-and-development units. Creativity, vision, adventurousness, and appetite for risk are not necessarily among their strengths. But these are precisely the qualities needed to create and introduce entirely new customer solutions and better ways of delivering them. Certain propensities to try crazy things and to be willing to take risks are required for this, and, as a rule, these attitudes show up in individuals or small groups of like-minded people. The managers of large-scale enterprises, by contrast, look after the money of other people, and have a difficult time investing this money in mad innovation projects whose chances of success are hard to predict—and even harder to explain to those who are paying for them. Individual entrepreneurs have the freedom to bet their money on high-risk projects. Their enthusiasm and the prospects of fame and wealth can lead them to doggedly pursue projects even when they have only minimal chances of success. The history of enterprise innovation, from early industrialization to the newest information technologies, is full of examples of the obsession and stubbornness we have to thank for a whole host of groundbreaking innovations.

While small-scale entrepreneurs hold the advantage in pursuing major innovations, large-scale enterprises have the advantage when it comes to minor innovations. The latter flourish within well-equipped research and development units and when there is a profound understanding of what is going on in the global market. This requires comprehensive investment and complex organization.

The main argument in favor of market socialism is that society should not end up being effectively dominated by a capitalist financial elite. But is there a place for individual entrepreneurs within this system at all? In a market economy, entrepreneurs may become rich, but as long as their enterprises are small, the wealth of the entrepreneurs has limits. There is thus no danger of a plutocratic degeneration of the polity as a consequence of the rising influence of small-scale entrepreneurs. As small and middle-sized enterprises contribute significantly to the flexibility and dynamism of the overall economy, they are still very valuable under market socialist conditions.

An obvious approach is accordingly to pass a law defining for each sector the conditions under which private enterprises are allowed. One might take the number of employees and their turnover as criteria and establish sector-specific limits for them. But this is not a good idea. Quite apart from the necessarily arbitrary nature of these limits, they elicit expensive attempts at circumventing them, such as bogus enterprises registered under the names of relatives or friends. Even more serious is the absence of incentives. If an entrepreneurial enterprise is not allowed to expand beyond a certain point, its founders have no incentive to keep improving it. And without the prospect of dramatic success, really major innovations do not happen.

A MECHANISM FOR TAKING OVER PRIVATE ENTERPRISES

Market socialism apparently requires an institutional framework that promotes private entrepreneurial activities and, at the same time, prevents the formation of large-scale private firms. But in our present-day capitalism, new and successful enterprises often end up being sold to older, larger enterprises that develop their ideas further and implement them on a larger scale. It is quite possible to take up this practice within market socialism, as well, although difficulties might result if a private owner of an enterprise simply refuses to sell it. This possibility raises the question of whether the sales could be based on an entirely voluntary arrangement, in which case an owner might simply not sell, and might try instead to create an economic empire and a capitalist dynasty. A new financial aristocracy would slowly emerge.

Thus, a mechanism must be designed to maintain the investment incentives for private enterprises while preventing the emergence of capitalist dynasties. This section describes such a mechanism, based on the idea that the foundation of enterprises should be voluntary and free, and that private enterprises should freely participate in market competition. It also, however, involves a commitment by entrepreneurs to put their enterprises up for sale regularly; through the setting of minimum prices they could be guaranteed to receive at least the value of the enterprises if they were sold. Let's assume such a mechanism is in place. How does it work?

Once a year, every private enterprise is required to name an amount of money it is prepared to pay to the government. We will call this the "enterprise contribution." It replaces all other existing taxation of profit for the private enterprise.

Soon thereafter, a list is published of all private enterprises showing their respective enterprise contributions. Payments are due after a specified period of time—let's assume in one month's time. During that month, all market socialist firms are eligible to place bids to acquire these private enterprises. Any bids are communicated confidentially to the authority overseeing the auction process.

For every auction a minimum price is set, below which an offer will not be accepted. This minimum is derived from the enterprise contribution announced by the owner. Thus, if a private enterprise announces a payment of B, only bids that exceed B by a given multiple are valid. This multiple, which we can represent as m, is set down in advance by law and is valid for all enterprises. For an enterprise that has announced a payment of B, any valid bid would then have to be higher than $m \times B$. To illustrate with real numbers, let's assume an enterprise announces an enterprise contribution (B) of one million euros, and that the law stipulates a multiplier (m) of 100. Only bids higher than one hundred million euros are accepted.

After the month has elapsed, all offers are examined by the authority. If there are no offers in excess of $m \times B$, the enterprise pays the treasury the contribution B, and ownership of the enterprise remains in the same hands. If, however, at least one acceptable bid has come in, the highest bid wins. The bidder who made it receives the private enterprise for the price that was offered by the second highest bidder, or at a price of $m \times B$ if there is no other valid bid. (This is, in other words, a second-price, sealed-bid auction.) The enterprise contribution of B is then paid to the treasury by the successful bidder rather than by the original private owner.

Thus, the private owner receives a sum of at least $m \times B$ as compensation for the takeover of the enterprise by a market socialist firm. The owner can always set the enterprise contribution B at such a level that, should there be a takeover, the sale will yield at least the sum corresponding to the value of the enterprise to him or her. If, for instance, $m=100$, the owner could name an enterprise contribution of one percent of the value he or she personally attaches to the enterprise—taking into consideration not only business expectations, but also any other factors that affect a personal valuation, such as the level of emotional involvement the founder has with the enterprise. If all relevant aspects are taken into consideration, the owner can only be content with the remuneration in case of a takeover by a market socialist firm.

There is a good reason, by the way, for the rule obliging the highest bidder to pay only the amount bid by the second highest bidder. This has the effect that the best option for each bidder is to offer the maximum sum he or she is willing to pay for the enterprise. The maximum sum a bidder is willing to pay results from the present value of future profits that bidder expects from the enterprise. Thus, the enterprise goes to the bidder best placed to profit from it.

This mechanism retains the investment incentives for private enterprises, and ensures that takeovers in the market socialist sector are efficient in terms of timing and the selection of the buyer. The investment incentives for the private sector are retained because entrepreneurs reap the benefits of their investments even if they are forced to sell. If an owner invested well, there are good prospects for profits. And in that case, the owner is also prepared to pay a high enterprise contribution. If the owner is nevertheless caught out by a bidder, the enterprise is sold, but at least the owner receives a satisfactory price for it.

Through this mechanism, a market socialist system allows firms to acquire dynamic private enterprises without damaging incentives to private initiative. The market socialist firm that is in position to make the most of a private enterprise makes the highest bid and incorporates the enterprise. If no public firm can be found that is prepared to pay the required price, but nationalization nevertheless makes sense from the perspective of the community, the government makes an appropriate bid, perhaps through its ministry of finance.

The size of the private sector within a market socialist economy can be regulated through the determination of the multiplier m. If the polity is of the opinion that private enterprises should play a more minor role, its parliament can lower m, thus lowering the required minimum for bids and making takeovers easier. If, by contrast, the hope is to stimulate the private sector, this can be achieved by raising m.

A nontrivial advantage of this mechanism is that it makes the current practice of taxing profits superfluous for private sector enterprises.

UNIVERSAL BASIC INCOME
AND BASIC CAPITAL

ALL THE STOPS SO FAR on our tour of alternative economic systems have had one crucial feature in common: public ownership of the means of production. But we have also seen that collective use of the means of production leads to significant difficulties. In the best possible case, shareholder socialism, these alternative economic systems turn out to require a complex new institutional structure; and even then, it is still not clear that they can to solve the cooperation and allocation problems.

We now set off to the last two destinations on our trip. In contrast to the economic systems we have looked at so far, these do not meddle with private ownership of the means of production. Still, they promise great things. One of the systems is based on a universally granted and unconditional basic income, and the other on universally granted and unconditional basic capital.

These two economic systems are related to each other, and both are simple to describe. In the first case, the state pays each individual the same monthly transfer, a sum that allows for a comfortable standard of living. Thus, everyone has a right to an income that may be spent as they please. In the second case, all people upon reaching a certain age receive the same one-time capital payment which they can use as they see fit.

Neither system seeks to abolish the market or private property, and so they remain, by definition, capitalist. Yet the ardent supporters of these, whether they favor basic income or basic capital, expect their innovation to create a truly free and egalitarian society, and thus to effect a kind of systemic change.

Public ownership of the means of production, as for instance in market socialism, socializes the profits of the enterprises, with the intention of limiting the concentration of income in a few hands and avoiding a degeneration of democracy into plutocracy. The aim is to curb the power of those who are at the top of the income scale. By contrast, basic income and basic capital aim to increase the power of those at the bottom. If everyone is granted the unconditional right to a sufficient income, then no one is forced to sell their labor for a wage. It follows that no one is subject to coercion by employers or by the market. The same emancipatory effect is claimed for the provision of basic capital.

A SHARED PHILOSOPHY

Basic income and basic capital are transfer payments from the public purse to individual citizens. In today's capitalism, public transfers, such as unemployment benefits or state pensions, are usually justified as instruments to achieve distinct social-policy goals: only individuals who are in situations of economic or social plight, or who have paid the relevant social contributions, are entitled to such transfer payments. Basic income and basic capital are different in this respect. Their ethical justification goes back to Thomas Paine and the intellectual climate around the time of the American and French revolutions. According to this ethos, each human being, as a child of the earth, has a natural right to enjoy its fruits, because what the uncultivated earth produces is not the result of anyone's labor and therefore should be the property of all. But today, the use of the earth's resources is subject to property laws that exclude those without titles to ownership from accessing them. Thus, individuals cannot exercise their natural rights, and as a compensation for the fact that they cannot immediately enjoy the fruits of the earth, the state should make an equivalent transfer payment to each of them.

This is the reason that basic income and basic capital are not conditional. Most strikingly, they are granted regardless of a recipient's level of need. An individual's income or accumulated wealth is irrelevant; a millionaire and a homeless person have exactly the same claim on these payments. Family situations do not matter either. It is of no consequence whether someone has children or not—or if there are children, what ages they are. Basic income and basic capital do not depend on contributions having been paid, and so there are no entitlements that first need to be earned. No willingness to work, or to take part in training schemes, need be demonstrated. Basic income and basic capital are simply universal transfers to which every person has a fundamental and inalienable right.

Although basic income and basic capital are not mutually exclusive, as a rule they are not advocated as a package but separately and by different groups of supporters. For that reason, we will consider them in turn as two different schemes. And, indeed, we will see that the proponents of these two approaches actually have different aims in mind.

UNCONDITIONAL BASIC INCOME

Another, shorter expression for an unconditional basic income is to call it a citizen's income. In the economic system that its proponents have in mind, the state grants all individuals who reside mainly within its boundaries an equivalent income. The state provides that income in increments, usually portrayed as monthly transfers, and the usual goal is for the income to cover the minimum sociocultural subsistence level—that is, this income should allow an individual to take part in the social life of a society, and therefore should not fall too much below the average total income of a citizen. If we really want to finally overcome the flaws of capitalism, the citizen's income needs to be generous.

Most proponents of unconditional basic income expect it to produce three main advantages over today's system: more individual autonomy, less greed, and the complete abolition of poverty. Let us take a closer look at these three supposed advantages.

More Autonomy

Having such incomes largely liberates people from the imperatives of the market, and especially of the labor market. Labor ceases to be primarily a means of securing a livelihood for oneself or one's family; instead, the intrinsic qualities of labor become more important to people. Individuals without much wealth no longer depend on employers who may or may not deem them worthy of a job. Rather, the employers are forced to create more attractive workplaces to retain employees or recruit new ones.

A basic income not only strengthens the position of employees in their relations with employers. It also provides more autonomy for individuals in general in their relations with bureaucrats, credit lenders, spouses, parents, and so forth. This shift in power relations may be welcomed for several reasons.

First, the newly gained autonomy can be a boon to creativity and the production of new ideas. Artists, authors, scientists, and inventors can all dedicate themselves to the pursuit of their ideas, regardless of whether these ideas attract a buyer, a financing institution, or a sponsor. History is replete with examples of ingenious products of the human intellect that came about quite in spite of the market or actions of the state or church. We need only remind ourselves of Socrates, Galileo, or van Gogh, and the exceptional perseverance demanded of them to pursue their paths.

Granting a citizen's income allows modern-day mavericks in the arts and sciences no longer to worry about how to finance their subsistence. It means they no longer have to adapt to the wishes of sponsors or backers. Instead of "networking" and formulating grant applications, they can concentrate on their ideas and their creative activity. Individual creativity is unleashed, and ultimately all of society profits from the diversity of ideas this yields.

Second, individuals, and especially young people, allow themselves longer periods for experimentation. They can afford to study for more advanced degrees or undertake new courses of vocational training if they are not happy with their first ones. Everyone has opportunities to dip into various professions as low-paid apprentices until they find what is right for them. Adults can take time out to prepare for entering a new profession. People are much more likely to find their true vocation.

Today, such experiments are possible only to a limited extent, because so few individuals have capital reserves at their disposal sufficient to support them over long periods. This is especially true of young people. If they apply for loans from banks, they must meet very strict conditions because of the high risk of default. In the end, only a few are adventurous enough to quit their jobs and try new things.

More experimentation can be beneficial, because a better knowledge of oneself means a more precise understanding of one's talents and preferences. This reduces both the likelihood of making the wrong decisions and their margin of error. It is possible, moreover, to learn from mistakes made by others. While the costs of experimentation are borne solely by the individual doing the experimenting, others also benefit from some of the insights thus gained; there is therefore potentially less experimentation by individuals than is optimal from the perspective of society overall. A citizen's income counterbalances this tendency.

Third, more independence improves social relations. Bolstering the positions of those who have been subject to coercion makes them less vulnerable to domination by others. In day-to-day life, superiors and their staff are more and more on equal footing. This promotes cooperation and a belief that authority must be grounded in competence. Conversely, individuals who strive to occupy positions of authority have a strong incentive to acquire "know-how" to succeed on that basis, rather than because of their sharp elbows or connections to old boys' networks.

Less Greed

Proponents of a citizen's income hope that it will lead to a sea change in people's values. Everyone is less focused on earning money, because they are entitled to their basic incomes. They pay more attention to the things that make life worth living, such as love, spending time with family and friends, helping those in need, and creative work in all its forms. More people do volunteer work, because there is no longer a need to pursue gainful employment.

This shift in priorities most likely leads to less conspicuous consumption and to more solidarity. Those out of work and those earning little are no longer stigmatized, since they might, after all, be geniuses who are concentrating their energies on great projects rather than earning filthy lucre. Thus, social status depends less on an individual's financial position, and fewer resources are wasted on ostentatious displays of wealth. There is less envy of the rich.

Fighting Poverty

The third advantage of having a basic income has to do with combating poverty. If the basic income covers the minimum required for sociocultural subsistence, the polity can abolish the social benefits that today seek to protect the population from poverty. Proponents of the citizen's income point to several merits in this regard.

Thanks to a citizen's income, avoiding poverty no longer involves potentially embarrassing visits to social security offices or humiliating means-testing. The problem of poverty is solved completely. When individuals who are entitled to state support do not claim it, either out of shame or out of ignorance regarding the complex laws governing benefits, there exists some level of hidden poverty. This does not happen with a citizen's income.

The administrative expense of fighting poverty is reduced, because the citizen's income is not dependent on any conditions that the state has to assess. The administrative costs of social security offices and of dealing with disputes over entitlements, which tend to be very high, are greatly reduced.

For people who are currently unemployed and in receipt of unemployment benefits, incentives to work increase. Today, these people usually gain little from taking on low-paid jobs, because any income earned is deducted from their benefits entitlement, almost in its entirety. The entitlement to a citizen's income, by contrast, remains intact even if a recipient gains additional income.

As opposed to today's benefits, the citizen's income does not have any undesirable impacts on the family life of the recipient. At present, entitlement is often tied in various ways to facts about the home life of the recipient; for instance, a woman with children to support may be better off living separately from the father of her children, as she can then cash in on a benefit for single mothers. There are no such incentives created by universal transfers such as the citizen's income. In particular, living together and with others in general is attractive because of the savings in accommodation costs it allows, without having any effect on the level of transfers received.

WHAT'S THE CATCH?

For many critics of capitalism, the idea of an unconditional basic income is like Columbus's famous solution for standing an egg on its tip— something unimagined before, but once it is glimpsed, suddenly simple and obvious. Let us see whether it stands up to closer scrutiny.

The term "citizen's income" emphasizes the recipient of this payment: the citizens receive the money. It is the government's duty to provide this financial payment to the citizens. The entitlement to a citizen's income therefore is accompanied by corresponding expenses for the state that ultimately must be financed by additional revenue from taxation or from the reduction of other public expenditures.

Thus, behind the citizen's income lurks a "citizen's sacrifice" that must be made to cover the fiscal burden caused by the introduction of the citizen's income. The appeal of an economic system based on a citizen's income depends crucially on what kind of sacrifice the citizens are asked to make.

The direct fiscal costs of a citizen's income depend on the level of the payment, and are easy to establish. The simplest case is that of a uniform citizen's income that every citizen receives regardless of age. To determine the associated public expenditure, all we have to do is multiply the amount of the citizen's income by the size of the population. The expenditure can also be expressed in terms of the proportion of the gross domestic product (GDP) it represents. If we want to have a citizen's income that corresponds to x percent of GDP per capita, the expenditure required would be x percent of GDP, assuming all citizens receive the citizen's income. Imagine we are in a hypothetical country, only marginally poorer than Germany, which has an annual GDP per capita of 30,000 euros. If we want a (tax-free) citizen's income of 1,000 euros per month—that is, 12,000 euros per year—the citizen's income represents 40 percent of the GDP per capita, and the corresponding overall expenditure represents 40 percent of the total GDP. If, however, we are content with a citizen's income of 750 euros per month, the expenditure represents 30 percent of GDP.

We can look at an actual transfer payment that is provided in Germany to the long-term unemployed, Unemployment Benefit II (UB II), as a contrast case here. It is paid to individuals out of work who are not entitled to the higher Unemployment Benefit I (UB I), and who have no other sources of income. In the case of a single person without a family, UB II assumes a monthly subsistence minimum of roughly 700 euros, a bit more in municipalities with high housing costs, a bit less in those with low housing costs. Thus, if the citizen's income is intended as an attractive alternative to the social market economy, it must certainly not fall below UB II.

To better comprehend the dimensions of the additional public expenditure associated with a citizen's income, we may compare them to some recent figures from Germany's public finances. The overall annual public expenditure for UB II does not equal even 1.5 percent of GDP. The overall annual public expenditure on education roughly corresponds to 5 percent of GDP. On the revenue side, the overall annual income from taxes corresponds to a good 20 percent of GDP.

Thus, the additional expenditures incurred directly by the state to provide an attractive citizen's income (as we saw, some 30 to 40 percent of GDP) would be exceptionally high. Even if the full citizen's income were to be granted only to the adult population, this would change very little. In a country like Germany, people under the age of eighteen make up only about 16 percent of the population. Were Germany to pay individuals under eighteen only half the citizen's income, the reduction in the state's expenditure would be 8 percent. For the possibility noted above of a citizen's income of only 750 euros per month, the associated costs would still be equal to around 27 percent of GDP, even if the state paid people under eighteen years of age only 375 euros instead of the full 750 euros. This is still an enormous burden for the public finances to shoulder.

Possible Savings to the Welfare Bill

The introduction of a basic income thus cannot be financed through additional taxation alone, as this will more than double the tax burden (in a country like Germany) and force the state to cut spending in other areas. But as the citizen's income provides all citizens with purchasing power, there is an obvious way forward: Can we not do without the other payments made to individuals by the state?

In the case of Germany, one might think of abolishing child benefits, or child allowances, upon the introduction of the citizen's income. As children are entitled to the citizen's income, and that income is more generous than the existing payments, this is unproblematic.

Removing other benefits, however, might make some people worse off despite the introduction of a citizen's income. These might include, in Germany, parental leave benefits, support for pupils and students under the Federal Training Assistance Act (BAföG), Unemployment Benefit II, housing benefits, basic security in old age, and some basic welfare benefits.

The removal of UB I in particular seems problematic. The level of this benefit depends on the wage the employee received prior to becoming unemployed. As opposed to UB II, it does not take need as a benchmark. It serves the purpose of an insurance against a decrease in standard of living in the case of temporary unemployment. Because the citizen's income is the same for everyone, it cannot fulfill this function.

The removal of UB I therefore means that the social need for protecting the standard of living of workers goes unsatisfied. We should note, moreover, that the market is ill equipped to provide solutions for insurance against unemployment risk. Due to substantial information barriers, many employed persons will not be offered insurance at all, and many of those who are offered insurance will be presented with unfavorable terms and conditions, because the private provision of unemployment insurance carries all sorts of increased administrative costs.

Further, the removal of UB I does not save the state much money at all, because the contributions to the unemployment insurance scheme must at the same time be removed. The only savings come from the tax-financed subsidy from the federal budget that covers the difference between the expenditures and the contributions of the unemployment insurance scheme.

One possibility for increasing the amount saved in connection with a removal of UB I is to abolish the contributions from employers and employees, while at the same time raising the wage tax to such a degree that the state receives more or less the same as before. Two disadvantages, however, come with this option. First, it would result in discrimination against wage laborers, as opposed to the recipients of other types of income, with regard to the personal income tax, as the former would pay higher taxes on the same level of income. Second, we know that taxes are economically more damaging than contributions, because of their more deleterious effects on incentives to work. The reason for this is that the payment of contributions entitles the employee to a claim, and the amount that can be claimed rises with the contributions to be paid. By contrast, an employee does not gain any entitlement in return for paying taxes.

If we're looking for places to seek savings to cover the citizen's income, perhaps we should look at the largest item in the welfare budgets of European countries, which is the provision for old-age pensions. In Germany, this amounts to roughly 9 percent of GDP. Certainly, if social security serves only the purpose of fighting old-age poverty—as is practically the case in some Anglo-Saxon countries—then the removal of public pensions is relatively unproblematic. Unfortunately, this is not always the situation; in Germany, for example, payments under the statutory pension scheme usually far exceed the subsistence minimum, and the amounts involved depend on contributions made by the insured across their entire lives.

In countries that are similar to Germany in this regard, the accumulated entitlements to a public old-age pension enjoy legal protections similar to those of property. Withdrawing old-age pensions upon the introduction of the citizen's income would do serious financial harm to many senior citizens—and also constitute a severe case of discrimination against those who depend on state pensions versus those who are privately insured. Cancelling statutory pension schemes is therefore not a realistic option in these countries.

It might nevertheless be possible to embark on a gradual reduction in public expenditures for old-age pensions so that, in the long term, the statutory pension scheme disappears. This means honoring existing pension entitlements, but not allowing further entitlements to accrue. Henceforth, generations entering the labor market receive no state pensions when they leave it, and in the long term the state reduces its expenditures on old-age pensions.

There are problems with this proposal, however, both in the transitional period and in its final aims. The catch of the transitional period is the fact that old-age pensions are administered through a pay-as-you-go system, whereby the old-age pensions paid out in any given year are financed by the contributions made by employees and employers in that same year. This is not a system in which accumulated capital yields returns, but a generational contract by which each generation is supported by the following one. Thus, if today's generation of employees, who have already made contributions, retain their entitlement to old-age pensions, these must be financed by a new generation of taxpayers. If the statutory pension scheme is discontinued, the majority of the next generation has to carry twice the burden of all previous generations; to maintain their standard of living in old age, its members have to pay into private pension schemes in addition to fulfilling their role as taxpayers and financing the pensions of the previous generation. The next generation of employees is thus clearly worse off than under the present system.

This brings us to the second catch. Even the aim of having each senior's income be a mix of a citizen's income plus an additional private pension scheme is not necessarily desirable—neither from an economic perspective nor from the perspective of those critical of capitalism. Economists have pointed out the various information problems that plague insurance markets, and especially regarding old-age pensions they disagree on whether the advantages of market competition outweigh its costs. Germany's sobering experience with its government-subsidized private pension scheme, called the Riester pension, comes to mind.

From the perspective of those critical of capitalism, at least two arguments speak against the privatization of social security. First, it forces people to concentrate on money even more. They need to spend a great deal of time thinking about how best to save for old age and where their savings should be invested. They need to track their capital returns constantly, and compare the cost of their insurer with that of other insurers.

Second, with private pension schemes, there is less solidarity among generations. Under the current pay-as-you-go system, a general rise in wages also benefits pensioners, because their state pensions rise in accordance with the level of wages. By contrast, in a system where the elderly ultimately depend on returns on capital to finance their livelihoods, it is rational for them to support cuts in wages—because any cost reduction that increases enterprise profits helps to boost their capital returns.

Imagine that, despite all this, the statutory pension schemes nevertheless wither away. The resulting savings are substantially less than the old-age pensions no longer paid out. The reason for this is the same as with cancelling UB I—namely, that abolishing insurance benefits also implies the loss of contribution payments. The only savings achieved would therefore come from eliminating the governmental subsidy to the pension scheme.

A Rough Calculation for Germany

A few years ago, the renowned social-policy expert Richard Hauser produced a study in which he estimated the fiscal cost of an unconditional citizen's income for Germany, taking into consideration the potential welfare savings. The savings he assumed included the complete removal of UB I, although he did not assume a cancellation of the corresponding social insurance contributions—a measure that would very likely be controversial for the reasons given above. His calculations also did not include the withdrawal of the statutory pension scheme.

Hauser's estimated overall savings from the cancellation of various social benefits, using 2005 data, came to 233 billion euros per year. It should be borne in mind, however, that 2005 saw record levels of unemployment in Germany, and overall payments to the unemployed were therefore especially high.

Hauser emphasized that additional savings could also follow from the reduction of the bureaucracy needed for administering the withdrawn benefits. It is difficult, however, to put a figure on such savings. In 2005, the overall costs of administering Germany's social insurance system were estimated at about 22 billion euros. But this rather impressive figure represents the very upper limit for all potential savings. Some part of that bureaucracy pertains to the statutory pension scheme, which is not withdrawn under this proposal; and administering a citizen's income also entails costs, which are difficult to estimate. Consider, too, that there is very likely a rise in costs associated with personal income tax collection. We can expect that legislators will probably lower the basic tax allowance upon the introduction of a citizen's income, or abolish it altogether; we know the government will be in dire need of additional tax revenues and, after all, a subsistence income is guaranteed by the citizen's income. Thus there will be an increase in the number of tax returns needing to be processed, as income tax must be calculated even for those on very low incomes.

Now let us turn to the direct costs of granting a citizen's income. They depend on the amount to be paid and on any possible differentiation according to age groups. The following two versions can give us an impression of the magnitude of these costs. In the first version, the citizen's income is set for an adult at 1,000 euros per month, and for a minor (under age eighteen) at 500 euros per month. In the case of Germany, this version implies public expenditures to the tune of about 900 billion euros per year. The second version grants each adult 750 euros per month, and each minor 375 euros per month. In this case, public expenditure for the citizen's income is reduced to about 670 billion euros per year.

If we subtract the savings in the state's welfare bill from the direct cost of the citizen's income, we arrive at the additional net expenditure required. Hauser's calculations show the total volume of savings from cutting benefits and administrative costs coming to 240 billion euros per year (in 2005), which translates to roughly 260 billion in 2013 euros. In our first version of a citizen's income—1,000 euros for adults and 500 euros for minors—this results in a net additional expenditure of 640 billion euros. In the second version—750 euros for adults and 375 euros for minors—the figure is 410 billion euros.

These are rough estimates of the revenue needed to finance an attractive citizen's income in Germany. Keeping other public expenditures fixed, and assuming that cuts in the region of the hundreds of billions would have catastrophic social consequences for the population, most of this must be generated through increases in taxation. Given that Germany's total revenue from taxation for the year 2013 is about 600 billion euros, this means tax revenue needs to be roughly doubled to finance an attractive citizen's income. Assuming a fixed tax base, this necessitates a doubling of tax rates.

Citizen's Income and Migration

The rough calculation presented above makes no assumptions about households' and firms' possible responses as a citizen's income is introduced, some benefits are removed, and tax rates are raised. But such reforms would of course change the behavior of economic agents, and these changes would, in turn, affect both the government's revenue and its expenditure.

In what follows, we will look at two central impacts of a citizen's income on economic behavior, one having to do with the labor market and the other with migration flows. Some assumptions are required here; let us assume that Germany is the only country to introduce the citizen's income, and that it is financed mainly by raising the rates of personal income tax and VAT (sales tax), the two taxes with by far the highest yields in Germany. Insights we gain here should also carry over to a scenario in which several European countries coordinate to introduce a common citizen's income.

We can expect an attractive citizen's income to encourage the immigration of individuals into Germany who are able to work, but do not wish to enter employment. Some Germans, for instance, who have been living abroad and would like to stop working for a few years, or even for good, will return to Germany. Small groups of people can be expected to economize by getting together, perhaps on the basis of their similar hobbies such as painting or gardening. With just their citizen's incomes they could afford to rent houses in nice but not too expensive areas and lead decent lives there.

Such effects on migration do, of course, raise the amount needed to finance the citizen's income. To mitigate this problem, perhaps it makes sense to pay a citizen's income only in proportion to how much of the recipient's life has been spent in Germany. This, however, implies some documentation as a requirement for receiving the citizen's income and thus takes away some of the simplicity that is one of its attractions.

Sooner or later, Germany's citizen's income also attracts other European citizens who wish to "drop out," especially if they speak the German language or already have contacts in Germany. Indeed, they would not necessarily have to give up their employment with the move to Germany, as the Internet makes remote work so possible.

To stem this flow of immigration, perhaps the citizen's income can be limited to individuals who either have German citizenship, or fulfill the current requirements for obtaining it. This idea has to be examined regarding its compatibility with EU law, though, as discrimination on the basis of citizenship is likely to contravene it. The social implications of such a regulation must also be considered. Many people already live and work in Germany who are not German citizens and are not entitled to citizenship. If the citizen's income is introduced for German citizens only, and current benefits are removed, these people cease to receive support from the government in the case of unemployment, and have greater risk of falling into poverty. It follows that Germany needs a system providing basic social security for those not entitled to the citizen's income. This, in turn, reduces the savings in the area of administration.

While, on the one hand, some people who want to drop out or top up their income will come to Germany, on the other hand, some so-called high flyers will emigrate to avoid the heavy tax burden, or choose not to immigrate to Germany from other countries. As a rule, small changes in taxation have only small effects on taxpayers' decisions about where to live. But a doubling of the tax rates makes the net incomes of high earners here versus abroad differ massively. Young and highly qualified employees in particular have strong financial incentives to turn their backs on Germany. The emigration of any high earners is bad news for the citizen's income, because these individuals, given the relatively large amounts of tax they pay, are crucial to financing it.

All in all, we may therefore expect the introduction of a citizen's income to invite and encourage new trends in cross-border mobility that further complicate the task of financing it.

Citizen's Income and the Willingness to Work

Let us now turn to the labor market. How does the population's willingness to work change in a country like Germany when a citizen's income is introduced? From a fiscal point of view, this is a crucial question, because in the end, income from work generates the most significant part of the tax base, and its level depends on the population's willingness to work for pay.

It is not possible to give a general answer to this question. Individuals' responses to such a reform in terms of their willingness to work are likely to differ widely, in large part depending on their household types. We must at least distinguish among three categories of people who are able to work: the unemployed, average earners, and high earners. And among the unemployed, we can further identify four different types of people.

First, there are the temporary recipients of unemployment benefits who find their way into the labor market fairly quickly. These people may be added to the category of average earners. Second, there are individuals who are voluntarily unemployed and exploit the welfare state. They do not take advantage of acceptable job offers and they successfully avoid sanctions the job center tries to impose. Among this group of people, the introduction of a citizen's income leads to an increase in willingness to work. Under current conditions, their potential regular income from work is subject to high implicit marginal taxation. This means that their disposable income increases by only a few cents for each additional euro earned, because their social benefits are correspondingly reduced. With a citizen's income, by contrast, the additional euro is taxed at the relevant income tax rate, which is lower than the current rate of transfer reduction. For this group of people, then, willingness to work rises when social benefits are replaced by a citizen's income.

Third, there are recipients of social transfers who have been given a low-paid job by the job center and do this job only to avoid sanctions. With the introduction of the citizen's income, some of these people who currently top up their benefits give up jobs that pay poorly or are otherwise unrewarding, simply because they can; the citizen's income is granted whether they work or not. Therefore, the overall volume of work done by this group most likely decreases.

Fourth, there are unemployed people for whom it is simply not possible to find jobs, independent of their willingness to work. They are involuntarily out of any paid work. The volume of work done by this group neither grows nor diminishes with the introduction of a citizen's income.

Let us now turn to the second category of household, the large group of average earners.

The introduction of a citizen's income brings about a reduction in the labor supply of this group. To begin with, the introduction of a citizen's income, together with a simultaneous increase in taxation, means that these households are roughly as well off as they were before. Their marginal tax rate rises, however, and that means that a small reduction in labor performed results in less of a loss in purchasing power than in the past. These households therefore have more incentive to reduce their working hours. Among those who are self-employed, the tax hikes may lead to expansions of undeclared work—although the opposite could also occur if, in connection with raising tax rates, the state also introduces more severe punishments for tax evasion.

Based on prior labor market research, we can expect the reduction of labor performed by households with average earners to take place mainly among married women who also have responsibilities caring for children or elderly family members. Some of these women change from full-time to part-time work, or leave the labor market altogether, to devote more time to those care duties.

How average earners respond to an opportunity to say goodbye to the labor market altogether—that is, simply to drop out of the workforce for the rest of their lives—is more difficult to predict. A citizen's income that offers people this option has so far never been introduced, and there are therefore no empirical studies on which to draw. Singles and couples without family to look after may, for instance, choose to travel the world. Others may move to the countryside and lead simple lives close to nature. Like-minded people who are not interested in paid work may gravitate to specific parts of a city and organize their neighborhoods to support their ideas of the good life that doesn't require a lot of money. Just how many people will take up these sorts of options is a crucial question. If it is just a handful, then the impact on the overall tax base is fairly irrelevant. But the larger the numbers of dropouts, the more difficult the financing of the citizen's income becomes.

The third category of employees we need to consider are the high earners. As noted above, some of them can be expected to emigrate because of the high tax rates. But let us look at those who stay in the country. Like the average earners, they see their marginal tax rate rise, meaning that their willingness to work potentially diminishes. For these individuals, however, the introduction of the citizen's income is associated with a clear reduction in disposable income. The additional taxes they must pay to finance the citizen's income are higher than the citizen's income they receive. If the high earners want to retain their old standard of living, they need to work more than before. Thus, there are two opposing effects, and the net change in the labor performance of this group is hard to gauge.

It needs to be stressed, though, that the positive effect on willingness to work is the result of a loss in earnings caused by raising taxes. The greater this loss, the greater will be the urge to compensate it through additional work. But one thing is clear: Those households who suffer the largest loss of income are also the most likely to decide to emigrate. We should expect, therefore, that the introduction of a citizen's income will have an overall negative effect on domestic high earners' willingness to work.

We are now in a position to combine the expected changes in willingness to work of all the various groups of households. It becomes abundantly clear that we should not expect an introduction of a citizen's income to bring about a rise in the total volume of work performed. If it creates a positive incentive at all, it is for just a subgroup of the people who have been unemployed—a subgroup characterized by low productivity and whose members pay the lowest taxes. For the large group of average earners, we may expect a reduction in the amount of labor they supply, and if dropping out establishes itself as a socially acceptable form of behavior, this reduction may happen on a large scale. Among high earners, there are no great changes to be expected, unless tax rates rise so much vis-à-vis other countries that many of them emigrate—a scenario that is not unlikely.

What does all this mean for the possibilities of financing an attractive citizen's income? The rough calculation for Germany presented at the outset of this discussion did not take into account likely changes in the behavior of economic agents. It suggested that the additional fiscal income required would require roughly a doubling of average tax rates. This assessment now looks overly optimistic, because a doubling of tax rates does not double income from taxation if overall income from labor goes down. As labor power becomes scarcer and thus naturally more expensive, capital income also decreases. Thus, the overall tax base declines, and a doubling of the tax rates does not suffice to generate the additional fiscal revenue needed. Can the citizen's income then be financed with an even more significant increase in tax rates? Unfortunately, from today's perspective it is not possible to give a reasonably certain answer to this question. If the tax rates are very high, a further increase does not necessarily lead to an increase in tax revenues, because behavioral responses are such that taxable income is greatly reduced by further increases in tax rates. It is therefore possible that an attractive citizen's income, whether or not it is politically viable, cannot be introduced because there is no tax system capable of financing it—at least as long as the polity does not introduce a duty to work and does not prohibit emigration.

This pessimistic evaluation does not change much if we take into consideration that the introduction of the citizen's income might have an influence on labor productivity, and hence on hourly wages and resulting tax revenues. On the one hand, productivity may benefit from the increase in autonomy, as people have more original ideas and choose professions that are better suited to their talents than is now the case. On the other hand, productivity may suffer because, when choosing careers or jobs, individuals pay less attention to levels of remuneration and more to the joys promised by certain work or training environments—and therefore end up working more often in places characterized by lower productivity. All in all, it is unlikely that a citizen's income leads to a noticeable increase in labor productivity.

Caution! Thin Ice!

To be an attractive alternative to today's economic system, an unconditional basic income needs to make possible the freedom its proponents desire. But if a sufficiently high citizen's income is introduced, it leads to enormous public expenditures. The additional fiscal income required for a country like Germany is on par with the current total tax revenue—that is, about 20 percent of GDP. At present, it is altogether unclear whether additional revenues of such a magnitude can be achieved at all. From the combination of a citizen's income and much higher tax rates we must expect a clear reduction in economic performance. The economy either finds a new balance then between the lower level of consumption and the greater amount of free time, or it collapses altogether.

This evaluation assumes that, alongside the payment of an attractive citizen's income, there are simultaneous (cautious) cuts to various benefits. An entirely different evaluation results if the citizen's income is set at a level below today's welfare benefits for the poor, alongside a program of savage cuts to social expenditure. An approach of this type is advocated by those proponents of a citizen's income who see in it a powerful political tool for rolling back the welfare state, restoring a sort of laissez-faire capitalism, and paving the way to a market society.

Conservative intellectuals, particularly in the United States (such as Charles Murray), made proposals in this vein in the years before the financial crisis, and these have been eagerly echoed by European experts. This neoliberal version sets the citizen's income at a low level, often assumes proportional income taxation to finance it, and demands the abolition of the welfare state, including the public statutory pension scheme and health insurance.

Because it stipulates the removal of most of the benefits provided by the welfare state, this neoliberal version of the citizen's income can be financed without a massive increase in taxation. If one is critical of capitalism, then, the danger for the project of a citizen's income is that it will start out being promoted and implemented with an emancipatory intent only to end up being reduced to something like this neoliberal version when financing it becomes difficult.

Concluding Thoughts on the Basic Income

One fundamental problem with the idea of a basic income has so far not been mentioned. For sake of argument, let us pretend that people have suddenly become twice as productive—maybe by swallowing a magic potion like the one in the Asterix and Obelix stories—and their income has doubled overnight as a result. Now it is easy to finance a generous basic income with the resulting increased tax revenues. Is it possible, however, that most people do not even want a basic income? What if it strikes them as fundamentally unfair, and they suspect it will disrupt the social ties of mutuality?

Behind this suspicion is the following line of thought. The citizen's income is financed through taxation. Because income from work constitutes the larger part of the national income, and because the scope for increasing capital taxes is limited due to the international mobility of capital, the citizen's income is mostly financed through personal income tax and through the withdrawal of other benefits. It is therefore mostly those who receive salaries or wages who are footing the bill. If there is no obligation to work, which would undermine the freedom that is so prized by proponents of a citizen's income, then people decide freely whether they will work or live off their citizen's income. If all people have the same preferences, then they all choose to spend the same amounts of time out of work and in work. But if people's preferences differ, there will be some who never work, others who work all the time, and others who oscillate between work and not working. At one end of the spectrum are idlers and at the other, hard workers. Assuming there is something like this split between idlers and hard workers, a citizen's income can hardly be justified: It boils down to the hard workers being exploited by the idlers. There can be no talk of solidarity here, and solidarity is a crucial aspect of any attractive social model.

The citizen's income thus allows for the emergence of a class of perfectly healthy loafers, who live only for themselves and are supported by the rest of society. The right of someone fit for work to live well off the work of others, without ever contributing anything, is a feature that distinguishes this economic system from all the other alternatives we have come across in the course of our journey.

From an economic perspective, this state of affairs is problematic because it threatens the system's capacity to pass the cooperation test, to which we have subjected all the other alternative economic systems. But what really pricks our conscience here is the violation of deeply rooted ideas about social justice. The rebellion of peasants and bourgeois citizens against the aristocracy and the clergy in medieval times, and the later rebellions of workers against industrial magnates, were uprisings by those who slaved away and toiled against those who lived off the fruits of other people's labor.

In today's world, similar tensions can be seen, for instance, in Israeli society. Israel offers ultraorthodox Jews the possibility of living off the state without performing any work themselves, an option that is chosen by an increasing proportion of the population. The rift between modern Israelis, who are solidly integrated into the world of work, and the ultraorthodox Jews supported by the state could hardly be deeper. The possibility that, in a multiethnic Europe, a citizen's income could lead to a comparable segmentation of society—that is, between those who contribute and those who profit—should give us pause.

All told, this potential for social conflict, the formidable financial and economic problems, and the political risk of a citizen's income degenerating into a neoliberal form combine to rob the citizen's income of almost all the appeal it seemed to have at the outset.

BASIC CAPITAL

The sister idea to unconditional basic income is the idea of basic capital. Here, the notion is for every citizen to receive a lump sum of money from the government without any restrictions on how it is to be used. As with a citizen's income, basic capital is a universal transfer payment that is not subject to means testing. In contrast to the citizen's income, however, basic capital is only paid once, upon reaching the age of maturity.

The proposals for basic capital currently on the table are less radical than those for a basic income. The amount of the transfer payment is far less than one would receive over a lifetime drawing a basic income, and therefore the provision of basic capital places a significantly lower burden on the public finances.

This two-hundred-year-old idea captured some attention in the United States in 1999, when two professors, Bruce Ackerman and Anne Alstott, suggested a basic capital transfer of $80,000. A little later, a sum of 60,000 euros was discussed for Germany. At today's prices, this represents about 65,000 to 70,000 euros, and would require an additional public expenditure of about 55 billion euros per year, or a solid 2 percent of GDP, assuming that the measure did not lead to any significant rise in the immigration of large families.

Basic capital has never been introduced, although there are several countries that could afford it. Governments that achieve significant revenues through natural resources, such as oil or gas, could allow their populations to participate directly in these by way of basic capital. There are, however, smaller programs that are modeled on the idea. The United Kingdom has its Child Trust Fund, a program that provides every newborn with a long-term savings account, into which the government pays a small amount of money. The child may use the money only after reaching the age of eighteen. In the meantime, the parents may make additional payments into the account, and the returns from the account are tax-free.

Seventy thousand euros is not enough to fund a life of idleness; in a system featuring a basic capital provision, most people still have to sell their labor to get by. Thus, in contrast to basic income advocates, the proponents of basic capital rather emphasize the importance of equal opportunities. This system has positive effects in that regard because it means that children of parents without means get the benefits that come with inherited capital, and at a time in their lives when many doors are still open to them. Thanks to this chunk of basic capital, an individual can choose to make investments such as enrolling in university or starting a small enterprise—projects that they cannot otherwise finance out of their own pockets and for which they would have to take out loans.

Basic capital gives young people more independence from their parents and, also, from social welfare and from lenders. While this sounds good from the perspective of the young person, it is not clear whether society overall stands to gain anything from it. On the one hand, the independence that is gained is in principle positive, because it creates more opportunities. And the fewer the options a young person has without basic capital, the more valuable the gained independence is. On the other hand, this independence may come at too young an age, when young people are not equipped to make good use of it. They no longer need to seek their parents' approval before laying down their money— to begin a degree course, enter a profession, start an enterprise, or, possibly, just buy a flashy sports car. They need not listen to the advice of banks or social services staff either. Therefore, more frequently, they make poor decisions and waste valuable resources. Proponents of basic capital typically counter this worry with the claim that the prospect of receiving it endows adolescent young people with greater sense of responsibility, which leads them to live their lives more cautiously and with more forward planning.

Financing Basic Capital

The gross sum required to provide basic capital in the amount mentioned above represents, again, a good two percent of GDP. As opposed to the citizen's income, the introduction of basic capital is not accompanied by the removal of other benefits for those threatened by poverty. The belief persists that one should help people in need—even if they have simply frittered away their basic capital. Probably there are fewer needy people, but nevertheless the savings from social benefits cover only a small part of the expenditure on basic capital. Some obvious thoughts are to abolish support for education and training (BAföG in the case of Germany), to raise university fees, and to discontinue programs supporting new business launches. It is likely, however, that basic capital needs to be financed mostly with money from taxes.

For a country like Germany, we can expect that the tax burden needs to rise by almost 10 percent (that is, about 2 percent of GDP) to finance basic capital. This is a significant increase, but not one that should have devastating effects on economic performance.

The proponents of basic capital usually demand that it be financed through inheritance taxes. But this alone is certainly not enough, especially in a country like Germany, where the revenue from inheritance tax amounts to not quite a tenth of the sum needed for financing basic capital.

A further problem is posed by the introductory phase of basic capital. An abrupt introduction on, let's say, January 1, 2018, means that anyone born on December 31, 1999, or before receives not a single cent from the state, while everyone born the next day receives seventy thousand euros. If that is not a lack of equal opportunity, then what is? To mitigate this problem, perhaps there is a transitional phase during which the amount of basic capital slowly increases and compensatory mechanisms are introduced to create a fair balance between the generations.

Criticism of Basic Capital

The proposal for basic capital is often justified with reference to the value of individual responsibility and the principle of equal opportunities. With respect to individual responsibility, the proponents of basic capital stress that its introduction makes it crystal clear to young people just how important the decisions they make are. It thus counteracts carelessness and lethargy.

It is plausible, to be sure, that a basic capital has such an effect. The need for this effect is not so obvious; there are no empirical findings that indicate that, in Germany, for example, young people tend to live for the moment or simply vegetate. To the contrary, they seem to begin worrying about their futures fairly early on and trying to prepare for them in good time. It is therefore not at all clear why a measure to strengthen the sense of individual responsibility deserves to be prioritized.

We should also not deny that a one-sided emphasis on individual responsibility has its drawbacks. If basic capital is granted, might we see a serves-them-right attitude taking hold? After all, if someone ends up poor despite having received their basic capital, it is his or her own fault. The basic tenor is clear: the person had his chance, but wasted it. This weakens solidarity and altruism within society.

As far as equal opportunities are concerned, the progress that can be made through the introduction of a basic capital scheme is limited and ideas about it are easily exaggerated. There is a risk, therefore, that other, more meaningful, measures for fostering equal opportunities are not pursued.

It is true that under capitalism, the distribution of inheritance and inter vivos gifts is extremely unequal. The majority of people receive no significant inheritance, while a very small minority of individuals inherit vast fortunes. But basic capital reduces this imbalance only marginally. It is much more effective to reform how inheritance is taxed. In most countries there is a tax on inheritance, but it is subject to so many loopholes and exemptions that it hardly fulfills its purpose.

Those who profit most directly from basic capital are the children of poor families. Nevertheless, the starting conditions are still much worse for these children than for children of the same age from wealthier backgrounds. Numerous empirical studies show that inherited wealth is only one of a number of factors that play a role in determining someone's life chances and, for most individuals, it is not even the most important one.

Individuals in a basic capital system receive their money at age eighteen. But by this time, so much has already happened that their life chances are not significantly affected by it. One's upbringing as a child and young adolescent are far more important. Any substantial disadvantages experienced in childhood can hardly be compensated for by the payment of basic capital.

The research in this area suggests that equal opportunities can be promoted in a more targeted way with different measures, such as high-quality education in early childhood, a school system that extends the phase of comprehensive schooling, and careful personal support from social workers for children with learning difficulties.

If the fiscal resources required for the payment of basic capital are instead invested in these areas, we can achieve far more in the way of equal opportunities. If in Germany, for instance, just fifteen billion of the estimated fifty-five billion euros per year were used for improving day care for children, we could roughly double the amount spent on early childhood education, and could thus expect an extraordinary improvement in the outcomes of disadvantaged youth.

1 0

MARKET ECONOMY PLUS WELFARE STATE

THE PREVIOUS CHAPTER MARKED the end of our tour of alternative economic systems. There is, at present, not really much else on offer. Anything else I might be able to suggest could only be either a closely related version of one of the systems already discussed, or a much more modest innovation that would not produce radical change.

Our trip has confirmed that it is not enough to state that capitalism is inefficient, unjust, and alienating. The true challenge is to raise the convincing prospect of a superior alternative to today's system. And no small amount of humility is called for in this quest, because while there is certainly no shortage of alternative designs, none stands out as clearly feasible and clearly superior to today's capitalism. In the end, we are unable to name such an alternative.

And yet, we should not resign ourselves to inaction. If we want to improve the world, we can take a pragmatic stance, and start with what we have. The economic system that exists today—and I am thinking here mainly of Germany's social market economy—is at least no longer a predatory form of capitalism. The question is how we might best harness its strong motivational forces to turn it into a more efficient, just, and humane form. This is the topic of the present chapter.

CAPITALISM WITH A HUMAN FACE

It is useful to take a short look at the roots and essential features of our present economic system, to be better placed to capture its potential.

The evolution beyond so-called Manchester capitalism, the capitalism of Marx's time, actually began in Berlin. At that time, bitter social unrest shook the industrial centers of Germany's burgeoning economy at the heart of Europe. As the carrot to go along with the stick that was the Anti-Socialist Law of 1878, Chancellor Bismarck introduced social insurance for ill and old workers. This turned out to be a political decision with extraordinarily far-reaching consequences. In retrospect, we might even say that this was the decisive moment that, together with the legal institutionalization of collective wage bargaining, ultimately reconciled the workers to capitalism, and thus pulled the rug out from under the proletarian revolution.

The German social insurance system was soon recognized around the world as a success, and increasingly copied in other places. In the United States, Roosevelt's New Deal led to a substantial expansion of welfare-state institutions. In western Europe, the Great War triggered strong desires for social reform. But the golden age of social reform began only after the end of the Second World War, and it lasted deep into the 1970s. Those decades gave western Europeans a hitherto unknown degree of formal and real freedom, an enormous increase in productivity, low income inequality, and a long-awaited modernization of social customs.

The ideal toward which this century of social reform was moving can be described as a model combining a market economy and a welfare state. The logic of this model lies in the division of labor between its two fundamental elements. The market economy, with its competitive markets and private initiative, sees to it that economic resources are used efficiently, and that products and production processes are constantly brought up to date and improved. It accomplishes this within a context of state regulations designed to ensure that monopolies and cartels cannot dominate markets and to prevent information asymmetries of various kinds from suffocating trade. And it accommodates, apart from capitalist enterprises, other kinds of goods and service suppliers such as municipal firms, cooperatives, and other nonprofit organizations.

Meanwhile, the welfare state does the work of advancing distributive justice and building buffers against the income uncertainty that comes with market processes. Its central instruments are a progressive tax-transfer system, social insurance for provision in old age and in case of unemployment, and free social services including health care, education, childcare, and care for the elderly. This welfare provision from cradle to grave liberates people from many worries and anxieties, and thus frees energies that they can better apply to finding personal fulfillment and enriching their social lives.

The market economy and the welfare state support each other and flourish on the foundation of a lively civil society that infuses both spheres with the vital resource of social trust. All in all, this model does relatively well with respect to all the evaluative criteria that we have stressed—efficiency, justice, and humaneness.

Although the potential of the market-economy-plus-welfare-state model has not yet been fully realized, it already has substantially changed the lives of millions of people for the better. The transfers and taxes of the welfare state, for instance, make a large contribution to the reduction of income inequality. Without them, the latter would be about seventy percent greater in a country like Germany.

BUDDING VIRTUES

What is often not recognized is the potential for the betterment of the human character that is inherent in the combination of market economy and welfare state. In the long term, a polity based on this model could get close to achieving a society in which financial self-interest has stopped being the main driving force behind people's economic decisions. Its place could be taken by motivations like those driving the mutual giving described earlier as we explored the system of common ownership.

To appreciate this claim, consider how the generosity of the welfare state might very well strengthen human inclinations toward reciprocity. One receives support from the state (which is to say, from one's fellow citizens) if one's needs clearly exceed one's earning capacity; and conversely, one supports the state (all other citizens) if one is able to work more than is necessary to make a living. Participating in such a system may cause nobler motives for economic endeavor to take root. One might, for instance, develop an authentic sense of obligation to the polity to perform the work that one is able to do, in the expectation that others will do the same. If the state helps an individual discover his or her talents, then the individual may in turn believe those talents should be used in service of the common good.

An intrinsic motivation to do the work one does could also become significantly more important over longer periods of time. The welfare state helps to keep various groups from being excluded from social participation; thanks to social inclusion, many workers have gained the ability to carry out more sophisticated work. And increasing numbers of people also expect to be offered more demanding jobs. Market mechanisms tend to match these resources and needs by gradually raising the quality of jobs. In future, a genuine passion for one's work may therefore become the most important motivational factor for all those who are economically active.

In turn, a stronger sense of duty toward the polity and a stronger personal motivation to work could lead to more income equality, without any negative impact on economic growth. If the economic performance of individuals is based on internalized values and genuine interest, it will be of only secondary importance to them that such-and-such a proportion of their income is redistributed via taxes and public expenditure. Two generations from now, a situation might exist in which incomes are subject to very high levels of taxation, but people work happily because they like their jobs and view the payment of high taxes as nothing short of a moral duty.

THE CURRENT RETREAT OF THE WELFARE STATE

The evolution of the welfare state after the Second World War can roughly be divided into three phases. The period up to the mid-1970s saw a substantial expansion of the welfare state. This was followed by a time of stabilization, without significant changes, which lasted until the beginning of the 1990s. Since then, the trend has reversed.

In Germany today, compared to twenty years ago, there are lower rates of taxation on high incomes and on company profits; old-age pensions and unemployment benefits are less generous; the government now subsidizes those on low wages and subsidizes private pension schemes; the private school sector has expanded; and there are numerous private-public partnerships providing public goods such as highways. The last two decades have also seen massive job cuts in the civil service, advancing privatization, a retreat of traditional trade unions, significant erosion of the proportion of employees covered by collective wage agreements, deregulation of the market for financial derivatives, growth in stock markets, and stronger orientation of large companies toward maximizing shareholder value.

The countermovement of the last two decades has even affected Sweden, a country recognized around the world as a strong market economy with an extensive welfare state, and therefore a model that is a thorn in the side of many a neoliberal. Following a severe recession in the early 1990s, the Swedish government began scaling back the welfare state. Benefits for the unemployed, sick people, and the elderly became less generous. The tax system was made less progressive, and capital income was taxed at a flat rate instead of progressively. Inheritance taxes and taxes on personal wealth were abolished altogether. The proportion of pupils attending private schools increased dramatically.

Compared to where it was in the 1980s, income inequality in Sweden has risen significantly in the last two decades. Income in the highest bracket, especially income from investments, has risen much faster than average incomes. Meanwhile, the risk of poverty has substantially increased. Recent empirical studies have also affixed a question mark to the claim that Sweden is a country of equal opportunity. Although they confirm that, as compared to the United States or most other countries, Sweden's income mobility between generations is higher—that is, the children of poor parents are more likely to break out of their income stratum by earning more—they also show that the economic elite in Sweden is pretty impenetrable. Despite having a strong welfare state, Sweden is a country with capitalist dynasties whose members form the very top of the income pyramid generation after generation.

Nevertheless, we should note that Sweden, together with other Scandinavian countries, internationally remains the most successful example of a market economy with an extensive welfare system.

If we look at the emerging economies, we see entirely different dynamics at work. In contrast to Western Europe, the countries of East Asia in particular have rapidly pushed forward with the construction of welfare systems. They set out from a low baseline, however, and the welfare benefits provided are still less generous than those of most European countries.

THE ROOT OF THE PROBLEM

Why did the last twenty years see a retreat of the welfare state? One answer to this question tends to dominate public opinion. It argues that this retreat was a necessary adaptation to changing circumstances. The reforms were the result of a painful learning process that showed that the societies of western European countries were living beyond their means; there was no way around making welfare cuts. According to this received wisdom, the welfare state in Europe has not only passed its peak, but it also faces further decline in the immediate future, as further budget cuts will be necessary to manage the consequences of the financial and economic crisis. The German welfare state ten years hence will look less like the Sweden of today, and more like Canada.

This dominant view is, however, quite one-sided. It is too simplistic to cast the retreat of the welfare state as just an accommodation to a less favorable set of circumstances. If that were the case, surely politicians, before beginning to dismantle the welfare state, would have attempted at least to draw on the substantial existing financial reserves they had to prop it up. The existence of these reserves cannot be denied. One need only think of the vast amount of public money wasted on misguided projects, of the potential sources for additional public revenues that are untapped, and of the numerous counterproductive regulations and privileges the state has introduced even though they reduce the tax base. If it had been the hope of rational and benevolent politicians to protect the social achievements of the welfare state against deteriorating framework conditions, they would have drawn on these reserves before declaring defeat.

A different story about the retreat of the welfare state may have more plausibility. This is the hypothesis that capitalism (the market system plus private ownership of the means of production) has the tendency to repel the welfare state as something foreign to it. The emergence of the welfare state was brought about by the unique historical circumstance of the threatening prospect of rebellion by industrial workers. And its expansion was helped along by further unique historical circumstances: the First and Second World Wars, the Great Depression, and the Cold War. During recent decades, no such uniquely favorable conditions for the development of the welfare state have prevailed. And thus, the structural mechanisms that tend toward eroding the welfare state gained ground again.

This interpretation of the current situation suggests that the deterioration of the welfare state will continue unless the polity seizes the initiative and confronts these mechanisms. If it fails to do so, capitalism's friendly mask will keep slipping, revealing its original face. It will return to its default operating mode—as a system in which most people are abandoned to their fates and exposed to the vicissitudes of the market without any protection, and in which there are no limits to economic and social inequality.

Implied by this line of thought is a need for constant work to defend the value of the welfare state. As the structural mechanisms of capitalism reassert themselves, it will not just spontaneously emerge, but will need to be fought for again and again in the political arena. To detect these mechanisms, we need to recall that the welfare state was and still is the result of political decision making. Like any other decision-making process, its results depend on the preferences of those making the decisions and on the options at their disposal. If under capitalism there are structural reasons why a generous welfare state has only a minimal chance of being a stable outcome of political decision making, then the reasons for this must lie in the *political preferences* of the polity and in the *economic conditions* that provide the framework for the activities of the state. Before we can outline a strategy for further developing the model of a market economy plus welfare state, we should gain a better understanding of both of these aspects.

Shaky Political Support

Measures aiming at a consolidation of the institutions of the welfare state need to prevail in the democratic process. Because these institutions directly represent the material interests of the working class, they were historically fought for by the social democratic and socialist parties, as well as by the labor wing of the Christian democratic parties. Today, in most countries, the responsibility for strengthening the welfare state still rests mainly with the social democratic parties. The term is not meant to refer specifically to parties who carry the words "social democratic" in their name, but to any party that sees itself as continuing the tradition of progressive reform. In most European countries, these social democratic parties constitute one of the strongest political forces, and they claim to represent the majority of the working population that, in turn, profits most from a well-functioning and generous welfare state.

Thus, the political stability of the welfare state depends essentially on the effectiveness with which social democratic parties represent the interests of the working population. This condition, in turn, contains two separate requirements. First, social democratic parties must have sufficient political influence on the legislature. Second, they must genuinely represent the interests of the majority of the working population. As we have already seen in our discussion of government failures in the context of Plato's work, it is anything but a foregone conclusion that these two requirements will be met.

Less Than Loyal Leaders

Let us first consider the attachment of social democratic parties to the working population. By "working population," we mean the vast majority who play by the rules and whose work and effort are what keep the great ship of society afloat. They are also those who would like to contribute but are not able to do so due to illness, or because they cannot find work, or because they have to care for family members. By contrast, those who do not want to make contributions to society, or who do so from an exceptionally strong position that they occupy perhaps by dint of getting a place at an elite American university, or because they inherited a flourishing business from their parents, are not part of this group.

Note that this "working population" is not the same as the traditional working class. Traditional working-class families have actually become ever more rare; the traditional sociological distinctions between manual and intellectual labor, dependent and independent work, and working class and middle class appear increasingly arbitrary, and have been rendered progressively less useful by changes to the world of work. It makes more sense to define groups by the economic sources and levels of their incomes. The term "working population," then, refers to people whose subsistence is overwhelmingly based on their own labor, as opposed to inherited wealth, and whose income does not diverge significantly from the median income that is typical for their generation. Also included in this category are people who are unable to work.

The working population thus defined is the natural core vote for the social democratic parties. But the relationship between politicians and their constituencies is much more complicated in the case of social democratic parties than in liberal or conservative parties. This difficulty affects the recruitment and motivation of their political leadership.

Politicians with successful careers become parliamentarians, party leaders, or ministers, or take on other important offices, such as heading regulatory authorities. This makes them part of a professional group that earns multiple times the median income. These individuals come into contact mainly with members of the upper class, both professionally and in their private lives. Thus, the brief of social democratic politicians in positions of leadership is to represent the interests of voters the likes of which they rarely encounter in their professional and social environments. In some cases, they have no direct experience of the needs of this reference group at all, and often, the interests of this group contradict their own material interests. Social democratic leaders should, for instance, be committed to heavy taxation of very large incomes, but they and their friends belong to the group that is hardest hit by progressive taxation.

This conflict of interests is further aggravated by revolving-door politics—that is, the movement of individuals from political offices to related, lucrative posts in the private sector. In Germany, several members of the supposedly left-wing Red–Green coalition government have changed sides and taken up well-paid positions in the world of finance and in the pharmaceutical and energy industries.

This divergence of interests has plagued the labor movement from its very beginnings, and is reflected in the divided loyalties of rebellious popular leaders in the present day. There is a general tendency for a small elite to maintain its position by winning over individual popular leaders who threaten its power—often by simply absorbing them into the elite—and social democratic parties are by no means immune from this tendency. When the same party figures, more or less, remain in place over many years, the loyalty problem can be even further exacerbated. Through the kind of evolutionary processes described in Chapter 4, once a party tolerates a few turncoats betraying the base, social norms of loyalty begin gradually withering away. Mutual backscratching and political patronage follow, eventually producing a corrupt network that cooperates with the financial elite, provides individual party leaders and their coteries with privileges, and finally eliminates the representation of the interests of the working population.

This can happen, but it does not have to happen, because the loyalty problem can be averted if political leaders retain their sense of duty and if the party base exercises sufficient control. Both these mechanisms, however, have snags. The first implies that faithfulness to principles and personal dedication should be the decisive criteria in selecting leaders—but if they are, professional expertise and political ability might be underemphasized. The second calls for stricter control by the party base, yet that might hinder decision making and deprive the party leadership of its necessary flexibility. There is a tightrope to be walked here, something social democratic parties have not always managed in their turbulent histories.

The loyalty problem also has an intergenerational dimension that should not be underestimated. As is true in many other professions, there is a tendency in politics for the children of politicians to pick up the skills of their parents and to follow in their footsteps. Here again, there are dangers for social democratic parties more than for parties who represent the interests of the upper class. As the children of successful politicians grow up among the upper class, the connection for them to the work of a social democratic party may be less obvious. If they nevertheless seek to do that work, it is reasonable to expect the tension they feel between their loyalties to be especially acute, having been socialized in a different environment than the children of the working population.

Less Than Fully Competent Voters

The second structural challenge that bears on political support for the welfare state is the maintenance of a broad constituency in the electorate that votes for the party that represents the interests of the working population. "Broad" here means a sufficient proportion of the electorate to give the party the parliamentary majority needed to form a government under social democratic leadership.

The part of the population that profits from a well-functioning welfare state includes the core voters of social democratic parties, and as a rule this part amounts to well over half of those with a right to vote. But, for several reasons we can name, it is perfectly possible for people to make misguided political judgments.

First, the areas in which political decisions are necessary mostly lie outside the expertise of individual voters (the expertise, for example, that they might have gained working in their own professions). Therefore, voters often find their particular knowledge strengths to be of little help as they try to form political judgments. Second, voters cannot learn very much from policies that are actually implemented, because the world is subject to rapid change, and a policy that was successful in one country will not necessarily be effective in another. Third, individual voters have barely any incentive to invest efforts into understanding which policies best serve their interests, because their votes, considered singly, make such a small contribution to the collective decision-making process. When political scientists speak of "rational ignorance," they are referring to this problem.

These insufficiencies provide a raison d'être for professional politicians, and especially for specialists with expert knowledge within the parties. If citizens were always able independently and instantly to recognize which policies were best for them, then clearly it would be best to have a pure system of direct democracy. That would save the polity all the costs of maintaining political parties and a parliament. Every question of collective interest could be answered by voters deciding with the click of a mouse. But in a world where knowledge and time are scarce, a certain division of labor is helpful. In principle, politicians help voters identify those policy options that are the best for them given their interests.

The fact that voters have limited powers of judgment has important consequences for the political support the welfare state receives. It has the effect that some portion of the electorate thinks about political matters mainly in an associative and affective fashion, and this makes them susceptible to influence through the kinds of methods deployed in consumer products marketing. Presidential elections in the United States are a prime example of how political advertising plays a role in a democracy. This is another structural reason that, under capitalism, political support for the welfare state is a fragile achievement.

The tabloid press and television can reach large sections of society that would fundamentally benefit from the maintenance and further development of the welfare state. But their political behavior can be influenced in such a way that either they do not cast their votes at all or they vote against welfare state agendas. By now, empirical research on voting behavior has been able to demonstrate the effectiveness of the media's political influence with concrete figures. A recent study of Berlusconi's electoral victories in Italy was even able to demonstrate that the kind of shows and feature films broadcast on television can have a significant influence on voting behavior.

National Policies and the Global Economy

We can find further explanation for the instability of the welfare state under capitalism in the economic conditions that constitute the framework for the activities of the state. Modern economies must all deal with a fundamental contradiction between trade's becoming ever more globalized and political power's remaining tied to the national level. The gradual decline of the welfare state is in part the result of this contradiction. On the one hand, a market economy made up of profit-maximizing enterprises encourages transnational developments that push, to the greatest possible extent, the advantages that can be gained by division of labor. There is nothing new in this tendency; it was manifest in the trade capitalism of antiquity in the Mediterranean. Today, however, globalization takes the intensity of foreign trade, the international transfer of technologies, investments abroad, and migration to unprecedented levels. On the other hand, the power to legislate remains with national states, and transnational agreements are mostly limited to the purposes of creating uniform global markets for goods and capital.

Globalization undermines the welfare state mainly by diminishing its capacity for redistribution. In a welfare state, an essential aspect of redistribution is relatively heavy taxation of large incomes, which consist in significant measure of capital income. But we are seeing dramatic increases in the transnational mobility of those who receive large incomes, of investments made by enterprises, and of financial capital. When a single state decides to hike taxes, the response is often simply a migration of individuals or assets to other states. No state surrounded by low-tax jurisdictions can therefore expect to finance ambitious redistribution programs simply through high taxation.

Meanwhile, some countries (particularly those with relatively small domestic tax bases) have an opportunity to raise their revenues significantly by engaging in the aggressive tax cutting that attracts multinational investments and rich taxpayers from other countries. This fiscal incentive has launched governments all over the world into a global race to lower their taxes, with each country effectively trying to gobble up elements of the others' tax bases. For the world as a whole, this is a zero-sum game in which only the wealthy and those who receive high incomes ultimately win. Even a cursory study of the development of tax systems over the last three decades reveals widespread and substantial tax-relief measures for capital incomes, coincident with rising taxation of income from work and on consumer spending. At the same time, governments have drastically reduced the tax rates they apply to very high incomes. In the aftermath of the financial crisis, despite needs for large amounts of additional revenue, the tax burden on high incomes and capital returns has only increased marginally in the last few years.

In tandem with this downward tax competition, globalization has also opened up new possibilities for the economic elite to lower their effective tax rates through illegal or semilegal means. So-called tax havens—that is, states that are prepared to engage in such practices—offer numerous services to multinational corporations and wealthy individuals, often through banks that operate internationally. Thus, it is not uncommon for banks that have been saved directly or indirectly with taxpayer money in the countries where they are headquartered to at the same time undermine the public finances of those countries by helping their domestic residents engage in international tax evasion.

Worldwide, the private wealth hidden in tax havens is estimated currently to be in the region of twenty trillion U.S. dollars. Recent studies show that the high-profile initiative launched by the G20 countries in 2009 to combat this phenomenon, which led to much bilateral information sharing between tax havens and other countries, has not managed to bring about a reduction in the amount of wealth stored in tax havens. It is estimated that, globally, the annual loss in revenue runs to the hundreds of billions. By way of comparison, the United Nations World Food Program has an annual budget of only four billion U.S. dollars.

Further, these losses in revenue represent only a portion of the fiscal damage caused by tax havens. To understand the full scale, we would need to add to them the revenue from multinational corporations that is lost due to their use of offshore companies based in tax havens. These losses also involve astronomical sums of money.

If this tax competition is not stemmed, things will reach a point where the only redistribution possible for a welfare state to bring about will be neutral reshuffling or, at best, shifts from average earners to poorer parts of the population. And we will see more of the result which has been evident in most welfare states for some time now, in the widening gap between rich and poor.

A META-REFORM

We have thus found that, for a variety of solid political and economic reasons, the model of a market economy plus welfare state may not be a stable configuration. Its structural problems essentially concern the loyalty of politicians, the mobilization of the electorate, and the effectiveness of redistributive policies in times of economic globalization. Any strategy that aims to further develop this European model must give priority to tackling these problems. The slow-motion crisis of the welfare state that has unfolded over the last two decades has left us with a strategy challenge that is actually quite urgent.

We should therefore think about "meta-reform" to create an institutional framework within which a well-functioning welfare state may flourish in the long term. In what follows, we will explore some concrete activities to accomplish such meta-reform. Each of the three problems mentioned above—loyalty of politicians, mobilization of the electorate, limits to redistributive policies posed by global competition—corresponds to an area of activity. We are not concerned here with country-specific details, but with the core of these political problems.

Transparency and Direct Democracy

The loyalty shown by political decision makers to the working population is undermined by three factors: influential lobbies, the information deficit of the citizens regarding their representatives, and the large volume of decisions that are delegated. Thus, three corresponding measures for rectifying these suggest themselves. Relationships and deals between politicians and political lobbyists should be made more difficult. The actions of politicians should be more transparent to the citizens. And the citizens should have the opportunity to take more political decisions themselves. Each of these measures deserves some discussion.

Politicians' Additional Incomes and Interim Periods

To make deals between politicians and lobbyists more difficult, politicians' second jobs should be subject to scrutiny, and the revolving door between politics and the corporate sector should be regulated in the case of the holders of public offices. Similar rules should apply to the leading group of politicians in all political parties. "Transparency International," for instance, has presented promising proposals for the effective design of such regulations. Work that politicians do on the side, such as consultancy or lectures, should be disclosed. In the case of possible conflicts of interest, there should be interim periods of several years after someone has left political office. Taking up any professional activity immediately after a time as an elected politician or a period in office should generally be subject to a process of approval by an authority, and the new professional activity should be publicly announced.

Transparency of Political Decisions

The transparency of political decisions is meant to make politicians accountable to the electorate. Who bears the responsibility for a particular political decision? On the basis of what evidence was it taken? What were its consequences? Given today's information technologies, it is for the first time possible to produce this transparency at almost no cost. The Internet may be used for providing citizens with the information they need to understand how well their representatives are working. There are already steps being taken in this direction, but these measures can be substantially expanded.

More transparency does not mean, however, that everything should go online. There is still a need for a sphere of privacy, and too much information can end up being confusing. The information must be selected and understood before it can be used for meaningful evaluation. What citizens need is useful information.

To understand the quality of a political decision, people need to be informed both about the situation at the time of a policy measure's formulation and about the situation after its implementation. Information serving the former need would include any expert reports that were drawn up for the political decision makers. In most countries, for example, a cost-benefit analysis is required for any large infrastructure project, to establish whether it is in the public interest and how best to carry it out from an economic point of view. These analyses, which are publicly funded, should be made immediately available to everyone on the Internet. We also need transparency regarding whether the measures that end up actually being taken achieve their aims. Whenever a policy measure is introduced, provisions should at the same time be made to collect the data required to evaluate the measure's effectiveness. This information should, as a matter of principle, be made available to the general public. Anyone should be able to use it to understand the consequences of policy measures, and the quality of the political decision making that informed them.

Direct Political Participation of Citizens

To provide more possibilities for citizens to participate directly in politics, the process of holding a referendum should be made easier. One indirect benefit of having more referenda would be a general improvement in parliamentary decisions—because the members of parliament would learn to anticipate that any ill-conceived law might later be repealed by the people. Reforms that would make referenda more frequent would include changes to reduce the number of signatures necessary to trigger a referendum, to reduce the proportion of votes cast required to make a petition quorate, and to expand the legislative scope of referenda.

Referenda motivate citizens to become better informed. On this front, too, much better use can be made of modern information technologies. Ahead of every referendum, an independent regulatory body should use the Internet to publish impartial content relevant to the decision to be made.

It should also be possible to dismiss the head of a government or a mayor by referendum—Thomas More, you may remember, already suggested this. Likewise, political parties should offer similar mechanisms to their members with regard to their leaders.

Direct and indirect democracy should be integrated by promoting the involvement of citizens in the parliamentary legislature. Draft proposals for new laws should be put online early enough for civil society to comment upon them, and the resulting suggestions for changes should be taken into consideration in parliamentary discussions.

Infrastructure and Public Services

The stabilization of the political basis for the welfare state requires the lasting and comprehensive support of the middle class. The foolproof recipe for achieving this support is to provide high-quality services by the state, especially in the areas of education and health, and to minimize the wasting of taxpayers' money. If a government efficiently spends money on high-quality services, then middle-class voters will respond with skepticism to any rival political parties trying to garner votes with promises of tax reductions. These voters will fear that their standard of living will suffer from the cuts to public spending that would eventually result. When the quality of governmental spending improves, there can also be a reciprocal effect on citizens' behavior, by which they become more willing to cooperate with the government by, for instance, honestly paying their taxes.

Advice, Auditing, Evaluation

In many countries, local jurisdictions who are all affected by some public project, or share a common need, can get more value from their public expenditure by working cooperatively. Regional authorities should work to foster such cooperation, and also be prepared to delegate their authority to central bodies when this would be prudent. An example in Germany would be transferring tax auditing responsibility from the states to the federal authorities to make coordination easier and create stronger incentives for tax inspections and tax investigations.

Cost-benefit analyses, transparency, and the ex-post evaluation of policies should be given higher priority. Audit offices should continue to support regional authorities in their decision making and should examine whether budgeted resources were used prudently and the best possible results achieved. But no audit office should act as both advisor and examiner for a given project—there must be sufficient incentive for the office to be thorough in its examination. As opposed to current practice, when there is a case of a responsible authority embarking on a public project without due consideration of economic feasibility, the contravention should be called out, and the consequences for that authority should be serious.

To promote accountability and a prudent use of public money in public schools, hospitals, and other public institutions, each institution could be assigned a controlling body with close ties to the local community. This body would consist of experts recruited from civil society who would oversee the use of public funds by these institutions on a voluntary basis and give support and advice.

Transparent comparisons of performance and benchmarking can be crucial in identifying weak points in the public sector and in creating effective incentives to follow best practice. The public administration should, as a matter of principle, be obligated to make all data relevant to the evaluation of the processes it carries out available to citizens on-line. The higher authority should coordinate the provision of information on the Internet and give advice about how it can be meaningfully used for comparing performances. Schools, public order and security, water services, regional public transport, railways, and postal services all constitute sectors where the publication of performance indicators could lead to substantial efficiency improvements. (In the case of railways and postal services, a comparison of performance at the European level may also be helpful.)

This culture of openness should include any nonstate organizations providing services of public interest. The resulting informed comparisons can help set process improvements in motion that make the provision of services by the sectors in question more efficient.

Access to information regarding the quality of public service providers will make citizens more capable of responsible and independent judgment. Citizens will then be able to make realistic demands and exert effective pressure to make sure these demands are actually met.

Civil Servants

In some countries, especially in Germany, there have been massive cuts to the public sector workforce over the past two decades. At the same time, the salaries of highly qualified public sector employees have substantially declined relative to those of employees with similar qualifications in the private sector. While the private sector, and especially the financial services sector, has comprehensively expanded and strengthened its workforce in terms of intellectual skills, the government has failed to recruit enough young, well-qualified employees. As a result, the know-how of employees in the public sector tends to be out of date. Making matters worse, some of the most proficient employees in the public sector have been headhunted by private employers. It seems obvious that the government is becoming less and less able to provide high-class services and to resist encroachments by the private sector.

Human capital is by far the most important production factor in the public sector, and the optimal use of talent is therefore of the utmost importance. A politically independent research center should therefore investigate the optimal employment structure and reward structure for the civil service.

In terms of professional development, one goal regarding state officials who are likely to take up leading positions is to deepen their knowledge of economics and finance. There should be prestigious institutions offering relevant Masters and PhD programs. Renowned schools in France and the United States, which run such training programs, can provide blueprints for this task. Given that national governments negotiate deals worth billions at international government conferences, it will pay to have representatives with first-class educations in one's own delegation.

Whenever there is an important deficit of in-house know-how, a government should try to find flexible solutions drawing on external advice. It could, for instance, temporarily employ a handful of cutting-edge researchers to work on a specific question. Take, for example, the questions raised about megabanks in the aftermath of the financial crisis: How should the "too-big-to-fail" problem be solved? Does it make sense to break up large financial intermediaries? Should banks be prohibited from operating both investment and commercial arms at the same time? Would a tax on the short-term debt of financial institutions be useful to reduce systemic risk? For each of these and other related questions, the government could pick three specialists who are considered to be independent and outstanding experts by their colleagues. These three individuals would then be employed by the government for a limited period of time and under competitive conditions. The agreement would be that, during that time, they would exclusively dedicate themselves to the specific question they were asked to address. And at the end of the stipulated period, they would present a solution. Using such specialist task forces, the state could cease to be the repeat victim of the monopolization of knowledge by experts who work for private interests.

Catching the Internationally Mobile Tax Base

The third area for a promising meta-reform to revitalize the welfare state is the international coordination of tax policy. The pronounced cross-border mobility of firms, financial capital, and people at the top of the income distribution severely limits the possible progressivity of national tax regimes. The solution is not to constrain this mobility, because mobility fulfills useful economic functions and represents an important element of personal freedom. Rather, individual countries need well-focused coordination in their tax policies. Larger countries especially have a duty to take the lead and make significant efforts toward effective coordination.

The Fight against Tax Havens

The taxation of capital income and inheritance becomes increasingly important thanks to two interconnected trends. First, the total net wealth of private households is growing faster than their total income. Whereas in the early 1970s, private wealth in western European countries was roughly two or three times the annual aggregate income, today it is about four to six times the aggregate income. And this trend is bound to continue. It follows from this that asset-based taxation has an increasing potential to raise revenue, and will become ever more important for financing the activities of the state. Second, inequalities in the amount of inherited wealth are becoming a key driver of the distribution of the life chances of individuals, because lifetime wages grow more slowly compared to inherited wealth. This means that asset-based taxation, and especially inheritance tax, has to play a decisive role if we want to establish distributive justice in our society.

These developments highlight the urgency of finding effective ways to combat the tax evasion by very wealthy individuals that is made possible by tax havens. This fight requires broad-based international coordination, which should include at least all OECD countries. The aim of an international agreement with countries that operate as tax havens should be to begin a process for the transnational exchange of information on the basis of automatic notifications from banks to the relevant national tax authorities. This is the only way to collect information on capital income and financial assets on an individual level, to be able to subject them to progressive taxation.

Such an agreement should be the outcome of an international conference at which all states concerned commit themselves to participate in the automatic exchange of information. The current practice of bilateral agreements, by contrast, should be rejected, because it creates possibilities for further evasion through the relocation of undisclosed assets from one tax haven to another. The G20 initiative of 2009 also suffers from this defect.

Those countries that sign up to the international treaty should agree on sanctions for nonparticipants. Financial transfers between participating and nonparticipating countries, for instance, could be made subject to taxation. Such an initiative's chance of being successful will be higher if those tax havens that immediately join it are rewarded—for instance, by being allowed to participate in the tax revenues made possible by their cooperation.

A Minimum Top Rate of Tax

Over the last two or three decades, the concentration of income has rapidly increased in Europe and the United States, while the tax burden on very high incomes has been reduced. This tax relief flies in the face of the increased need for distributive justice, and can partially be explained as the result of international tax competition. Governments fear that those who receive very high incomes will emigrate if they have to pay high taxes. A clear indication of the importance of this problem is the number of countries introducing tax relief for foreign individuals with high qualifications. Among them are Belgium, Denmark, Finland, the Netherlands, Portugal, Spain, Sweden, and Switzerland.

To stop this race to the bottom, the OECD countries should agree on a uniform minimum top marginal tax rate, meaning that, in each of the signatory states, personal income above a particular threshold is taxed at no less than some internationally agreed rate. The agreement could, for example, stipulate that all annual incomes above 250,000 euros are subject to a tax rate of at least 48 percent. This minimum rate would decrease the incentive for individuals with large incomes to relocate for tax purposes. And the managers of multinational corporations would have less incentive to select headquarters locations based on tax considerations.

Ideally, all signatories should use the same methods for calculating their national income tax. As far as very high incomes are concerned, the most significant deviation from this ideal occurs in the treatment of capital income, which some countries exclude in part or in whole from personal income tax. To slow down the increasing concentration of income, all signatories should include capital income in the definition of income that is subject to personal income tax.

To take into account the differences in overall levels of income in the various OECD countries, one could determine the income threshold beyond which the minimum top tax rate applies in relation to the average income in each country. The income threshold could also be lowered for countries that do not tax income from capital, since they are subjecting only a part of personal income to taxation.

Corporate Taxation in Europe

The most pronounced effect of tax competition in Europe is on levels of corporate tax rates—that is, taxes on the profits of incorporated firms. In Germany, for example, the corporate tax rate has plunged from 56 percent in the 1980s to 15 percent today.

As firms enjoy complete freedom of cross-border movement within the EU, a common European policy for their taxation is urgently required. It is puzzling that we face a collective problem (the mutual undercutting of tax rates) and that an appropriate means for solving it is available (the EU), and yet no use of this means has been made. Especially today, when many people are doubting the European project, the introduction of a European-wide corporate tax would be an opportunity to show citizens that the political construction of the European Union has very concrete advantages for them. They could easily recognize how increased revenue from taxing corporations could translate to lower labor and consumption taxes and provide the financing for better public services.

This step would require relinquishing national legislative authority on this matter to a European institution such as the European parliament. Ideally, this would take place within the framework of a broad political process that gradually introduced the structures of a democratic federal system in Europe.

The uniform taxation of corporate profits across Europe would not only generate additional revenue but also improve the performance of our economic system in terms of the allocation test. Note that, under the current system, the business-location decisions that are motivated by tax considerations do not direct resources to the places promising the highest productivity; rather they direct them to the places where the fiscal burden is the lowest. Also consider the highly talented individuals currently trained to tackle the complex task of international tax optimization, whose skills could surely be used far more productively.

THREE PRIORITIES FOR META-REFORM

A pluralist market economy with an effective and generous welfare state represents the best economic system that is immediately available to us. But over the last two decades, we have moved away from it. The scaling-back of the welfare state was not always necessary, and certainly the thoroughgoing dismantling of it was not warranted. A long-lasting, revitalized welfare state requires a political program that is specifically committed to bringing about a certain kind of meta-reform. The purpose of such meta-reform should be to create a justified trust in the state and to stop the mechanisms that lead to the instability of the welfare state under capitalism. There are three crucial areas of activity in this regard: more transparency and direct democracy, higher quality of public spending, and the international coordination of tax policies. These should be priorities for all progressive political forces.

EPILOGUE:

A FATHER AND DAUGHTER COME TO TERMS

QUITE SOME TIME HAS PASSED since the father sent his daughter the last attachment, on the market economy and the welfare state. The two now meet up at a university. In a seminar room that has just been vacated by a group of students, they pick up their conversation where they left off.

Daughter: Did I mention that, in the copious spare time I've had between reading all your very long postcards from your alternative states, I have also been reading *The Divine Comedy*? I can't resist mentioning that after Odysseus returns to Ithaca, Dante sends him on a final journey—beyond the Pillars of Hercules. It seems like you don't share any of Odysseus's longing to be off again. Here you are, at the end of our trip, comfortably settled between your two certainties. First, you're certain now that there's no clearly superior alternative to capitalism. Second, you're certain that our best bet is a strategy that breathes new life into social democratic reform with some basic democratic principles and some new help from the Internet. The problem is, I'm still not convinced—and I'll tell you why.

I'll start with your second certainty. You're trying to sell me on this model of a "market economy plus welfare state" by claiming

it holds out the prospect of a qualitative change in our way of life.
Despite markets and private property, you expect the next generation of Europeans to develop an entirely different mind-set
compared to today's generation. Thanks to the welfare state, Europeans will be good, committed Kantians who take pride in their
work and are happy to pay their high taxes. And that will make it
possible, using the state's budget, to reverse the whole income
disparity trend, yet still have a flourishing economy.

I just can't see things playing out that way. You're talking about
a spontaneous spread of solidarity and trust that realistically can't
happen if there are still some number of mega-rich tycoons around.
These people occupy an entirely different world! They don't know
anything about the worries and needs of ordinary people, and
will never identify with the polity. And in the meantime, leading
their splashy lives, they only encourage others to try to be like them
and separate themselves in the same way from the rest of society.
So how can this improvement in human nature you describe ever
come about? Kant's categorical imperative can only flourish in a
society where all citizens are equals.

And then there's your first claim. Based on what you yourself
have written to me, I don't see how you arrive at the conclusion
that there is no superior alternative to capitalism. On our journey
beyond the social market economy, we did come across an economic system that passed both the cooperation test and the allocation test: shareholder socialism. It promises a level of prosperity
comparable to the social market economy, but doesn't lead to an
oligarchy. It empowers people in their workplaces. And it achieves
more egalitarian income distribution. Surely that constitutes a
better system, doesn't it?

So I continue to stand by my original call for the overthrow of
capitalism. It should be replaced by one of the three versions of
shareholder socialism.

Father (with mild irritation):   Steady on. You cannot simply pick an
economic system off the shelf like a product in a supermarket.
Maybe on purely theoretical grounds shareholder socialism isn't
inferior to the present economic system—I grant you that. But in

practical reality, we don't know that because it does not exist. You need to consider that implementing market socialism would require the creation of entirely new institutions—and we just have no idea whether they will eventually work. And on top of that uncertainty, introducing market socialism would have high transitional costs. It is highly likely that, once you factored in those costs, people would not actually profit from it at all. So do me a favor: stop indulging in fiction. Let's deal with facts.

Daughter: Hey! Ever heard of domination-free discourse?! Just listen to me for a minute. We have to consider the matter without any prejudices. Progress always involves change and therefore never comes without a certain risk—we have to accept that if we want to make the world a better place. And I am not prepared to accept transitional costs as a counterargument, because, by definition, society would have to bear them only in the short term, while society would profit from market socialism over the very long term. Don't you care at all about your grandchildren?

Father: Of course I do. But I think you massively overrate the advantages of market socialism compared to a social market economy. Market socialism would only marginally reduce today's economic inequalities, because its effects would depend on the compensation that today's shareholders would receive when their enterprises were taken into public ownership. If that compensation corresponded to the current market value, there would be no effect on the distribution of wealth at all. And even if we made an unrealistic assumption that nationalization would take place without any compensation, we still could not expect any substantial reduction of inequality.

Daughter: Wait, I'm not following you. Capital income represents a significant part of the national income overall, and these assets grow faster than income—you said it yourself. Doesn't that suggest that socializing the means of production would have far-reaching distributive effects?

Father: Look, the annual national income for Germany amounts to roughly 2,000 billion euros, and wages make up about two-thirds of that. So the income from capital amounts to about 650 billion euros.

But today's capital income consists mainly of returns from assets that would not be socialized under a system of market socialism, such as savings accounts, government bonds, company pensions, and rental apartments. Currently, private households in Germany receive around 300 billion euros every year in the form of dividends and withdrawals from the enterprise sector. But even this figure overestimates market socialism's potential for redistribution, because it contains incomes from many small enterprises that would remain in private hands even in a market socialist system.

So we have to deduct the dividends paid by small and medium-sized enterprises, and the compensation to be paid to shareholders, from that annual figure of 300 billion euros. And we also have to deduct the costs involved in creating the new state institutions that will administer the public property. Now, how much do you think will remain for paying a social dividend? If you were being optimistic, you might say 100 billion per year. That would allow the state to pay everyone a social dividend of about 100 euros per month. But is it really worth all the pain of turning an entire economic system—one that functions, after all—upside down for 100 euros a month?

Daughter: OK, you might have a point. But reducing income inequality is not, in my opinion, the primary reason why market socialism is a desirable system. The crucial argument, in my mind, is getting rid of the social and political distortions that are caused by the capitalist elite, and that ultimately corrupt all of society. I'm talking about money fetishism and the emphasis on material possessions. The exploitation of the weak. The corruption of politicians and the erosion of democracy. And I am talking about the unacceptable consequences all this has, like states getting involved in murderous wars.

Father: Regarding money fetishism, a certain degree of that is going to be inherent in any monetary economy, because most goods and services will be measured in terms of money. Market socialism would merely reduce this effect, as economic power would be less a measure of success if there were no longer any billionaires.

I am also less confident about how well democracy turns out to function under conditions of market socialism. Wouldn't we see dangers arising from the top managers of market socialist enterprises that are very similar to the ones created by capitalists? Shareholder socialism also dangles incentives for managers to get payments tied to the profitability of their firms. This means they personally profit if the government treats their firm preferentially. It's possible they would engage in even more lobbying than capitalists do. After all, capitalists spread their assets across several investments, but under market socialism, the greater part of a top manager's income would be the incentive payments resulting from the financial performance of the firm that hired him.

Daughter: True enough. But under market socialism, measures will be taken against this danger. These might be similar to the ones you referred to as meta-reform: making deals between politicians and lobbyists more difficult, creating more transparency, and strengthening direct democracy.

Look at it in a broad historical context. The introduction of shareholder socialism would mean a unique expansion of economic and political rights. This would make it one of Europe's biggest contributions to the development of civilization—one of those things that makes this continent distinct from the rest of the world, like Athenian democracy, the Enlightenment, and the welfare state. The creation of a functioning system of shareholder socialism would be the next achievement in that grand history of inventions.

You know better than me that the European model of society has, by now, lost a lot of its appeal. Europe is in steady decline compared to China, or, to a certain extent, the United States, whether we are talking in political or economic terms or about research and culture. If we don't want to see European values and the European understanding of democracy lose relevance, we need a renaissance based on these values. And shareholder socialism could be the beginning of such a renaissance.

Father: But a generous and efficient welfare state would also accomplish that. And maybe we could agree on assigning a key role to shareholder socialism—as a credible threat.

Daughter: What do you mean, a key role as a threat?

Father: You might know that it was only after the Second World War that the creation of the welfare state really gathered momentum. But back then, a lot of people in Europe actually wanted to see a transition to a socialist economy, and quite a few experts thought it very likely that socialism would win the day. The prospect of that happening led to an alliance being formed of the major popular parties, the trade unions, and some enlightened captains of industry, and it was because of that alliance that the social programs, public education, health care, and progressive taxation of the modern welfare state ultimately emerged.

I'm thinking, therefore, as we're seeing the welfare state fading away today, that maybe if there were a credible alternative to capitalism, that would help to stabilize the welfare state, just as socialism did after 1945. It seems plausible that shareholder socialism could be such an alternative system.

In other words, given the high transitional costs, the introduction of market socialism does not look to most people like a rational strategy as long as the social achievements of the European model still exist. But if the dissolution of the welfare state continues—and if, as a consequence, more and more Europeans have to deal with precarious working conditions, low wages, poverty, bad public schooling, insufficient medical care, weak social cohesion, and a mediocre cultural life—well, then it won't seem so unreasonable to a lot of folks to shoulder the high transitional costs of introducing market socialism. That would be a threat the elites would have to take seriously, and I think we'd see them making efforts to put a stop to the erosion of the welfare state.

Daughter: That sounds very much like the wishful thinking of old-fashioned social democrats to me! I'd say the social reforms of the postwar years came about not because of elites worrying about an alternative approach, but thanks to pressures exerted by a well-organized labor movement and the bourgeoisie's fear of a militarily successful Soviet Union.

Father: Yet the labor movement and the Soviets were inspired by ideas in a pamphlet, published around 1847 to 1848 by two young German intellectuals . . .

Daughter: Fair enough. But don't you think market socialism would only be an effective threat today if there were concrete examples of cases demonstrating it could actually work? And the government would need to be viewed as a skillful economic agent. But the exact opposite is the case today. If you brought up the competence of the state with anyone who reads the newspapers in Germany today, for instance, their thoughts would likely go to those regional state banks who bought up toxic assets all over the world, and funneled taxpayer money into the pockets of Wall Street bankers. Not to mention the financial disasters that are Stuttgart 21 and the new Berlin airport. With stuff like that going on, it's hard to imagine getting people excited about the introduction of market socialism.

Father: Then let's leave that aside. I just told you that . . .

Daughter: No, wait, I have another idea! At the moment, of course, there is no broad political support for market socialism. But maybe we could persuade citizens to give it a fair hearing if we adopted an open-ended approach. Here's what I'm thinking.

First, we introduce those measures for increasing transparency and citizens' direct political participation we've already been talking about. They would serve the purpose of providing more solid foundations for the democratic infrastructure we need for the program to be successful.

Second, we create an independent institution, like the one you described in your "x percent" version of market socialism. That kind of institution—you called it the "federal shareholder"—would represent the public interest as a collective investor.

Finally, we nationalize a certain percentage—let's say 51 percent—of the capital of some of the large-scale enterprises and banks. You're following me, right? The idea is for these share assets to be transferred to the federal shareholder. The experts of this institution then represent the polity on the supervisory boards of the enterprises under their control.

With these three steps, we set in motion an evolutionary process—and then we can wait and see whether the collective management of capital turns out to be superior to its capitalist management.

(She stops and thinks for a moment, then continues.)

And, you know what: it *will* be superior! Because, if you think about it, capitalists also use their economic empires to pursue their personal dreams of power, and they often have incompetent heirs who take over their businesses despite having no qualifications to do so. Or they enjoy the easy life and ignore the fact that, all the while, their enterprises are being plundered by greedy managers. The point is, the capitalist class is really nowhere near as efficient as you and your colleagues assume in your economic theories. If the federal shareholder did a good job, and I assume that would be the case, and thus maximized the collective "shareholder value," then the market socialist sector of the economy would be the more profitable one, and its share of the overall economy would gradually increase.

And there would be another crucial factor. Thanks to the increased transparency of the state, it would become more and more difficult for capitalist corporations to buy into the political class to increase their profits by circumventing the market. Cartels, monopolies, and various kinds of hidden subsidies would therefore gradually disappear. The artificially high returns of capitalist corporations would therefore be drastically reduced. And that means capitalist cliques will die out, and over time we get closer and closer to the full version of x percent shareholder socialism!

(She leans back and looks triumphantly at her father.)

Father (after taking a long look at her and pausing to think): You know, I really think you are on to something here. I especially like it because it combines an evolutionary process of discovery with social engineering. If the independent institution—that is, the federal shareholder—failed to deliver normal market returns, the polity could always close it down again without much effort. The government would simply sell off its shares again. If, however, it achieved *better* returns than the capitalist firms, this would show the polity that, in economic terms, the capitalists were superfluous. And so our economic system would slowly be transformed, and would become more humane, more just, and more efficient.

Daughter: Exactly . . . but don't stop there. What does the financial aspect of this excellent program look like? I am not really clear about this. I read a while ago that an enterprise like BMW has a total market cap of about 40 billion euros. To bring it under the control of the federal shareholder would have to cost more than 20 billion euros. If you wanted to take over a dozen of such enterprises, it would be a pretty expensive undertaking, especially if not all EU countries joined in.

This is expenditure for investment, so surely the government should finance these nationalizations through borrowing. But in these times of financial crises, this sounds pretty problematic, and I am really no expert . . .

Father: Actually it's not a problem. If the firms to be nationalized are well chosen, then economically speaking it is not objectionable to finance their purchase with new borrowing. Capital costs are relatively low in the case of solvent states such as Germany. While in the long term the government refinances its debt at an annual rate of about 3 or 4 percent, the firms produce annual returns of roughly 8 percent. This means the government is in a position to borrow to buy shares, and then ensure that the dividends that are achieved are sufficient to cover the interest that accrues on the debt.

Of course, this only works if the federal shareholder manages the firms at least as well as they are managed under the present ownership structure. It would therefore make sense to begin by nationalizing just those sectors of the economy where the state already has some experience of ownership and management. That would reduce the risk of the returns falling below the capital costs.

Daughter: And what about the famous—or should I say infamous— debt brake?

Father: The German debt brake relates to the annual budget deficit of the public sector. As long as the returns achieved by the market socialist firms remain above the costs for refinancing the public debt, we'll have no problem at all. Quite the opposite. Each year, the budgetary situation of the public sector would improve by the difference between the returns from the capital invested in the firms and the cost of refinancing it, multiplied by the value of capital held by the federal shareholder.

Daughter: And what about the Maastricht criteria?

Father: That's a good question, and a delicate issue. Let me put it this way: A bit of creative accounting might be necessary. This is because, at the European level, it is gross debt and not the net debt of the country that matters, and the gross debt would of course rise due to the nationalizations. A popular method used by local and national jurisdictions that want to conceal their additional borrowing for investment projects is to enter into so-called public–private partnerships. Something similar could also be used in the context of nationalization. However, public–private partnerships are not an ideal solution, because they burden the state with unnecessary and high transaction costs that benefit bankers and consultants. It would therefore be better to negotiate an agreement with the EU that excludes the costs for the purchase of enterprises from the gross debt concept that is employed by the European budgetary rules.

Daughter: Well, let's assume this will wash: the EU agrees to this exemption, and the government raises the money for the purchase of companies on the financial market. Wouldn't it then be financially dangerous if the volume of government-issued bonds circulating on the market increased dramatically? Wouldn't the financial markets respond by panicking and forcing Germany to pay horrendously high interest rates?

Father: I think such a response would be unlikely. The government's additional borrowing, under the scenario we are considering, would go hand in hand with an increase in the stocks held by the public sector. These stocks function like securities that can be sold off, should this ever turn out to be necessary. But to repeat: what is absolutely crucial is that the government not let the firms go to the wall. The structure of incentives around the federal shareholder is therefore extremely important.

Daughter: What I still worry about is whether we would find enough investors willing to buy all these additional government bonds.

Father: No, that will be all right; there will be an excess of liquidity in the markets due to the takeover of the firms by the state. This liquidity could ultimately be invested in the government bonds.

And there are more and more small savers who are desperately looking for investment opportunities to secure their old age. Long-term bonds issued by a solvent state that are indexed to inflation are exactly what they need.

Daughter: Right. So, you're happy with this idea?

Father: Yes, I am. It really could be the start of a better world. And I'd also call it a good day's work on our part—so honestly, I could go for a coffee about now. Care to join me?

A TWO-STEP PROPOSAL TO ENHANCE THE ROLE OF PUBLIC CAPITAL IN MARKET ECONOMIES

The case for enhancing the role of public ownership of capital in current advanced economies can best be made by referring to the recent evolution of the wealth distribution. The central importance of this trend is suggested by a number of empirical findings—in particular, the increase of top-wealth fractiles and aggregate wealth-income ratios over the last decades in several countries. In the United States, for instance, the share of overall wealth commanded by just the top 0.1 percent wealthiest people has grown from 8 percent in the mid-1970s to 22 percent in 2012, according to Emmanuel Saez and Gabriel Zucman.[1] During the same period, the aggregate wealth-income ratio grew by almost one-third, according to Thomas Piketty and Gabriel Zucman.[2] Such findings have aroused various concerns, chief among them the following ones:

(1) The effect of wealth inequality on income inequality is magnified by unequal access to financial returns: large portfolios have access to substantially higher returns than smaller ones. Similar to the

This appendix draws on my Policy Paper "Inequality, Public Wealth, and the Federal Shareholder" for the Forschungsinstitut zur Zukunft der Arbeit (Institute for the Study of Labor), published in October 2016 and accessible at http://ftp.iza.org/pp115 .pdf. I repeat here my gratitude to Leonardo Becchetti, Angela Cummine, Massimo Florio, Volker Grossmann, Thorsten Hens, Olivier Jeanne, Katharina Jenderny, John Roemer, and Paolo Vanin for their helpful comments and suggestions on that work.

labor market, there is an insider / outsider divide in financial markets which makes the dollar of an ordinary saver earn less than the dollar of a billionaire.[3]

(2) A large and increasing fraction of household net wealth is inherited rather than self-made. In turn, inheritances are very unequally distributed.[4]

(3) The rise of wealth concentration increases the incentive and the ability of the wealthy to buy political influence, which in turn is used to further increase the concentration of economic power.[5]

Point (1) suggests that the bulk of the population faces restricted access to financial markets and foregoes efficiency gains from pooling wealth together so as to reduce the sunk costs of financial investment and share its risk. Point (2) suggests that the birth lottery is gaining importance relative to individual merit as a determinant of the distribution of economic welfare in society. Point (3) suggests that incomes at the top of the distribution often result from rent-seeking activities rather than from creating value for society. Taken together, those points cast serious doubts on the benign view of capitalism that has long been popularized by classical liberalism.

Both the details about (1)–(3) and their interpretation are controversial—which is unsurprising given limited data and the uncertainty about the right models to use to interpret them. There is, however, relatively wide consensus that they deserve appropriate policy responses and that such responses should not wait until all scientific controversies are resolved. The subsequent policy debate has mainly focused on Thomas Piketty's proposal to dramatically increase capital taxes. As cautioned by many economists, capital taxes pose a number of subtle issues in terms of incentives and shifting via general-equilibrium effects. It seems fair to say that we currently cannot predict with confidence the consequences of a large increase of capital taxes. Careful empirical simulations of the Laffer curve of capital taxation by Mathias Trabandt and Harald Uhlig suggest that unintended consequences of raising capital taxes are likely unless the tax increase is moderate.[6]

The problems associated with the rise of wealth inequality can better be tackled by enhancing the role played in our economies by the public ownership of capital. Public capital can be used, namely, to reduce inequality in the distribution of primary capital incomes and therefore make high capital taxes superfluous. As argued below, provided a sound governance structure is put in place, public ownership of capital of a certain kind has the potential to solve the problems raised by (1)–(3) above. It can break the vicious circle of increasing wealth concentration and political capture, contribute to more equality of opportunity, and reduce the transaction costs of financial investment.

My proposal borrows ideas from the literature on shareholder socialism discussed above and blends them with insights from republicanism and the civil-economy tradition.[7] Public capital in this proposal does not refer to infrastructure and utilities. It refers to forms of collective property grounded in democratic participation and designed to limit inequality among members of the community.[8] The management of such public capital requires suitable institutions that differ from existing ones and from those used for related purposes in the past. Admittedly, the institutions I sketch in this proposal require an environment characterized by sufficiently high-quality government and a sufficiently high level of social capital. These certainly do not exist everywhere, but several countries are currently endowed with such environments, making this blueprint relevant for them.

I propose that the public capital to be used as a tool for redistribution mainly take the form of stocks of publicly-quoted companies. Those stocks should be acquired by the government by means of market transactions to make up a diversified, international portfolio. Initially, such public capital should entirely be managed by a sovereign wealth fund. The next section describes the qualifying features of its governance structure, which include rules to prevent unethical investment. The sovereign wealth fund would help reduce inequality by distributing its returns to citizens equally through a social dividend. While a sovereign wealth fund would merely act as a collective rentier, concerns for democracy call for some activation of public ownership inside firms. Here is where the novel public institution referred to as the "federal shareholder" in Chapter 8 of this book enters the picture. That institution would replace private corporate control in some large firms, enable civil society to monitor those firms, and promote worker participation in their management. Its scope in the overall economy would not be determined in advance; rather, it should be the outcome of a collective learning process about the costs and benefits of such a public-democratic control of companies in contrast to private-capitalistic control. Of course, before public capital can be used as a tool to reduce inequality and foster participation, it must be accumulated. The final part of this appendix describes how a relatively large amount of public capital can be built at small costs—using proceeds from privatizations, government bonds, and an inheritance tax.

A SOCIALLY RESPONSIBLE SOVEREIGN WEALTH FUND

Suppose that a polity owns, through its government, a large and diversified portfolio of stocks of publicly-quoted companies. Initially, the responsibility for managing such public capital should rest entirely with a novel sovereign wealth fund (SWF) explicitly created for that purpose.[9] SWFs have been around for more than sixty years now; at present, there are more than fifty SWFs worldwide, including those in Australia, New Zealand, Norway, and Alaska. SWFs are state-owned financial vehicles that manage public funds. Generally speaking, they operate like passive investors seeking to secure high rates of return by making appropriate portfolio decisions, without assuming control of business enterprises.

The main goal of the SWF I propose is to allow every citizen to share in the high rates of return generated by the stock market. This should occur in a direct and transparent way, by earmarking the income of the SWF to finance a *social dividend*—that is, a monthly or quarterly universal transfer payment received by every citizen, which all are free to use as they see fit.[10] This social dividend, as a novel redistributive tool to be employed by the polity, would be tax-exempted and would not be credited against benefits to which people are otherwise entitled by social legislation. The income of the fund would consist of its returns after subtracting administration costs and a reinvestment quota to stabilize the ratio of fund size to GDP in the long run. The SWF can be expected, given its opportunities for diversification and the fact that it would not pay taxes, to yield above-average returns on capital for citizens over the long term. This means that even those who have no private means of their own would benefit from the high returns generated by the stock market, since every citizen would be an equal shareholder, through the state, in the investments of the SWF.[11]

The social dividend would make a significant contribution to reducing inequalities both of outcomes and opportunities. It is not realistic, however, to expect that it would be as large as a basic income. Assume, for example, that over a time lapse of twenty years, the polity builds up a SWF that gradually amounts to 50 percent of GDP and that such a level is maintained forever.[12] If the rate of return delivered to the public budget is 7 percent, total expenditures for the social dividend will equal three and a half percentage points of GDP. For the United States this would imply today a social dividend of about two thousand dollars per person per year.[13] This is far from sufficient to cover the cost of living but, especially for earners at the bottom of the distribution and large families, it would substantially contribute to improving living conditions. The poverty rate would mechanically decrease by about one-third. Using household data from the PSID and the NBER's tax-simulation model (called TAXSIM), we see that in 2012 the share of the U.S. population living below the U.S. Census Bureau's officially defined poverty lines was about 9 percent—and that a social dividend equal to three and a half percentage points of per-capita GDP would have reduced this to 6 percent.

In addition to directly affecting income distribution, the social dividend would reduce inequality by strengthening low-skilled workers' bargaining power vis-à-vis employers. Since the social dividend especially improves the fallback option of the working poor, they can be expected to strike better pay bargains. This would empower vulnerable groups that are often left behind both economically and politically.

Setting up this SWF would require an institutional framework that ensures both efficiency and democratic accountability.[14] I propose that the SWF display the following three distinctive features. First, it should be so transparent that the citizens can easily monitor its investment strategy and its performance relative to that of other funds. Second, the SWF should be a faithful expression of the aspirations of the citizenry.

Those aspirations are not limited to increasing the purchasing power of individuals. They also mirror deep concerns about the quality of human relationships in society and of humanity's relationship to nature. This broader view of the common good should be acknowledged by subjecting the fund's investment decisions to ethical requirements determined by a democratic process. This means the SWF would be prohibited from investing in companies that violate those ethical standards.[15] This would entail a recurring debate on endorsed values and social goals that would counteract political apathy and strengthen feelings of communality. As far as its portfolio management is concerned, the SWF would be similar to the socially responsible investment funds that have proliferated worldwide over the last two decades. While this may come at some cost in terms of financial returns, that cost would be minimized by a sufficiently large universe of investable stocks.[16] The large size of its portfolio would make this ethical SWF a prominent financial investor. Thus, its ethical criteria would not merely be the expression of a collective identity. They would also powerfully influence companies to pay more attention to the impact of their decisions on things like peacekeeping, environmental sustainability, and respect for human rights. Third, the SWF should be shielded from interference by both the government and the corporate sector; the necessity to avoid capture is obvious. I will discuss the need for independence from the government more fully below, since it arises even more acutely with regard to a second institution I will propose.[17] In terms of the prospect of capture by the corporate sector, the danger is that large enterprises and the financial industry will see opportunities to profit by manipulating the SWF's investment decisions. This suggests that the SWF's staff should include civil servants and that strict rules must be designed to minimize the risk of capture through revolving doors. Depending on country-specific conditions, it might make sense to put a relatively low cap on the investment of the SWF in domestic firms or, at least, in domestic firms that are large relative to the domestic economy. This raises issues of definition and measurement—for example, of ownership chains—that are not new to existing SWFs and can be tackled.[18]

The social dividend received by citizens would originate in the uncertain returns earned by the stock portfolio managed by the SWF.

While stock returns are volatile, introducing a social dividend need not increase the income risk carried by citizens. For one thing, the SWF would distribute its income to the government, and the government's budget could be used to smooth the payments to citizens. For example, in times of supernormal returns these could be used by the government to buy back the country's public debt and build a reserve to ensure the payments of stable social dividends in times of subnormal returns.[19] For another, a parliament could instruct the SWF to maximize its risk-adjusted return, assessed from the viewpoint of a representative private household. To the extent that the SWF was able to invest in stocks whose returns were negatively correlated with the country's national income, the social dividend would actually reduce volatility in private households' total incomes.

I recommend granting citizens the option to reinvest their social dividends in the SWF through personal accounts instead of having them paid out on a regular basis. In this way, one could finance sabbatical years during the middle part of one's life and an annuity in old age.

Setting up a sabbatical account could be a choice offered to every citizen upon reaching adulthood, which would entail allowing social dividends to accumulate for some specified number of time—perhaps nine years. During that period, the social dividends that would otherwise be paid out are instead reinvested in the SWF.[20] At the end, the holder of the account would receive the capitalized social dividends, a sum that would roughly suffice to finance a sabbatical year. This could be spent volunteering in the social economy, engaging in politics, or gaining new knowledge as part of a commitment to lifelong learning. As a result, pursuits such as these might become more usual in most people's lives and generate far-reaching positive externalities. Protections could be put in place to ensure that employees could return to prior jobs after taking unpaid leaves to engage in such sabbatical activities.

Starting at a later age—say, forty—citizens might choose to reinvest their social dividends in old-age-provision accounts instead of sabbatical accounts. The SWF could offer accounts with different lock-in periods; options might include twenty, twenty-five, and thirty years. Countries especially determined to fight old-age poverty might even decide to make such old-age-provision accounts compulsory. At the end of the stipulated period, the accumulated amount would be transformed into an annuity, yielding income the citizen would receive along with the social dividend; both would be tax-exempted and not to be credited against social benefits. In countries severely hit by demographic aging, this form of saving would complement existing pay-as-you-go pension systems and avoid the high asset-management fees typically demanded by private insurance companies. Furthermore, as this method of providing retirement income would not be linked to employment and the payment of social security contributions, it would not suffer from limited coverage. It would be available to everyone.[21]

Establishing such an ethical SWF and distributing a social dividend would thus not only help reduce inequality but also rejuvenate public spiritedness, foster social freedom, and support universal old-age provision. At the same time, it would inaugurate a collective learning process about the management of public wealth. The institution of the SWF suits this learning process well because its task is relatively well-understood. Moreover, international experiences already exist upon which the polity can draw as it sets up the institution and learns to manage public wealth efficiently. I mentioned above the passive role that public capital plays in firms the SWF chooses for its investment portfolio. Once the polity has learned to properly manage the SWF, public capital should start playing an active role. A novel institution should be created that challenges capitalists on their own terrain, by contending with them for the control of large firms.

FEDERAL SHAREHOLDER

A well-managed SWF can effectively counteract the developments (1) and (2) mentioned at the outset of this blueprint. But changes would not necessarily follow with respect to (3). That is, it would not be a safeguard against the gradual subversion of democracy by a wealthy oligarchy. Large corporations and banks, and the lobbies that represent them, are also the main devices employed by the members of the moneyed elite to coordinate their endeavors and foster their interests in the public debate and the political arena. If the polity were only to own a few shares but not to exercise any control in those corporations, the moneyed elite would still be able to translate its wealth into political power, thus fundamentally undermining the democratic ideals of equality and participation.[22]

Therefore, the second stage of the strategy I propose entails the activation of public ownership in selected domestic companies. The beginning of that stage would be determined by a law setting up a novel public institution explicitly designed to control business enterprises. I have coined the term *federal shareholder* to refer to such an institution.

The federal shareholder's initial financial endowment would stem from the SWF, from which it would likely also inherit some of its staff. The federal shareholder would use its endowment in order to acquire a majority stake in selected companies. Its first task would thus be to identify the companies that were amenable to public control. These would mainly be publicly-quoted companies that were under scrutiny by the SWF for some time, were found to be relatively badly managed, and became targets of hostile takeovers by the federal shareholder. Badly managed corporations often survive thanks to lobbying and political protection, and usually have plenty of technically competent employees who are dissatisfied with the current management and thus lack proper motivation. Hence, these are corporations where there is high potential to raise economic value, curb rent-seeking activities, and combat plutocracy. The process of activating public ownership in the economy should be based on efficiency considerations and occur gradually. Therefore, the parliament should cap the initial capital endowment made available to the federal shareholder for taking control of the firms. In its first years, only a tiny fraction of the sector of large firms would come under the control of the federal shareholder.

The federal shareholder could also acquire firms that were not publicly quoted and could also create new firms—for instance, in oligopoly-dominated industries. For reasons to be explained shortly, all firms of the federal shareholder should, however, go public within a certain time frame. After some time, the federal shareholder's ownership stakes in those firms should equal 51 percent of their capital and that level should be maintained as long as the firm is under public control. The corresponding shares would be frozen in state ownership while the remaining ones would be freely traded in the stock market. This is similar to the "x percent" version of market socialism; the firms of the federal shareholder would display a mixed ownership structure and the federal shareholder would be their majority shareholder. Under the terms of the law governing stock corporations, the federal shareholder would exercise leadership in the boards of directors or supervisory boards through its own personnel. The federal shareholder would require well-trained specialist staff: it should be a center of excellence for issues of corporate governance, investment analysis, financing, and risk management. It should offer its staff interesting long-term career prospects and foster a sense of belonging and mission.

The mission of the federal shareholder should be clearly stated: profit maximization. Its firms are not utilities operating under natural monopoly but players competing in global markets. Hence, profit maximization is called for on efficiency grounds. The dividends from shares owned by the federal shareholder would accrue to the government's budget and be earmarked for the social dividend—along with the income generated by the SWF.

It might seem strange that the federal shareholder should retain the same profit goal that capitalists have—although its profits benefit the whole citizenry via the social dividend—and not pursue any other social goal. But the experience of public firms in several countries shows that charging them with social goals usually means confronting their managers with vaguely defined and ever-changing objectives. This erodes managers' accountability, makes it almost impossible to evaluate their performance, and deprives them of a sense of responsibility. In competitive markets, insisting that public firms be controlled by politicians is a proven recipe for financial and economic disaster. It is much better to incorporate social and environmental desiderata in the general legal frameworks—the regulatory and tax systems—that apply to all firms, regardless of their ownership. Furthermore, it is advisable to cultivate a pluralistic economic environment that supports widespread entrepreneurship, small firms, and not-for-profit entities and that is responsive to people's varying demands for socially responsible forms of work, consumption, and investment. Crucially, while the *objective* of the firms under the federal shareholder's control should be the same as the alleged objective of capitalist firms, the firms' *behavior* would be systematically different in the two sectors. I will take up this point shortly.

The firms of the federal shareholder would be quoted on the stock market and the federal shareholder should retain only 51 percent of their shares. Private ownership of the remaining 49 percent has a key role to play in creating an incentive structure that leads those public firms to maximize profits. Since private investors would be free to buy and sell shares in the companies of the federal shareholder, the share price would reflect the market view of how well these enterprises' managers were performing. Hence, the information contained in the movement of share prices could be used to encourage the managers of the public firms to pursue profit maximization. The novel stake of the polity in this matter implies that much more attention than today would be devoted to a careful regulation of the stock market and the design of appropriate incentive schemes for managers. That is, the reliance of the polity on the stock market for managing its capital would foster regulatory attempts to fully exploit the stock market's potential to act as a discovery and information-generating device.

The second reason for having private minority ownership of the federal shareholder's firms relates to the need that any pluralistic society has for an array of checks and balances. Private shareholders could form associations, and those associations would constitute influential interest groups putting pressure on the management of the federal shareholder's firms to operate as profitably as possible.

If the federal shareholder is to fulfill its mission of maximizing long-run profits, it must be insulated from political pressures exerted by the government of the day. For instance, if a public firm were making losses and mass layoffs were necessary to restore its ability to compete, the federal shareholder should be free to restructure the firm even if the government opposed it.[23] Granting the federal shareholder this type of autonomy would require a set of constitutional norms concerning the appointment and removal of its trustees and staff as well as their duties and prerogatives. I suggest that the federal shareholder be endowed with a degree of political independence similar to the one enjoyed by some central banks—for example, the Bundesbank in Germany. This would ensure that public firms under the federal shareholder's control could not be abused by the government to accommodate special interests in view of the next election. This combination of clear mission and political independence is a necessary precondition for successful management of the public capital invested through the federal shareholder.

Since the federal shareholder contributes to finance the social dividend, every citizen is a stakeholder of that institution. Hence, it would be in the public interest to scrutinize the federal shareholder's performance, implying a duty of transparency on the federal shareholder's part. Supporting its monitoring by the media and general public there should be an institutional supervision by an already existing authority—for example, the central bank or the ministry of finance. In particular, that monitoring agency would publish the financial results of the companies under federal shareholder control along with the results achieved by relevant benchmark groups of companies. Furthermore, a portion of the remuneration paid to the federal shareholder's staff would be performance-related—that is, dependent on the relative performance of the controlled companies.

All arrangements described so far aim at enforcing profit maximization by this novel public institution in charge of controlling firms. But for profit maximization to be good for society as a whole, it should not be pursued at the expense of employees or consumers or to the detriment of the natural environment; it should be the result of increased production efficiency and successful innovations. Regulations designed to internalize externalities and enforce fair-market competition (and thereby protect employees, consumers, and the natural environment) should be enforced with respect to both public and private firms. But firms under the federal shareholder's control should be subject to additional checks by trade unions, consumer protection agencies, and environmental associations—all acting as watchdogs on behalf of civil society. This would help to avoid instances of political protection in favor of public firms. By way of example, more intense monitoring by consumer protection agencies would counteract a government's temptation to increase public firms' profits by adopting a lax attitude toward anticompetitive behavior; more intense monitoring by environmental associations would make it harder for a government to neglect the manipulation of emission tests by a state-owned car producer.

The additional information rights of civil society would be defined by a law granting its organizations easier ways to monitor the federal shareholder's firms and assess their compliance with regulatory norms. For that monitoring purpose, trade unions could enter a labor syndicate, consumer protection agencies a consumer syndicate, and environmental associations a natural-environment syndicate. Each syndicate would autonomously elect representatives to be sent as watchdogs to the various firms of the federal shareholder. The task of those representatives would be to inform their syndicate about firm behavior in possible violation of existing regulatory norms—so that the syndicate's members could initiate opposition to that behavior. Those watchdogs would also have the right to transmit to their syndicates information on firm behavior that, while not technically illegal, might be objectionable from a civil society point of view. For instance, they might reveal that a federal shareholder firm operates utterly unsafe production plants in a foreign country that lacks proper security standards. They would be prohibited, however, from revealing any business secrets gleaned by their monitoring activities that could be used by a firm's competitors. In such a case, the syndicate that sent the watchdog at fault would also be held responsible and could be sued by the damaged firm.

I now come to another key behavioral difference between the firms under the control of the federal shareholder and the capitalist firms, which explains why the firms of the federal shareholder may reasonably be described as *public-democratic firms*. Recall that the federal shareholder's instruction to its firms to maximize their profits is the same instruction capitalists give to their firms. The behavior of the public firms would differ, however, in the extent to which they involved and empowered their employees in firm governance. The federal shareholder staff representatives on supervisory boards would seek to revive the role of worker participation and to foster employees' sense of identification with their firms and the federal shareholder—the public institution embodying the polity's endeavor to rid itself of capitalist dominance. This participation by workers in the management of public firms, through works councils and other agencies of codetermination, would be a major difference between public and private firms.

It is often true that a capitalist firm tries to increase its employees' identification with the firm. But, as a rule, firms make no deep appeals to the common good or to a project of social transformation. The employees of publicly-owned firms can thus be expected to exhibit more altruism than the employees of private firms towards their employers.[24] That is, the employees of a federal shareholder's firm would be especially willing to exert extra efforts to help their firm thrive. High levels of identification with a firm can in turn mitigate the problems so often associated with mechanisms to engage workforces by giving them more voice. Typically, capitalists give worker institutions within firms less power than is socially optimal because of this desire not to be "held up" by them. At the margin, granting more codetermination to workers in a capitalist firm is likely to increase labor productivity by improving communication flows inside the firm. But codetermination also improves the ability of workers to self-organize for bargaining purposes and, ex post, it allows them to reap a larger share of the surplus generated by the firm. Therefore, capitalists fail to set up institutions of worker participation that maximize production efficiency, and even in this narrow sense they empower workers too little.[25]

Enhanced altruism toward employers, in the case of the federal shareholder's firms, works as a commitment device that lessens the hold-up problem by reducing the share of the pie demanded ex post by the workers. Since the extent of worker participation in capitalist firms is inefficiently low, once one of them is acquired by the federal shareholder, productivity can be increased by setting up institutions that generate greater worker involvement. At the same time, public ownership makes employees identify more closely with the company they work for. Since this reduces the share of the surplus demanded by employees in wage negotiations, establishing more codetermination also ultimately pushes up firm profits. Therefore, the requirement that the federal shareholder put special emphasis on promoting worker participation is not an additional, competing goal of that institution but rather a distinctive channel through which it should pursue the primary goal of profit maximization—and a means by which the federal shareholder's public-democratic firms might well be able to outperform capitalist firms.[26]

The capitalists thus deprived of corporate control would no longer be in a position to exert major influence on political decision making. This would help to break the vicious circle of increasing wealth concentration and political capture. However, the *economic power* formerly enjoyed by capitalists and their managers does not dissolve once control is transferred to the federal shareholder. That power simply takes a new form. Private controlling shareholders are replaced by representatives of the federal shareholder; the firms' managers now cooperate with works councils; and trade unions, consumer protection agencies, and environmental associations have supplementary information rights.

Despite these changes, one might be concerned that the federal shareholder's firms would be large organizations instructed to maximize profits, and that such organizations might be tempted to use their economic power to distort the political process in much the same way capitalist firms do. Large firms under the control of the federal shareholder would indeed be likely to exert some special influence on the political process, but it would markedly differ from the power exerted by today's corporations. Capitalist firms, coordinated by their associations and lobbies, devote considerable resources to advancing the interests of the capitalist class in the political arena. An example is the generous contributions they make to politicians and think-tanks that actively promote the repeal of estate taxes. The federal shareholder staff who replace the capitalists in firm supervision would expend virtually no effort on such an objective. Given their different social backgrounds and personal economic situations, the federal shareholder's representatives would not disproportionately gain from estate tax repeal. More generally, it is not only the owners of capitalist firms who hail from the wealthiest fractiles of the population; the CEOs these owners recruit also tend to be similar to them, drawn also from the upper class. In public firms and public institutions the social backgrounds of board members tend to be much more diverse.[27] We can expect therefore that the endorsed values and political ideals of those in control of public-democratic firms would be more progressive than those of capitalists and the managers they hire. Their impact on the political process would thus also be more progressive in nature.

Nowadays, corporations often buy political influence to secure policy measures that increase their profits. Examples include polluting industries demanding to be exempted from ecological taxes, banks demanding light capital regulations, agricultural conglomerates demanding protection through tariffs, oil companies demanding military interventions in oil-rich countries, and car producers demanding no reductions of highway speed limits. The increase in profits comes with an increased amount of some public bad. The lobbying firms get the profits, and society at large carries the costs associated with the public bad. Would firms under the federal shareholder's control lobby less for policies that would increase their own profits at the public's expense? I think so. The federal shareholder would be a public institution with a raison d'être that transcended profit maximization; it would exist to help create a society where equal democratic participation was not thwarted by the overwhelming economic power of the wealthy. Thus, one might expect the federal shareholder staff on the boards of firms to have internalized the value of democracy and therefore to experience feelings of guilt if and when they tried to subvert democracy to boost firm profits. They would also condemn such behavior in others, including their colleagues. This implies that the firms of the federal shareholder would be less prone than their capitalist counterparts to buy political favors that would do no favor to the majority of the population.

One might argue that the public-democratic firms' reduced propensity to lobby would backfire by negatively affecting their competitive edge relative to the capitalist firms. This need not be the case for two reasons. First, socially responsible consumers would likely recognize lobbying as socially harmful and therefore decide to vote with their wallets in favor of public-democratic firms—knowing those firms would be unlikely to lobby for a public bad. The same individuals, as investors, might similarly discriminate in favor of public-democratic firms' stocks when making portfolio decisions. By the same token, their voting with their wallets might more than cover the costs for public-democratic firms to provide extra information to trade unions, consumer protection organizations, and environmental groups. Second, lobbying typically triggers an increase of profits at the level of an entire industry rather than for a single firm, and firms cannot be excluded from industry profits on the basis of their lobbying efforts. For instance, the lack of general speed limits on Germany's highways benefits all producers of relatively fast cars, independent of their connections to the German government. This means that the federal shareholder's firms refraining from lobbying would still free-ride on the lobbying efforts of their capitalist competitors.

A priori, it is unclear how well the public-democratic firms would perform in comparison with capitalistic corporations. The establishment of the federal shareholder should therefore be viewed as an open-ended challenge to determine the polity's ability to replace capitalist control of large firms with public-democratic control. Conventional wisdom takes for granted the superiority of private control of firms, but this belief is grounded in the perceived behavior of owner-entrepreneurs in small and medium-sized businesses. As far as large firms are concerned, claims of such superiority are far-fetched.[28] Capitalistic corporations are often plagued by governance problems. They are sometimes run by incompetent heirs who love to exert power on other people, occasionally they are preyed upon by their own managers, and in general they fail to reap the full gains they could by empowering their employees and giving them voice. It is by no means obvious that large firms under active public ownership and governed by well-designed incentive structures could not beat capitalists on their own ground—that is, in terms of rates of return.

The final partition of the corporate sector between private-capitalist and public-democratic control should not be set in advance. Rather, it should be the outcome of a collective learning process. Once the federal shareholder was established and the first few corporations placed under its control, a market-driven selection process would follow that would lead in time to an optimized partition. Given a level playing field where both forms of governance could compete fairly on even terms, and externalities were internalized, their relative profitability would mirror their relative efficiency. The more profitable governance form would expand and the other would shrink, until the efficient partition was arrived at. In the course of this process, the more efficient companies would be more profitable, and the higher returns they offer would mean that their shares were more in demand; consequently more capital would flow into the more efficient companies, and their market share would grow. If these were the public-democratic firms, this would help prevent democracy from turning into plutocracy and promote worker participation in the management of firms.

Should the federal shareholder eventually turn out to be too successful—that is, if a large fraction of the corporate sector became public-democratic—the polity might want to reform the institutional framework of public ownership so as to dilute the economic power embodied in the federal shareholder and foster pluralism in corporate control. At that stage, various routes could be taken. One possibility would be to distribute the stocks of the federal shareholder to myriad municipally-owned investment funds, as proposed by Leland Stauber. Those locally-owned funds would then act independently in a competitive market for corporate control. Another possibility would be to distribute the stocks of the federal shareholder directly to the individual citizens—however, in a way that prevents the resurgence of capitalistic dominance. John Roemer figured out how to accomplish this by redenominating the stocks in a special currency used only in the stock market, distributing that currency equally among the individuals when they enter adulthood, and socializing their stock portfolios when the individuals pass away.

BUILDING A STOCK OF PUBLIC CAPITAL

Readers who think that the evolutionary approach sketched above could contribute to solve problems (1)–(3) may want to step back and consider the problem of putting in place the initial level of public capital. The novel SWF should be endowed with a stocks portfolio amounting to some thirty to fifty points of GDP. How might the government finance the corresponding public expenditures? Assuming no windfalls from natural resources, I propose that the government turn to three main sources of financing: privatizations, government bonds, and an inheritance tax. As argued below, this would allow the government to gradually build the required capital stock at small social costs.

The first source of financing would be proceeds from *privatizations*—which might include sales of emission rights, licences for the use of airwaves, and gold reserves. Its relevance would be highly country-specific and dependent on circumstances. In some countries, various assets are in public ownership because of historical reasons that are no longer compelling. As an example, seeing strong trends in urbanization, several countries built large public capital stocks in the form of flats to be rented at special conditions to the needy. Today, that kind of public ownership may be no longer warranted to the same extent and the size of the stock may be considerably reduced. Other countries still have significant public ownership in manufacturing and infrastructure industries. To the extent that the strategic reasons that motivated it are no longer valid, some of that property may be used to endow the SWF.

As a second source of financing, the government should consider issuing new *public debt*. Globally, the real interest rate has declined over the last three decades and in triple-A countries the long-run real interest rate on government bonds is now close to zero.[29] This makes government debt a valuable option to finance the SWF. As long as the interest rate paid by the government remained lower than the growth rate of GDP, the debt incurred to endow the SWF would keep decreasing relative to GDP; it would eventually vanish in relative terms if that situation persisted indefinitely. In this case, the issuing of new public debt would raise no concerns of debt sustainability.

If the current low level of interest rates proved temporary, the interest rate on government bonds would likely be higher than the growth rate in the future. But even in that case, countries with a high financial standing might increase their gross public debt to endow the SWF without affecting debt sustainability. Why? Because the interest rate on government debt could be expected to be considerably lower than the rate of return earned by the SWF on its stocks. Then, the government could announce that the income of the SWF would be prioritized to cover its interest payments. If, for example, the stocks in public ownership yielded over the long term a rate of return of 8 percent and the interest paid on government bonds was 2 percent, one-fourth of that rate of return would suffice to cover the government's refinancing costs. With some GDP growth, this implies again that the incurred debt would asymptotically vanish in relation to GDP. Since the difference between the rate of return on the stocks and the interest rate on government debt would be used for the social dividend, this strategy is tantamount to socializing the equity risk premium. According to Rajnish Mehra, the equity risk premium in the past century used to be in the range of 7–9 percent.[30]

If this were not enough to maintain a country's financial reputation, the government could announce that the obtained net financial return would be prioritized for paying down the debt incurred to set up the SWF. After a period of fifteen to twenty years, the new borrowing to purchase the stocks would almost certainly have been repaid and the gross public debt of the country would then have returned to its initial level. Only then would citizens begin receiving the social dividend.

The three scenarios depicted above entail no increase of the debt-to-GDP ratio in the long run. Alternatively, the formation of public capital could come along with a permanent increase of that ratio. In several countries, demographic change brings about long-lasting increases in private households' demand for safe assets to finance consumption during retirement. It is plausible that this rise of savings could not be matched by an equal increase of economically meaningful real investments and should be accommodated by means of a higher public debt.[31] Liquid, inflation-indexed long-term government bonds would offer households a reliable instrument to smooth their consumption over time, while being a cheap form of debt financing for the government.[32]

In the case of a large country, such an issuance of new public debt could have a first-order effect on the worldwide supply of fixed-income securities, causing the equilibrium level of the risk-free interest rate to increase.[33] Under present conditions, this effect would likely be moderate. The risk-free interest rate is close to zero and at that level the demand for risk-free assets is almost flat. By continuity, this suggests that a first-order addition to the offer of risk-free financial assets would likely produce a small effect on the interest rate.[34] In turn, a moderate increase of interest rates would likely generate positive macroeconomic effects by reducing the risk that monetary policymakers would be constrained by the zero lower bound on the nominal interest rate, and by decreasing the risk of financial instability.[35]

A progressive *inheritance tax* is the third source of financing I suggest. Its yearly revenues could be earmarked to endow the SWF until it reached the desired size. Especially because of demographic change, the revenue potential of the inheritance tax is predicted to increase faster than GDP in many advanced economies over the next few decades.[36] In that time span, even a moderate average tax rate would allow the polity to build a relatively large SWF.

A highly progressive inheritance tax would directly reduce the concentration of wealth. Since an inheritance tax hits wealth that is inherited rather than self-made, it expresses the meritocratic values that underpin modern democracies and that are endorsed by most people across the entire political spectrum. Instead of accruing just to a minority of lucky heirs, a share of each of the largest estates would thus be used to form public capital for the benefit of all.

The proposed tax would have a generous exemption threshold shielding the vast majority of small inheritors from taxation, and would feature a rising marginal tax rate, depending on relatedness, that might get close to fifty percent for the top bracket. Empirical investigations suggest that such an inheritance tax could be designed such that it scarcely affected the accumulation decisions of individuals. This would be due in part to the fact that most superrich do not keep accumulating wealth in order to allow their heirs to lead more comfortable lives. Their primary driver is rather a desire to excel in comparison to other superrich. This drive to accumulate wealth would barely be affected by such an inheritance tax.[37]

Finally, a highly progressive inheritance tax would play a useful role as a stabilizer of the stock market. Especially in the case of a large country, stock purchases on the order of some GDP points could generate a stock-market bubble. Moreover, by reducing the returns on the purchased stock, a rise of stock prices would reduce the government's net financial gain from issuing debt to acquire stocks. A highly progressive inheritance tax would counteract this effect by increasing the net supply of stocks in the market. Stock ownership at death is highly concentrated in the largest estates. Hitting them with a high tax rate would prompt inheritors to sell a part of the inherited stock to pay their taxes, which would negatively affect the price of stocks and diminish the risk of a stock-market bubble.

Summing up, putting in place a SWF would not need to strain public finances. A mix of privatizations, new government debt, and a progressive inheritance tax could be used to gradually build a substantial amount of public capital at negligible social costs. Needless to say, different countries might want to choose different combinations of those financing sources, depending on country-specific circumstances.

A high level of wealth inequality is a threat to both shared prosperity and democracy. Public capital can play a crucial role in counteracting that threat. It can generate a social dividend for every citizen and it can spur individuals' participation in their workplaces and the political arena. By doing these things, public capital can break the vicious circle of increasing wealth concentration and political capture, contribute to more equality of opportunity, and reduce the transaction costs of financial investment. The role of public capital should be enhanced through a carefully designed evolutionary process of institution-building. That process should start with the creation of a socially responsible SWF that acts as a collective rentier, investing worldwide in stocks so that every citizen shares in the high returns generated by the stock market. If this institution proved successful, a second one should be introduced that activates public ownership by contesting capitalists' control over some large firms. I have called that institution the federal shareholder. It would empower the employees of the firms it controls, enhance their transparency, and inject a more progressive mood in the political discourse. Together, the socially responsible SWF and the federal shareholder would considerably rebalance people's access to material goods, social recognition, and autonomy and lead to a more pluralistic market economy—one more attuned to the democratic values of a truly open society.

NOTES

1. Emmanuel Saez and Gabriel Zucman, "Wealth Inequality in the United States since 1913: Evidence from Capitalized Income Tax Data," *Quarterly Journal of Economics* 131 (2016): 519–578.

2. Thomas Piketty and Gabriel Zucman, "Wealth and Inheritance in the Long Run," in *Handbook of Income Distribution*, vol. 2B (Amsterdam: Elsevier, 2015).

3. See, for example, Thomas Piketty, *Capital in the Twenty-First Century* (Cambridge, MA: Harvard University Press, 2014), chap. 12; and Anthony B. Atkinson, *Inequality* (Cambridge, MA: Harvard University Press, 2015), chap. 6.

4. See Piketty and Zucman, "Wealth and Inheritance in the Long Run."

5. See, for example, Lawrence Lessig, *Republic, Lost* (New York: Twelve, 2011); Joseph E. Stiglitz, *The Price of Inequality* (New York: Norton, 2012), chap. 5; John Nichols and Robert W. McChesney, *Dollarocracy* (New York: Nation Books, 2014).

6. Mathias Trabandt and Harald Uhlig, "The Laffer Curve Revisited," *Journal of Monetary Economics* 58 (2011): 305–327.

7. See, in particular, Richard Dagger, "Neo-Republicanism and the Civic Economy," *Politics, Philosophy & Economics* 5 (2006): 151–173 on republicanism; and Luigino Bruni and Stefano Zamagni, *Civil Economy: Efficiency, Equity, Public Happiness* (Oxford: Peter Lang, 2007) on the civil-economy paradigm.

8. This perspective on redistribution has received scant attention by public economics, which rather focuses on how taxes and transfers should be set to solve the equity-efficiency tradeoff. The role of public ownership is investigated by the literature on incomplete contracting, but its focus is on issues of micro-governance rather than society-wide inequality.

9. Giacomo Corneo, "Public Capital in the 21st Century," *Social Europe Journal* (2014), Research Essay 2 discusses the potential role of a SWF from a European perspective. Anthony B. Atkinson, *Inequality* (Cambridge, MA: Harvard University Press, 2015) proposes a SWF for the UK. A related proposal was put forward by Nobel laureate James Meade in *Efficiency, Equality, and the Ownership of Property* (Cambridge, MA: Harvard University Press, 1965). An overview on existing SWFs is offered by Alberto Quadrio Curzio and Valeria Miceli in *Sovereign Wealth Funds: A Complete Guide to State-Owned Investment Funds* (Petersfield, UK: Harriman House, 2010).

10. The entitlement may be contingent on a minimum number of years of main residence in the country. Persons under the age of eighteen could be entitled to half of the regular social dividend.

11. Private households in their majority do not invest in stocks despite their high mean return—which constitutes a "participation puzzle" from the viewpoint of traditional models in financial economics. The literature has put forward various explanations for this puzzle: beyond fixed participation costs, lack of familiarity, loss aversion, narrow framing, and limited cognitive ability contribute to explain why many households are unwilling to participate in the stock market. See Nicholas Barberis and Ming Huang, "The Loss Aversion / Narrow Framing Approach to the Equity Premium Puzzle," in

Handbook of the Equity Premium, ed. Mehra, Rajnish (Amsterdam: Elsevier, 2008); Luigi Guiso, Paola Sapienza, and Luigi Zingales, "Trusting the Stock Market," *Journal of Finance* 63 (2008): 2557–2600; and Mark Grinblatt, Matti Keloharju, and Juhani Linnainmaa, "IQ and Stock Market Participation," *Journal of Finance* 66 (2011): 2121–2164.

12. By comparison, the market value of Norway's SWF is about twice that country's GDP.

13. This is a similar order of magnitude as the social dividend that is currently paid out by the Alaska Permanent Fund. That SWF was set up in 1976 by a liberal Republican governor, who introduced it after a referendum. Meanwhile, Alaska has gone from being the state with the most unequal income distribution to being one of the states with the lowest poverty and inequality in the United States. See Scott Goldsmith, "The Economic and Social Impacts of the Permanent Fund Dividend on Alaska," in *Alaska's Permanent Fund Dividend,* ed. K. Widerquist and M. W. Howard (New York: Palgrave Macmillan, 2012); and Guy Standing, *A Precariat Charter* (London: Bloomsbury Academic, 2014).

14. Abdullah Al-Hassan, Michael Papaioannou, Martin Skancke, and Cheng Chih Sung, "Sovereign Wealth Funds: Aspects of Governance Structures and Investment Management," Working Paper 13/231 (International Monetary Fund, 2013), discusses various alternative governance structures for SWFs.

15. This is already the case in Norway. There, a Council of Ethics assesses whether specific companies should be excluded from the universe of potential stocks available for investment. Contributing to violations of human rights, promoting war, causing environmental damage, and fostering corruption are among the reasons that may lead a company to be excluded.

16. This is suggested by empirical findings in John Nofsinger and Abhishek Varma, "Socially Responsible Funds and Market Crises," Mimeo, 2012; and Leonardo Becchetti, Rocco Ciciretti, Ambrogio Dalo, and Stefano Herzel, "Socially Responsible and Conventional Investment Funds: Performance Comparison and the Global Financial Crisis," Working Paper 04_14 (Rimini Centre for Economic Analysis, 2014). The latter also discuss informational reasons why, adjusting for risk, socially responsible funds perform similarly to conventional unconstrained funds.

17. Shai Bernstein, Josh Lerner, and Antoinette Shoar, "The Investment Strategies of Sovereign Wealth Funds," *Journal of Economic Perspectives* 27 (2013): 219–238, shows that SWFs exposed to political influences are likely to exhibit major deviations from long-run return maximization.

18. See, for example, Erik Dietzenbacher and Umed Temurshoev, "Ownership Relations in the Presence of Cross-Shareholding," *Journal of Economics*

95 (2008): 189–212; and Victor Dorofeenko, Larry Lang, Klaus Ritzberger, and Jamsheed Shorish, "Who Controls Allianz?," *Annals of Finance* 4 (2008): 75–103.

19. As a by-product, this would help to stabilize the stock market.

20. The rate of return would be the one used by the government to set the social dividend. Hence it would depend on expected future returns rather than on the actual returns earned by the SWF. This would substantially reduce the risk burden carried by persons who chose to have their social dividends accumulate in their accounts.

21. Empirical findings on lifetime earnings inequality in Germany (Timm Bönke, Giacomo Corneo, and Holger Lüthen, "Lifetime Earnings Inequality in Germany," *Journal of Labor Economics* 33 [2015]: 171–208) and long-term earnings inequality in the United States. (Wojciech Kopczuk, Emmanuel Saez, and Jae Song, "Earnings Inequality and Mobility in the United States: Evidence From Social Security Data Since 1937," *Quarterly Journal of Economics* 125 [2010]: 91–128) suggest that younger cohorts find it increasingly difficult to save for retirement out of their wage income, especially the low-skilled.

22. Randall Morck, Daniel Wolfenzon, and Bernard Yeung, "Corporate Governance, Economic Entrenchment, and Growth," *Journal of Economic Literature* XLIII (2005): 655–720, discusses why political influence depends on what one controls, rather than what one owns, and surveys the literature on the economic distortions it creates.

23. I assume that decent unemployment benefits and effective labor market policies are in place.

24. This may occur because altruists self-select in the public firms and / or because altruism is increased by the sense of mission attached to the federal shareholder.

25. See Richard Freeman and Edward Lazear, "An Economic Analysis of Works Councils," in *Work Councils,* ed. J. Rogers and W. Streeck (Chicago: University of Chicago Press, 1995). Mandatory codetermination in Germany is an example of far-reaching worker empowerment that has been forced upon companies having more than five hundred employees. The empirical literature suggests that it has small but positive effects on productivity and innovation—as measured by patents—and no negative effects on profitability. See John T. Addison and Claus Schnabel, "Worker Directors: A German Product that Did Not Export?," *Industrial Relations* 50 (2011): 354–374.

26. Since the optimal extent of worker participation is likely to be firm-specific, the firms of the federal shareholder should be free to choose the institutions through which they want to implement more worker participation. For instance, the federal shareholder could offer a menu of codetermination charters

from which each firm may select the one that is expected to generate the highest profit over the long run.

27. See, for example, Michael Hartmann, *Eliten und Macht in Europa* (Frankfurt: Campus, 2007).

28. Acknowledging this, the OECD has recently released guidelines on the governance of public firms (*OECD Guidelines on Corporate Governance of State-Owned Enterprises* [Paris: OECD, 2015]).

29. See, for example, Mervyin King and David Low, "Measuring the 'World' Real Interest Rate," Working Paper 19887 (National Bureau of Economic Research [NBER], 2014).

30. Rajnish Mehra, *Handbook of the Equity Premium* (Amsterdam: Elsevier, 2008). Retrospectively, stocks have very rarely underperformed bonds over periods of time of two or three decades. Of course, the time at which the SWF purchases its stocks should be a matter of concern. The power to tax allows a government to credibly promise to repay an incurred debt even in case of low stock returns, which explains why the same financial strategy cannot be adopted by individuals. As pointed out by Hal Varian in "Redistributive Taxation as Social Insurance," *Journal of Public Economics* 14 (1980): 49–68, income-related taxes work as an insurance device, spreading risks in a way that can be superior to incomplete financial markets. Capital-market imperfections—including the factors that explain the "stock market participation puzzle" mentioned above—imply that the bond-financed equity investment performed by the SWF can be welfare-increasing. See the general-equilibrium analyses in Simon Grant and John Quiggin, "The Risk Premium for Equity: Implications for the Proposed Diversification of the Social Security Fund," *American Economic Review* 92 (2002): 1104–1115; and Peter Diamond and John Geanakoplos, "Social Security Investment in Equities," *American Economic Review* 93 (2003): 1047–1074.

31. See Carl Christian von Weizsäcker, "Public Debt and Price Stability," *German Economic Review* 15 (2014): 42–61.

32. See, for example, John Campbell, Robert Shiller, and Luis Viceira, "Understanding Inflation-Indexed Bond Markets," Working Paper 15014 (NBER, 2009).

33. Under conditions of Ricardian equivalence there would be no effects as long as private investors had stocks in their portfolios that could be sold to buy the additional public debt. But in reality, various kinds of transaction costs severely constrain the financial investment of small savers and their ability to take risks. Ricardo J. Caballero and Emmanuel Farhi, "The Safety Trap," Working Paper No. 19927 (NBER, 2014). Mimeo, MIT and Harvard formalize the idea of a deflationary safety trap and show that swapping private

risky assets for public debt can stimulate the economy. Anat Admati and Martin Hellwig recommend forestalling various instances of moral hazard that characterize the behavior of financial intermediaries by requiring high levels of equity funding (*The Bankers' New Clothes* [Princeton, NJ: Princeton University Press, 2013]). The creation of a SWF that was financed by public debt and invested in stocks would promote such a change in the capital structure. It would also reduce the incentive for financial intermediaries to satisfy savers' demand by creating assets that were safe only on paper, which is to say, given an implicit state guarantee.

34. By way of an example, between 2008 and 2010 the level of the gross public debt of Germany increased by almost one-fourth or some fifteen GDP percentage points. During the same period of time, the financial costs of the German government did not increase, they decreased.

35. See, for example, Narayana Kocherlakota, "Public Debt and the Long-Run Neutral Real Interest Rate" (speech, Bank of Korea Conference, Seoul, South Korean, August 19, 2015).

36. See Piketty and Zucman, "Wealth and Inheritance in the Long Run."

37. See, for example, Wojciech Kopczuk's "Economics of Estate Taxation: A Brief Review of Theory and Evidence," *Tax Law Review* 63 (2009): 139–157, and "Taxation of Intergenerational Transfers and Wealth," *Handbook of Public Economics, Vol. 5.,* ed. Alan Auerbach, Raj Chetty, Martin Feldstein, and Emmanuel Saez (Amsterdam: Elsevier, 2013).

REFERENCES

QUOTED AND ADDITIONAL WORKS

More information on the topics covered in this book can be found in the references listed here.

CHAPTER 1

Bergstrom, Theodore. 1995. "On the Evolution of Altruistic Ethical Rules for Siblings." *American Economic Review* 85: 58–81.

Campanella, Tommaso. 2007. *The City of the Sun.* New York: Cosimo Classics.

Caraman, Philip. 1976. *The Lost Paradise.* New York: Seabury Press.

Gothein, Eberhard. 1883. *Der christlich-sociale Staat der Jesuiten in Paraguay.* Leipzig: Duncker & Humblot.

Nichols, John, and Robert McChesney. 2013. *Dollarocracy.* New York: Nation Books.

Persson, Torsten, and Guido Tabellini. 2000. *Political Economics.* Cambridge, MA: MIT Press.

Plato. 2006. *The Republic.* Translated by R. E. Allen. New Haven: Yale University Press.

CHAPTER 2

Kreps, David. 1997. "Intrinsic Motivation and Extrinsic Incentives." *American Economic Review* 87: 359–364.

Laffont, Jean-Jacques, and David Martimort. 2002. *The Theory of Incentives: The Principal-Agent Model.* Princeton, NJ: Princeton University Press.

More, Thomas. 2002. *Utopia.* Edited by George M. Logan and Robert M. Adams, rev. ed. New York: Cambridge University Press.

Pitzer, Donald. 1997. *America's Communal Utopias*. Chapel Hill: University of North Carolina Press.

Sutton, Robert. 2004. *Communal Utopias and the American Experience: Secular Communities*. Westport CT: Praeger.

CHAPTER 3

Alger, Ingela. 2010. "Public Goods Games, Altruism, and Evolution." *Journal of Public Economic Theory* 12: 789–813.

Bergstrom, Theodore, and Oded Stark. 1993. "How Altruism Can Prevail in an Evolutionary Environment." *American Economic Review* 83: 149–155.

Bester, Helmut, and Werner Güth. 1998. "Is Altruism Evolutionarily Stable?" *Journal of Economic Behavior & Organization* 34: 193 209.

Bowles, Samuel, and Herbert Gintis. 2011. *A Cooperative Species: Human Reciprocity and Its Evolution*. Princeton, NJ: Princeton University Press.

Boyd, Robert, and Peter Richerson. 2005. *The Origin and Evolution of Cultures*. Oxford: Oxford University Press.

Camerer, Colin. 2003. *Behavioral Game Theory: Experiments in Strategic Interactions*. Princeton, NJ: Princeton University Press.

Corneo, Giacomo, and Olivier Jeanne. 2010. "Symbolic Values, Occupational Choice, and Economic Development." *European Economic Review* 54: 237–251.

Fershtman, Chaim, and Yoram Weiss. 2000. "Why Do We Care What Others Think About Us?" In *Economics, Values and Organizations*, ed. A. Ben-Ner and L. Putterman. Cambridge: Cambridge University Press.

Frank, Robert. 1987. "If Homo Economicus Could Choose His Own Utility Function, Would He Want One with a Conscience?" *American Economic Review* 77: 593–604.

Fudenberg, Drew, and Jean Tirole. 1991. *Game Theory*. Cambridge MA: MIT Press.

Kolm, Serge-Christophe. 1984. *La bonne économie, la réciprocité générale*. Paris: Presses Universitaires de France.

Ostrom, Elinor. 2010. "Beyond Markets and States: Polycentric Governance of Complex Economic Systems." *American Economic Review* 100: 641–672.

Roemer, John. 2015. "Kantian Optimization: A Microfoundation for Cooperation." *Journal of Public Economics* 127: 45–57.

CHAPTER 4

Basu, Kaushik. 2000. *Prelude to Political Economy.* Oxford: Oxford University Press.

Frey, Bruno. 1997. "A Constitution for Knaves Crowds Out Civic Virtues." *Economic Journal* 107: 1043–1053.

Gneezy, Uri, and Aldo Rustichini. 2000. "A Fine Is a Price." *Journal of Legal Studies* 29: 1–17.

Kropotkin, Peter. 2015. *The Conquest of Bread.* London: Penguin Classics.

LeGuin, Ursula. 1974. *The Dispossessed: An Ambiguous Utopia.* New York: Harper and Row.

Leijonhufvud, Axel. 2007. "The Individual, the Market and the Division of Labor in Society." *Capitalism and Society* 2: Issue 2, Article 3.

Varian, Hal. 1978. *Microeconomic Analysis.* New York: Norton.

CHAPTER 5

Albert, Michael. 2003. *Parecon: Life after Capitalism.* London: Verso.

Arrow, Kenneth, and Leonid Hurwicz. 1960. "Decentralisation and Computation in Resource-Allocation." In *Essays in Economics and Econometrics in Honour of Harold Hotelling,* ed. R. Pfouts. Chapel Hill: University of North Carolina Press.

Barone, Enrico. 1908. "Il ministro della produzione nello stato collettivista." *Giornale degli Economisti* 37: 267–294 and 391–414.

Carlin, Wendy, Mark Schaffer, and Paul Seabright. 2013. "Soviet Power Plus Electrification: What Is the Long-Run Legacy of Communism?" *Explorations in Economic History* 50: 116–147.

Green, Jerry, and Jean-Jacques Laffont. 1979. *Incentives in Public Decision Making.* Amsterdam: North Holland.

Heal, Geoffrey. 1973. *The Theory of Economic Planning.* Amsterdam: North Holland.

Kornai, Janos. 1980. *Economics of Shortage.* Amsterdam: North Holland.

———. 1986. "The Hungarian Reform Process: Visions, Hopes, and Reality." *Journal of Economic Literature* 24: 1687–1737.

CHAPTER 6

Ben-Ner, Avner, and Egon Neuberger. 1990. "The Feasibility of Planned Market Systems: The Yugoslav Visible Hand and Negotiated Planning." *Journal of Comparative Economics* 14: 768–790.

Chilosi, Alberto. 1986. "Self-Managed Market Socialism with 'Free Mobility of Labor.'" *Journal of Comparative Economics* 10: 237–254.

———. 1999. "At the Origin of Market Socialism: Dühring's 'Socialitarian' Model of Economic Communes and Its Influence on the Development of Socialist Thought and Practice." *Economic Analysis* 2: 187–207.

Dow, Gregory. 1986. "Control Rights, Competitive Markets, and the Labor Management Debate." *Journal of Comparative Economics* 10: 48–61.

Kremer, Michael. 1997. "Why Are Worker Cooperatives So Rare?" *National Bureau of Economic Research,* Cambridge, MA: NBER Working Paper no. 6118. http://www.nber.org/papers/w6118.

Pencavel, John. 2012. "Worker Cooperatives and Democratic Governance." Institute for the Study of Labor, Bonn, IZA Discussion Paper no. 6932. http://ftp.iza.org/dp6932.pdf.

Ward, Ben. 1958. "The Firm in Illyria: Market Syndicalism." *American Economic Review* 48: 566–589.

CHAPTER 7

Bardhan, Pranab, and John Roemer. 1992. "Market Socialism: A Case for Rejuvenation." *Journal of Economic Perspectives* 6: 101–116.

Chilosi, Alberto. 1992. "Market Socialism: A Historical View and a Retrospective Assessment." *Economic Systems* 16: 171–185.

Salanié, Bernard. 2000. *Microeconomics of Market Failures.* Cambridge, MA: MIT Press.

Shleifer, Andrei, and Robert Vishny. 1992. "The Politics of Market Socialism." *Journal of Economic Perspectives* 8: 165–176.

Tirole, Jean. 2006. *The Theory of Corporate Finance.* Princeton, NJ: Princeton University Press.

Yunker, James. 1990. "Ludwig von Mises on the 'Artificial Market.'" *Comparative Economic Studies* 32: 108–140.

———. 2007. "A Comprehensive Incentives Analysis of the Potential Performance of Market Socialism." *Review of Political Economy* 19: 81–113.

CHAPTER 8

Roemer, John. 1994. *A Future for Socialism.* Cambridge, MA: Harvard University Press.

———. 1996. *Equal Shares: Making Market Socialism Work.* London: Verso.

Stauber, Leland. 1987. *A New Program for Democratic Socialism.* Carbondale, IL: Four Willows Press.

———. 1993. "A Concrete Proposal for a Market Socialism for Large Enterprises." *Coexistence* 30: 213–235.

CHAPTER 9

Ackerman, Bruce, and Anne Alstott. 2000. *The Stakeholder Society.* New Haven, CT: Yale University Press.

Corneo, Giacomo. 2011. "Stakeholding as a New Development Strategy for Saudi Arabia." *Review of Middle East Economics and Finance* 7, Issue 1, Article 1.

Elster, Jon. 1986. "Comment on van der Veen and Van Parijs." *Theory and Society* 15: 709–721.

Hauser, Richard. 2006. "Alternativen einer Grundsicherung–soziale und ökonomische Aspekte." *Gesellschaft–Wirtschaft–Politik* 3: 331–348.

Murray, Charles. 2006. *In Our Hands: A Plan to Replace the Welfare State.* Washington, DC: AEI Press.

Van der Veen, Robert, and Philippe Van Parijs. 1986. "A Capitalist Road to Communism." *Theory and Society* 15: 635–655.

Van Parijs, Philippe. 1992. *Arguing for Basic Income.* New York: Verso.

CHAPTER 10

Atkinson, Anthony B. 2015. *Inequality: What Can Be Done?* Cambridge, MA: Harvard University Press.

Bach, Stefan, Giacomo Corneo, and Viktor Steiner. 2012. "Optimal Top Marginal Tax Rates under Income Splitting for Couples." *European Economic Review* 56: 1055–1069.

Björklund, Anders, Jesper Roine, and Daniel Waldenström. 2012. "Intergenerational Top Income Mobility in Sweden: Capitalist Dynasties in the Land of Equal Opportunity?" *Journal of Public Economics* 96: 474–484.

Carens, Joseph. 1981. *Equality, Moral Incentives, and the Market.* Chicago: University of Chicago Press.

Durante, Ruben, Paolo Pinotti, and Andrea Tesei. 2015. "The Political Legacy of Entertainment TV." Centre for Economic Policy Research, London, CEPR Discussion Paper no. 10738. http://cepr.org/active/publications /discussion_papers/dp.php?dpno=10738.

Elster, Jon. 2013. *Securities against Misrule: Juries, Assemblies, Elections.* Cambridge: Cambridge University Press.

Enikolopov, Ruben, Maria Petrova, and Ekaterina Zhuravskaya. 2011. "Media and Political Persuasion: Evidence from Russia." *American Economic Review* 101: 3253–3285.

Johannesen, Niels, and Gabriel Zucman. 2014. "The End of Bank Secrecy? An Evaluation of the G20 Tax Haven Crackdown." *American Economic Journal: Economic Policy* 6: 65–91.

Kirchgässner, Gebhard. 2016. "Direct Democracy: Chances and Challenges." *Open Journal of Political Science* 6: 229–249.

Kleven, Henrik, Camille Landais, Emmanuel Saez, and Esben Schultz. 2014. "Migration and Wage Effects of Taxing Top Earners: Evidence from the Foreigners' Tax Scheme in Denmark." *Quarterly Journal of Economics* 129: 333–378.

Nolan, Brian, Wiemer Salverda, Daniele Checchi, Ive Marx, Abigail McKnight, István György Tóth, and Herman van de Werfhorst, eds. 2014. *Changing Inequalities and Societal Impacts in Rich Countries.* Oxford: Oxford University Press.

Piketty, Thomas, and Gabriel Zucman. 2014. "Capital Is Back: Wealth-Income Ratios in Rich Countries, 1700–2010." *Quarterly Journal of Economics* 129: 1255–1310.

Shaxson, Nicholas. 2011. *Treasure Islands.* London: Vintage Books.

Wright, Erik Olin. 2010. *Envisioning Real Utopias.* London: Verso.

Zucman, Gabriel. 2015. *The Hidden Wealth of Nations.* Chicago: University of Chicago Press.

INDEX